Training and Conditioning for Judo

AURÉLIEN BROUSSAL-DERVAL

Library of Congress Cataloging-in-Publication Data
Names: Broussal-Derval, Aurélien, author.
Title: Training and conditioning for judo / Aurélien Broussal.
Description: Champaign, IL : Human Kinetics, [2021] | «This book is a revised edition of La prépa physique judo, published in 2017 by 4Trainer Editions.» | Includes bibliographical references.
Identifiers: LCCN 2019058510 (print) | LCCN 2019058511 (ebook) | ISBN 9781492597940 (paperback) | ISBN 9781492597957 (epub) | ISBN 9781492597964 (pdf)
Subjects: LCSH: Judo--Training. | Weight training.
Classification: LCC GV1114 .B745 2021 (print) | LCC GV1114 (ebook) | DDC 796.815/2--dc23
LC record available at https://lccn.loc.gov/2019058510
LC ebook record available at https://lccn.loc.gov/2019058511

ISBN: 978-1-4925-9794-0 (print)

This book is a revised edition of *La Prépa Physique Judo*, published in 2017 by 4Trainer Éditions.

Managing Editors: Julie Marx Goodreau and Miranda K. Baur; **Translator:** Terra Sumstine; **Copyeditor:** Rodelinde Albrecht; **Proofreaders:** Emmanuel Charlot, Antoine Frandeboeuf, Olivier Remy; **Graphic Designers:** Sen No Sen, Dawn Sills; **Cover Designers:** Sen No Sen, Keri Evans; **Cover Design Associate:** Susan Rothermel Allen; **Photographs:** Emmanuel Charlot, Aurélien Broussal-Derval, Johann Vayriot; **Printer:** Versa Press

Printed in the United States of America
10 9 8 7 6 5 4 3 2 1

Human Kinetics
1607 N. Market Street
Champaign, IL 61820
USA

United States and International
Website: **US.HumanKinetics.com**
Email: info@hkusa.com
Phone: 1-800-747-4457

Canada
Website: **Canada.HumanKinetics.com**
Email: info@hkcanada.com

E8062

Contents

Acknowledgments

Thanks . . .

To Emmanuel Charlot, who taught me so much about transferring my knowledge to the page in a comprehensible way, and who entrusted me, when I was still so young, with a platform that is still just as popular 15 years later. I hope that I've proved him right and that I demonstrate everything I learned from him in every issue of *L'Esprit du Judo*.

To the entire *Esprit* team, particularly Olivier Remy and Antoine Frandeboeuf for their invaluable and now daily collaboration.

To the great coaches who shared so much with me and who had the courage to place their trust in me. Jane Bridge, Patrick Roux, and Ezio Gamba, thank you.

Let's not forget that the best trainer is first and foremost the one with the best athletes. Thank you to all of the sportsmen and women who trusted me, particularly the champions and friends who assisted in the writing of this book: Clément Delvert, Kilian Le Blouch, Walide Khyar, Marie-Eve Gahié, Pierre Duprat, and Alexandre Iddir.

And finally, to my father, to whom this project meant so much.

Foreword

It was likely on a judo mat that I met Aurélien Broussal-Derval for the first time, and it was likely his remarkable ground fighting skills that I first got to see up close. Back then, he was teaching Brazilian jiu-jitsu at the Cercle Tissier, the legendary club in Vincennes where the top martial arts experts in all disciplines can be found. Aside from the players and their world-renowned instructors, and thanks to the generous and warm welcome provided by Christian Derval, who rules the roost there, you can—at all hours of the day (and until late at night)—bump into athletes from a variety of sports, not just martial arts, sweating through their training sessions in preparation for an upcoming competition. You might also see a few French action film stars, who come for a tune-up on the mats or in the wonderfully equipped weights room that adjoins the dojos. It was in this temple in the Paris region devoted to physical effort, power, flexibility, and self-control that Aurélien started off. He fought there when he was little, he developed there, and he had ample opportunity there to test, develop, and gain an in-depth knowledge of his area of study: physical training. For transferring theory to practice, fine-tuning concepts, and adjusting exercises he was extremely fortunate to have at his disposal a wonderful testing ground in which to experiment freely on himself and on others. That's why, despite his young age, he already boasts impressive acumen and great influence in sport-focused physical training. But that would not have been enough to trace such a significant path had Aurélien not also been such a brilliant student in a daunting domain, was willing to draw upon all the latest American developments in an area that is constantly evolving, and work so hard, exhibiting a keen intellect and the mind of an educator, as I quickly realized when I asked him to start writing articles for *L'Esprit du Judo* magazine. This partnership, which dates back to the first edition—already12 years ago—has personally taught me a lot and has contributed to (of this I'm convinced) changing the mentality of French and European judokas over the years by providing them with the best possible source of information. All of those articles form the basis of this book.

EMMANUEL CHARLOT
Editor-in-chief, *L'Esprit du Judo*

History

ATHLETES, WEIGHTLIFTERS, BODYBUILDERS, GYM TEACHERS, PHYSIOTHERAPISTS . . . TODAY, A NUMBER OF SPORT FIGURES ARE SURFING A FASHIONABLE WAVE: THE PHYSICAL DIMENSION OF ATHLETIC TRAINING. IT HAS GONE SO FAR THAT, FOR SOME TIME, IT HAS BEEN VERY DIFFICULT TO TELL WHAT'S HIDING UNDER A TRAINER'S TRACKSUIT, AND WHAT THE ORIGINS OF THIS PRACTICE—NOW AN INTEGRAL PART OF JUDO TRAINING—ACTUALLY ARE.

Legend has it that Bernard Laporte, while working at the French rugby club Stade Français in the 1990s, was one of the first professional coaches to make use of external physical trainers. Already highly developed in the Americas, physical training only had a few formally recognized representatives in France back then. It is thanks to the intuition of certain enlightened coaches that physical culture has slowly started to break through to the sporting domain.

At the time, Laporte decided to call on the services of specialists in energy expenditure, who focused on the primary movement in rugby: running. Brought in from INSEP (France's National Institute of Sport), these track-and-field coaches would contribute to the great history of physical training, of which rugby still remains one of the main hubs of innovation. It is important to point out that, since the 1980s, track-and-field coaches have given a lot of time to consulting in other disciplines, mainly because they are well versed in notions of energy sources, which are often obscure in other sports. Professional clubs, mainly rugby or soccer, that use running as the preferred method of movement and of training were practically the only ones who could hire these coaches. Furthermore, the wide range of athletic movement meant that any athlete's running technique could be improved.

Track and field was one of the exclusive and predictable disciplines that forced its coaches early on to introduce as much variety as possible to their training approach. Consequently, they then had a huge amount of training content that could be rapidly shared with and adapted to numerous sports.

There are disciplines with a predictable (in other words, stable) environment, in which there are no external factors likely to influence performance. Athletes are solely responsible for their results, for example in track and field or swimming. On the other hand, there are activities in which performance is rendered unpredictable by an unstable environment, such as judo, rugby, and open-air sports.

Athletes laid the practical foundations for physical sports training, which were gradually supplemented by other energetic disciplines like cycling and swimming, especially in terms of tapering. At the same time, the PES (Physical Education and Sport) movement (many of whose representatives came from track and field) contributed to the theory of this emerging practice. The notion of internal logic, which would later become internal athletic logic, or even the fundamental problem, enabled apprentice physical trainers to pinpoint, as quickly as possible, disciplines of which they had little knowledge but in which they ended up getting involved.

DIFFERENT COUNTRIES, DIFFERENT CULTURES

It's fascinating to take a look at what happens on other tatami mats. Is the physical training approach completely different from one culture to the next? Let's take an athlete and offer them a physical training session. While in France they might turn up with a pair of running shoes, ready to work with cones and hoops, in Britain and in the U.S. they'll have their weight lifting shoes on, ready for some clean-and-jerks. A Brazilian, meanwhile, will be expecting natural body weight gymnastics, while a Japanese physical trainer, in Asia's hygienist culture, is actually closer to a naturopathic physiotherapist than to a Western trainer.

But in its exclusive role as a support service, track and field would prove unable to meet the endlessly growing variety of physical training demands for the following reasons:

- **The athletes, who were not experts in strength training, often demonstrated their limits in the weight room.**
- **The systematic use of running to improve physical attributes was gradually discredited, particularly for judo, which does not use that type of movement.**

Authorities on energy (and by extension, on endurance), athletes encounter a variety of competition that enriches physical training, starting with strength-training specialists. This is entirely logical when you consider the time devoted to muscle-strengthening exercises, particularly in combat sports.

Bodybuilders (expert in analytical muscle strengthening) and weightlifters (expert in explosive strength and preventing back injuries while performing full-body movements) as well as powerlifters also positioned themselves very early on. Historically focused on a fitness and well-being approach, specialists in these disciplines swiftly established themselves as physical training consultants in sports in which strength can make a significant difference. Consequently, in the final third of the 20th century, weight rooms began to appear progressively in fitness centers, even though the concept of physical training was not emphasized. Athletes who were ahead of their time and got involved in this type of complementary training claimed that they were developing their muscles or engaging in physical fitness. Even today, weights are seen as a key part of sports conditioning. Just like track-and-field athletes, these contributors appear to be ultra-specialists in strength and power, while their knowledge of energy-related aspects is seen as less comprehensive.

Another group of sports stakeholders were involved in the development of physical training, a discipline with varied and parallel origins. Let's file them under the heading "medical." In fact, doctors got involved in the physical aspect of the practice at an early stage, especially by implementing numerous research protocols on physical attributes and establishing benchmark tests. Physiotherapists now claim credit for developing physical training, and quite rightly so. But their contribution came later, because their involvement in sports conditioning coincided with the emergence of a prophylactic dimension to training. We owe a debt to them for a large part of the preventive, kinesthetic, and proprioceptive work (particularly balance work), as well as the advancement of core-strengthening techniques, which are essential in judo.

Finally, let's recognize the influence of gymnastics on certain areas within physical training, such as strength training without equipment, the bio-informational dimension, risk-taking (although that belongs more in the area of mental training), and—in a different way from the physiotherapists—proprioception and core strength.

This multifaceted history, featuring multiple changes and parallels, gives us a good understanding why many sports professionals today call themselves physical trainers. These trainers leave their field of expertise to become more versatile and to cover all of the physical and preventive aspects of their domains. Up to now, the goal was to master all or part of the discipline in which you were involved, or which you had practiced yourself. Unless you have represented your country at judo, can you really call yourself a judo physical trainer if you have never put on a kimono or had a taste of the adrenaline produced as you face an opponent who determines the physical pain he or she inflicts on you?

Judo at the Cutting Edge in the 1990s

Although, earlier in this section, I chose rugby to illustrate my point, don't be fooled into thinking that judo was just sitting twiddling its thumbs. For example, while, from the 1980s onward, the portion of the training sessions devoted to physical work increased considerably, the French national judo team imposed a physical dimension on the world that had not been witnessed up to that point. Of course, the best coach is the one who has the best athletes. And with a French contingent that boasted David Douillet, Stéphane Traineau, Jamel Bourras, and Darcel Yandzi, among others, a mix of genetics and frenzied training created an exceptional team. On the fringes of these public developments, an athlete had been working at INSEP for several years: Michel Pradet, the founding father of the discipline in France, who gave us the book *La Préparation Physique*. At the time, he advised a number of judokas on the French national team and contributed to the training of certain veterans like Laurent Del Colombo, who would go on to anchor the culture of judo-related physical training at INSEP.

Four Influences

Without questioning the origins, training, or convictions of a physical trainer, the examples shown in the figure illustrate the following two absolute necessities:

1. **Updating your expertise to adapt your intervention capabilities to the expanded set of modern physical needs**
2. **Building all of your acquired expertise around the central content of judo**

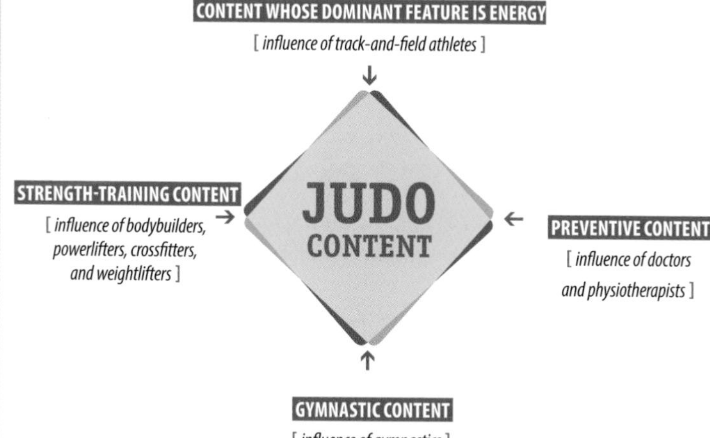

The diagram to the left shows the various sources of inspiration for physical training. These influences shaped the trainer's areas of focus more precisely.

What Comes Under the Heading of "Physical"?

When designing assignments intended for the physical training of an athlete, I always keep in mind five major fields of action that fall within the expertise of a physical trainer.

Prevention and Return-to-Sport Programs

Without encroaching on the territory of the physiotherapist and an athlete's rehabilitation, or the period in which they return to top form once they are no longer in the recovery phase, return-to-sport programs are part of physical training. But well before that, physical training must be incorporated into judo training via preventive content such as proprioception, core strengthening, body rebalancing, muscle stretching, recovery protocols, and so on.

Developing Endurance

This essentially involves an energy-focused calibration of the workout and the training program, through the methodical organization of effort around specific objectives, delimited by energy systems. Planning and maximizing effort in training—in terms of power and ability—therefore falls under the auspices of physical training, depending on whether you are pursuing objectives related to the improvement of the alactic, lactic, or aerobic systems.

Enhancing Muscle Parameters

This is a key area that influences an athlete's performance and safety. Bringing these two into harmony comes through physical training: increasing general strength peaks, developing local strength, balancing the body, creating a protective armor, increasing power, and so forth.

Planning and Scheduling Training

An athlete's physical training program must be devised methodically and organized around a strategy that features regular competitions. Drawing up a training plan involves combining technical, tactical, and physical training.

Recovery

The busier the competition schedule, the higher the level and degree of physical engagement, and the more the level of physical performance is likely to skyrocket. Above all, the trainer must optimize the athlete's rest periods.

In view of the packed competition schedule and the intensity of each competition, the current evolution of judo sometimes sees the physical trainer become a veritable physical recovery assistant.

GLOSSARY

internal logic: "Incorporating the constituent rules, spirit, and essential meaning of sport and physical activity" (Parlebas 1976).

fundamental problem: The essential problem that the type of activity (training or competition) causes the player.

analytical strengthening: Strengthening limited to a single muscle or to peripheral muscles, or to a single joint (for example, strengthening the biceps).

general strengthening: Strengthening a muscle chain (for example, strengthening the upper body push chain, the posterior chain of the arms).

overall strengthening: Working on exercises that link muscle chains together, sometimes from the tips of your fingers to the tips of your toes, like a snatch in weightlifting.

From the Demise of General Training to Its Resurrection in Specific Training

The demands of physical training are constantly changing with the development of competition and practices—less and less time, more and more competitions, needs that are always closer to the discipline in question, and so on. The time when a strength training program alone was enough to ensure that an athlete made significant progress is over. When you add to that the stricter definition of basic training periods (I'll come back to basic training limits later on in this book), the entire concept of general physical training is called into question, and could even be described as obsolete.

The renowned physical trainer Frédéric Aubert now distinguishes among three categories of physical training, which are used at different points of a training program.

1/ DISSOCIATED The content is external to the discipline. This is the case for cardio on an exercise machine or bodybuilding.

2/ ASSOCIATED The session alternates between discipline-related content and external content. For example, alternating between muscle strengthening and *nage-komi*.

3/ INCORPORATED The training activity or drill is actually the discipline itself. As an example, the judoka uses *tandoku-renshu* and *uchi-komi* to work on cardiovascular endurance.

The selection of exercises then varies, from general situations (applicable to any discipline) and guided situations (performing athletic judo moves to better control the intensity or amount of work) to specific situations (maximum relevance to judo).

Judo and the Judoka

OFTEN IT TAKES NO MORE THAN A GLANCE TO RECOGNIZE A POSSIBLE TRAINING PARTNER. IN THE STREET, THE LOOK, ATTITUDE, AND MORPHOLOGY OF THE JUDOKA REVEAL THE SECRET. ANY LINGERING DOUBTS VANISH FOR GOOD WHEN YOU SEE HIM OR HER TAKE PART IN ATHLETIC ACTIVITY: THEIR MUSCULATURE AS WELL AS THEIR STRENGTH, ENDURANCE, AND HEIGHTENED SENSE OF BALANCE—PHYSICAL CHARACTERISTICS THAT CLEARLY STEM FROM JUDO TRAINING—SET JUDOKAS APART FROM THE CROWD.

The Whole Package

Judo is, no question, one of the most complete sports out there. In fact, it constantly works all the muscles of the body, whether you're pushing, pulling, or blocking. That's why you need all kinds of muscle contraction workouts. Is there a marked difference between the upper and lower parts of the body, as in cycling? Absolutely not. In judo, the balance between the two is almost total. How about laterality, as in tennis? Although judo players do often favor one side for attacking, the other side never stops defending.

While some imbalances persist at a local level, these are due more to bad training habits than to the discipline itself (see the section on preventing knee injuries). Just in case it hasn't dawned on you: In judo, you work from your toes to your fingertips!

As Strong as a Judoka

Are judokas really all that strong? Yes, but not in the sense we normally understand it. In fact, judokas are among the most powerful athletes out there. That is, their muscular profile combines high levels of strength and significant speed. This benefit from participating in judo—because you obviously have to be strong and fast to throw an opponent—even makes our fighters exceptional in top-level sports: Whereas mere mortals engaging in strength training might limit their power exercises to 6 repetitions*, judokas can often go up to 8!

A V12 Engine Under the Hood

One thing is certain: Judokas don't run on diesel. Their endurance attributes are very specific to what they experience on the mat. Their energy system enables them to be particularly dynamic and to repeat intense actions for the relatively long duration of a match, which far exceeds four minutes if we take the *matte* into account. That's why judokas are particularly at ease with short, high-intensity exercises, as well as with staggered exercises.

The Agility of a Cat

The ease with which judokas pick up sliding or balance sports is well established. Whether it's skiing, surfing, or even gymnastics, daily participation in judo also improves the ability to process information and to adapt movement to all sorts of situations. A number of studies have highlighted judokas' excellent balance, whether they have access to visual information or not, giving them a level of efficiency practically equal to that of gymnasts (Mégrot, Bardy, Dietrich 2001; Mégrot, Dietrich, et al. 2004; Mégrot and Bardy 2005). This aspect is strengthened primarily by their level of coordination and enhanced by a relationship to risk that is optimized by their athletic activity. They are, in fact, better able to assess the risks of a situation without actually being afraid of it.

This profile is the result of constant adaptations to the intensive and enthusiastic practice of judo. To better understand the specifics of our discipline, it is useful to explore the factors that influence performance before thinking about how they interact with each other.

Modeling Judo Performance

We can't talk about specific physical training without fully understanding what we are trying to achieve. What are the implications of physical training for judo? In plain language, it's about examining the peculiarities of judo to better define the specifics, and then tailoring the training accordingly. One possible exercise is to model judo performance, representing the various factors that influence it and how they interact.

**A classic method consists of working at top speed with an average weight (around 60 percent), up to 6 reps maximum. If you don't follow these instructions, your speed of execution drops, fatigue takes over, and you end up working more on endurance.*

Six categories are constantly interacting during a bout:

1. Technique
2. Bioinformational parameters
3. Strategy and tactics
4. Psychology and emotion
5. Physiological parameters
6. Energy parameters

The figure shows this information in the form of a performance model.

JUDO PERFORMANCE MODEL

Energy parameters

The effort lasts for 5 minutes intermittently at high intensity; two important energy systems here are **power** and the **anaerobic-lactic capacity.** There are also numerous very intense and very short bursts of effort requiring the anaerobic-lactic processes (a bout can sometimes last for only a few seconds). But because these efforts are repeated during several matches on a single day of competition, all systems need to be developed, starting with **aerobic power.**

Bioinformational parameters

Interpreting the in-fight information (such as the opponent's characteristics or potential openings) and **updating it** constantly

Continually taking in information related to distance, so that you know what you can do and are aware of the risks involved

Keeping a clear head when receiving information by others involved in the bout (your coach, the opponent's coach, the referee, and so on)

JUDO PERFORMANCE

Win by *ippon*, win on points, or withdrawal over 5 minutes, interspersed with *matte*.

Psychology and emotion

Resisting pain inflicted by your opponent

Managing direct confrontation

Taking risks

The importance of competition

Your opponent's identity (nationality, record of wins, etc.)

Traditional factors (confidence, activation, motivation, imagery)

Strategy and tactics

Adapting and creating opportunities offered by your opponent's immediate reactions

Different objectives that lead to victory, such as *ippon*, two *waza-ari*, forcing your opponent to receive a penalty, hanging on until the end with a points advantage, submission

Adapting the way you fight to the adversary's strong points, and to certain moments of the match, such as dominating attack or defense, or extending certain phases

Adapting to the opponent's morphology: size, guard (right-handed or left-handed)

TECHNIQUE

Muscular parameters

The essential use of **power, endurance, and skill** because the actions are dynamic and high-intensity, repeated over the course of 5 minutes

Engaging all of the muscle chains in all forms of muscle contraction

SPECIFIC MUSCLE STRENGTHENING

Should We Put Away Our Weights?

IS THE TYPE OF TRAINING THAT TAKES PLACE IN A WEIGHT ROOM OLD-FASHIONED? CAN WE IMAGINE WORKING SOMEWHERE ELSE THAN ON A TATAMI WHILE STILL REMAINING JUDO-SPECIFIC? DON'T PUT YOUR DUMBBELLS AWAY JUST YET.

The evolution of modern judo toward an all-out trial of strength has not pleased everyone—far from it. While recent rule changes appear to reposition technique at the heart of things, as its grand return during competitions in Japan has proved, should we be looking to ban any practice not done on the *tatami*? The fact remains that for technique to come to the fore in a competitive environment, it must be built on foundations of solid physical aptitudes. And while specific endurance abilities can generally be improved on the judo mat, the development of other physical attributes such as strength, speed, flexibility, or even balance will remain incomplete if judokas do not temporarily step away from the confines of their sport, which no longer suffice when it comes to placing the body in appropriately demanding situations that will help them reach those final milestones.

After considering these factors, trainers must use their imagination to keep things specific to judo: They need to figure out a connection to judo, even when their judoka is lifting weights. That, in a nutshell, is the challenge of integrated training! There are a number of tools and methods that can help with this kind of work, some of which you will find in the text that follows.

Resistance Bands

Judokas were among the first athletes to use resistance bands for muscle strengthening. The idea, which has been somewhat forgotten in recent years, is actually extremely specific: In a large number of throws, opponents have the time to adapt their stance and resist vigorously, up to the breaking point where their resistance dwindles quickly and completely. This is exactly the type of resistance you encounter when you pull on a resistance band. In addition, muscle strengthening with a resistance band offers more freedom of movement and enables you to perform exercises that are even closer to the discipline. Finally, these bands also offer a certain functionality, because they not only allow you to effectively strengthen all areas of the body but can also be easily carried wherever you go.

Traditional Weights

Dissociated traditional strength training essentially depends on the use of free weights. The difficulty arises at the start of the motion, because you must overcome the initial inertia to continue more freely afterward. This type of work should not be neglected for two main reasons:

1. **No other method allows you to work at an equivalent intensity (particularly for the development of maximum strength).**
2. **This type of resistance is often encountered in judo, especially when facing an opponent you need to lift off the ground: It's a question of overcoming the inertia so that resistance disappears once the motion begins.**

For all that, traditional weight training needs to be adapted so that it can be properly applied to judo. Let's take the example of one of the better-known moves: the bench press. Will any judoka ever really need to lift one-and-a-half times their own body weight up into the air, while supine and using both arms? Even when we're comfortably stable on a bench, can we think of other ways to develop pushing strength that are as relevant and specific as possible to judo? There are two parameters we can play with here: dissociation of the arm work and the angles we use.

There are two benefits to dissociating arm work:

1. **It helps to balance the athlete and avoid compensation (weak side vs. strong side).**
2. **It is relevant to the judoka, who usually pushes differently with each arm.**

KEY POINTS

→ **Vary the exercises and movements.**

→ **Always keep judo-specific needs, both general and individual, in mind when selecting exercises, particularly from one weight category to another.**

A number of variations can make the bench press more specific to judo. Among them are the bench press with alternating arms (lift one arm after the other rather than both at the same time) and the dumbbell bench press.

It is now acknowledged that gains in strength are mainly transferable in fighting scenarios where the angle of the limbs is closest to that used during exercises. But we know that during a judo bout, the fighter must develop strength in all spatial fields. Even though we are just talking about pushing, you have to be able to push just as effectively upward and downward, when standing up and when lying down, when extremely close to your opponent (closed angle, arms bent) and when there is distance between you and your opponent (open angle, arms straight). It is therefore essential that training varies the working angles as much as possible. The traditional bench press, which is too limited, must be enhanced by working on an incline and a decline and by using different degrees of arm extension.

Grip Trainers

This innovation comes to us from Brazil. Not content with modernizing the *ne-waza*, the Brazilians based their judo practice on floor work (where strengthening the upper arms is even more important than when upright) and created a very simple but incredibly effective tool: the grip trainer. Mimicking the traction you get when you grip a *judogi* uniform (after wrapping your jacket around the bar), grip trainers are just rectangles of *judogi* equipped with a strap, which means you can hang or attach them wherever you want (on a bar, machine, dumbbell, resistance band, etc.). In fact, Adidas recently followed in the footsteps of the Brazilians by launching their own range of grip trainers.

This material offers multiple benefits for those who do judo, including these:

- **→ The possibility of incorporating a judo-style grip into almost all muscle-strengthening exercises**
- **→ The ability to develop endurance in the forearms throughout the workout, thereby avoiding tedious exercises and saving time**

If you do not own such a tool, you can always use towels, which are less judo-specific but are nonetheless effective.

Working Under Unbalanced Conditions

One of judo's principal features is the fact that an opponent can introduce instability via a series of weight transfers and imbalances. The key is to be constantly aiming to regain a stable position when an opponent tries to throw you off balance, and, under these same conditions, to try to make your opponent lose his or her balance and dismantle the opponent's defense. To achieve this, novel working methods—such as the use of balance discs, exercise balls, and balance boards—have emerged recently. These types of work require proprioception. With or without equipment, the idea is to engage the various receptors in the body that continually send information to the areas in the central nervous system that control movement and posture. These bring different contraction and relaxation reflexes, postural control, and dynamic balance into play.

Associating this type of work with traditional muscle strengthening involves the following:

- → **Developing reactive and intelligent muscles, capable of adapting and protecting themselves (gains in efficiency and prevention)**
- → **Strengthening the muscular system in a way that's as similar as possible to the practice of judo, using precarious balance**
- → **Calling upon the deepest muscles more quickly and more intensely; this saves time during a session by reducing the number of sets and repetitions**
- → **Devising varied and fun exercises for all types of judo athletes**

proprioception: This is the ability to position your body (or some of your limbs) in space, even without a visual stimulus, whether your body is moving or not.

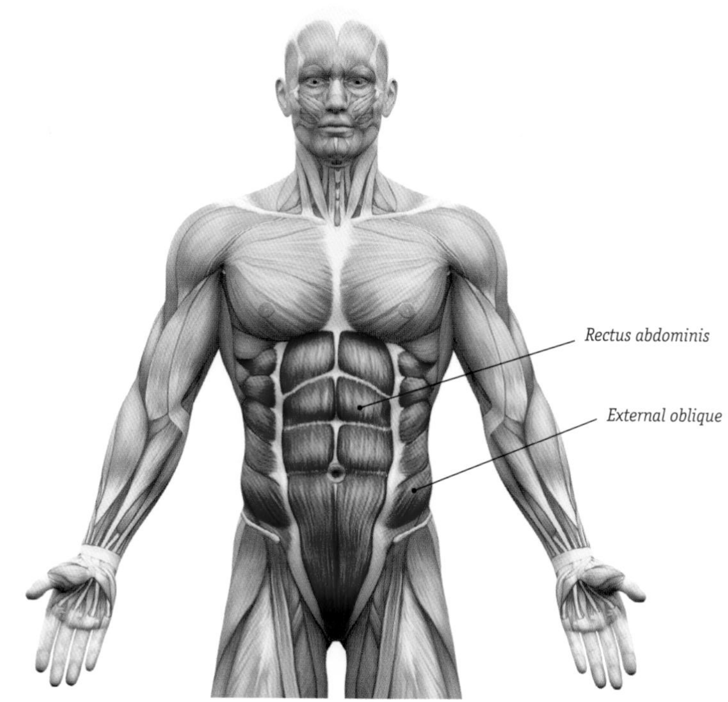

Building Abdominal Muscles for Judo

IN ABDOMINAL WORK, MORE THAN IN OTHER AREAS, OLD HABITS DIE HARD. HERE ARE SOME POINTERS FOR MAKING SURE YOU GET A SIX-PACK RATHER THAN A FOUR-PACK, AND THAT THIS HELPS YOU WITH YOUR JUDO.

Modern trainers have been ringing alarm bells for some time now: The approach to strengthening abdominal muscles often lacks prudence, sometimes going as far as to endanger an athlete's physical integrity. While some specialists today occasionally recommend static strengthening exclusively (such as core strength exercises), the range and the demands of judo, particularly the numerous twists, bends, and extensions of the trunk, compel us to pursue the more traditional torso bending over the leg work. This should not pose a problem if you adhere to the key principles that follow.

Knowing Your Muscles and Their Role

The problem with strengthening the abdominal muscles is mainly related to anatomy, because we tend to quite simply forget to mobilize and strengthen deep muscles! As a priority, we mobilize our rectus abdominis muscle, which is responsible for the six-pack. This term refers to the visual aspect of the abdominal muscles, whose cardinal function is flexing the torso. We are all familiar with the internal and external oblique muscles, which help us to rotate, bend from side to side, or bend forward when we lock our pelvis. But we are less aware of the transverse abdominis, a deep muscle. This muscle contracts when we cough or when we suck in our stomach. A postural muscle, it is also responsible for supporting internal organs and the abdominal area. A neglected transverse abdominis often results in the abdominal muscles looking swollen rather than flat (which is actually one of the desired objectives). Finally, locking down the pelvic floor and the perineum (which support the internal genital organs, especially in women) will complete this deep contraction of the abdominal wall; prolapse (slippage of body parts) is often linked to fragility in this area.

WHAT'S THE PURPOSE OF THE ABDOMINAL MUSCLES?

→ They help digestion and contribute to breathing.

→ They energize and strengthen the junction between the upper and lower parts of the body, a strength transfer relay point.

Therefore, before any abdominal work, the judoka must take care to do the following:

→ Tilt the pelvis back*

→ Suck in the stomach

→ Tighten the perineum by producing the same contraction that you feel when you stop yourself from urinating

The notion of sets of ab exercises doesn't make much sense: the muscle requires one long set that consists of doing different exercises together without stopping so as to saturate the muscle.

Remember that you can work different areas by focusing on the upper part of the body (chest raised) or the lower part (legs raised).

Pull in your buttocks to bring your pelvis forward and contract your abs to push your low back out.

1

HIGH UPPER ZONE

JUDO MOVE

Pull yourself back up to the guard position while facing your training partner.

THE IDEA

Focus of work: upper subumbilical area.

Without anchoring your feet, return to a sitting position with or without your training partner.

First use your partner's sleeves to pull yourself up, then work only with your abs.

BUILD YOUR ABS SESSION

When?
At the end of a warm-up for a normal-intensity workout, or in a dedicated session.

How?
By following a progressive order: by gearing the work first to the high upper *[set 1]* and low upper *[set 2]* parts, then to the upper *[set 3]* and lower *[set 4]* oblique portions, and then rounding things off with the deep abdominal muscles *[set 5]*.

By varying the tempo, speed, and type of contraction, in this order: lifting your torso *(concentric)*, holding the position *(isometric)*, and slowing down *(eccentric)*.

2 LOW UPPER ZONE

JUDO MOVE
Leg straddled, apart in the air

THE IDEA
Straddle your legs as high as possible, controlling the slow return to the floor.

Focus: the lower subumbilical area.

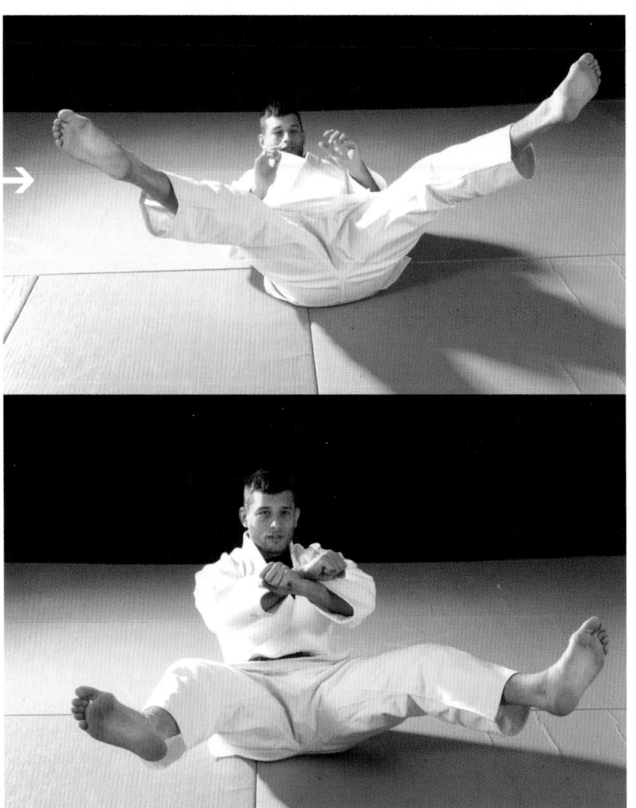

3 HIGH OBLIQUE ZONE

JUDO MOVE
Spring back up and launch an *ude-garami* attack between your training partner's legs.

THE IDEA
Sit, leaning to one side and placing your elbow on the floor. Use your elbow for support to lift your glutes, and then repeat on the other side.

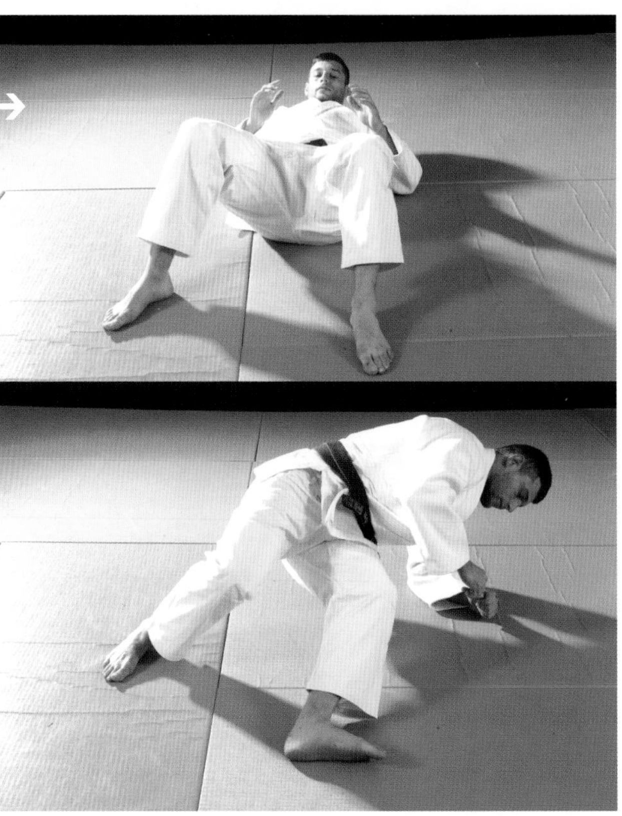

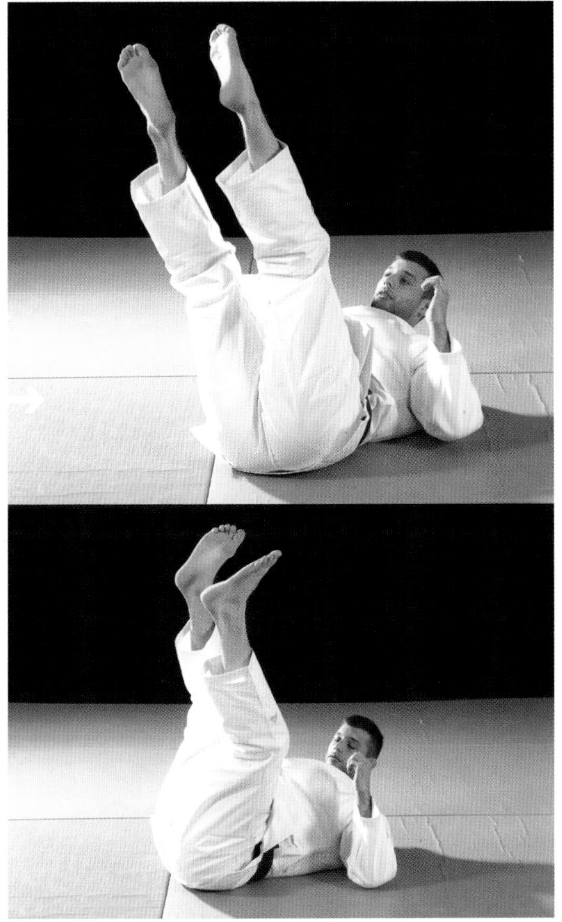

4

LOW OBLIQUE PORTION

JUDO MOVE
Hip mobility

THE IDEA
Keeping your legs together and up in the air, pivot your hips to the left and right.

5

DEEP ABDOMINAL MUSCLES

JUDO MOVE
Introduction to the face-on *sankaku*

THE IDEA
Lie back on your shoulders with your head and neck flat on the floor (candle position), lift your legs, open your hips, and then bring your legs together to form a triangle, keeping your core engaged. (Don't lower your glutes.) Support yourself with your elbows if you wish.

POINTERS

Don't forget

- Systematically protect your back (no hyperextension or arched back)
- After the ab sequence, always stretch your abs and the iliopsoas (hip flexor), a muscle that tends to get tight with regular abdominal work (despite efforts not to use it) and thus can be prone to inflammation

Try to avoid

- Using momentum to lift your torso, because this is dangerous for the lumbar vertebrae and also ineffective, because it limits abdominal muscle recruitment (If it becomes impossible to lift your torso, this means that the muscle is saturated.)
- Pulling on your head to help lift your torso (This is harmful to the neck and ineffective.)
- Repeating the same abs exercises (Within two to three sessions the muscles adapt, and it will just become routine.)
- Kicking your legs close to the ground (The position is detrimental to the lumbar vertebrae due to the tension from counterbalancing the weight of your legs. It feels like you're working hard, but it's actually the hip flexors that are being engaged. There is a risk of groin injuries over the long term.)
- Losing heart (Willpower plays a huge role in progress, because really working your abdominal muscles makes them burn.)

Developing Core Strength

WHETHER YOU ARE THROWING OR FALLING, EFFICIENCY AND SAFETY CAN ONLY BE ACHIEVED THROUGH IMPECCABLE CORE STRENGTH. IN FACT, THE JUDOKA IS ALREADY AN EXPERT IN CORE STRENGTH. HERE ARE A FEW TIPS SO THAT JUDOKAS CAN FINALLY HAVE A CORE STRENGTH CHALLENGE THAT MEETS THEIR NEEDS.

If you feel a slight weakness in your lower back, if you're not happy with your posture, or if you want to develop rock-solid blocking strength, perhaps you have already had core-strengthening exercises recommended to you. Extremely fashionable ever since physiotherapists (largely inspired by gymnastics) got involved in physical training, core strengthening might already be part of your daily routine. In general, athletes start core-strengthening exercises because of muscle weakness, often localized in the back or in the pelvic or abdominal areas. The objective is thus purely preventive. But you also find this type of exercise in bodyweight muscle-strengthening sessions. The work here is geared toward enhancing performance, and especially toward increasing strength.

These two different objectives often make us lose sight of the primary purpose of core strengthening, which is—as the name suggests—to build a protective casing around the core of your body: in anatomical terms, the spine and the pubic symphysis.*

Strengthening the abdominal muscles is thus just one piece of the puzzle, in addition to the muscles in the lumbar region and the deep muscles of the spine, to name just a few.

In the collective imagination, core strengthening is often limited to an extended hold, with the body in a horizontal position. For many, the term refers to isometric strengthening of the abdominal muscles (muscle contractions without movement). However, core strengthening is a necessary resource for optimal performance: transferring power from one joint to another or anchoring the body to the ground. It's also a priority to prevent injury; after all, the dictionary definition of *core* is "a central and often foundational part surrounded by effective protection." It might help to think of the outer covering of an electric cable, which protects the fragile wire responsible for transmitting electric current without limiting its mobility: Extremely flexible, it bends to adapt to different situations. This is the approach we must take to core strengthening in sports, and even more so in judo: protection and adaptation.

So you can see why simple core strengthening on your elbows in the plank position doesn't make much sense in judo: It's nonspecific, rigid (and so the opposite of adaptable), focused on the abdominal/lumbar region, and, let's be honest, really too easy for judokas, who are accustomed to more demanding situations.

So that judokas are not forced to do endless core exercises before they start to actually feel the benefits, we have to consider the complexity of their sport and their capacity to train. Clearly, we have to set the bar much higher. To begin with, there is no reason to limit our approach to the abdominal muscles. Though they are the main focus, they are not the only muscles involved. That is why you hear about core strengthening for the shoulder blades, the arms, the neck, or even the lower limbs.

Over the past several years I've developed three types of core strengthening in my work that you should consider when dealing with a complex discipline like judo.

***pubic symphysis:** *Secondary joint of the pelvis, located in front of the bladder and above the external genitalia*

1. Static Core Strengthening

Fundamental and basic, this is the starting point for all training, return-to-sport programs, and postural reeducation. As soon as possible (when it is evident that the judoka has the physical and postural resources to move on to more advanced exercises), it should be complemented by other types of core strengthening.

One of the fundamental rules when advancing in these exercises, but keeping the same general theme, is to maintain the alignment of the body's parts and of the body as a whole. Using the example of static core strengthening, judokas will be ready to move on to the next stage once they are capable of holding the position for the suggested time without significantly adjusting the body's position, such as

- **falling out of alignment,**
- **hyperextending the back (impossible to maintain alignment due to fatigue), or**
- **overly curving the upper spine (cheating to relieve the abdominal muscles of some of the weight).**

If one of these three things happens during the exercise, it means that the judoka is not quite ready to advance. In this way, judokas can progress from one level to the next as safely as possible.

You Need to Know

→ **In judo, you encounter this type of strength in certain holds or completions. Even for complete beginners, it is judo-specific and should remain a part of their workout for the rest of their career as a judoka. In addition, due to the reasonable level of motor skill complexity involved, it enables us to enhance our control over muscle recruitment by focusing on the transverse muscle or the pelvic floor, for example.**

BEGINNER

Exercises 1, 3, 5: 20 sec, **Exercises 2, 4:** 3 times per side *(work on opposite arms and legs)*. Keep the knees, pelvis, and shoulders aligned. Do 2 or 3 sets. Recovery time: 1 min.

INTERMEDIATE

Exercises 1, 3, 5: 15 sec, **Exercises 2, 4:** 10 sec per side *(work on opposite arms and legs)*. Keep the knees, pelvis, and shoulders aligned. Do 2 or 3 sets. Recovery time: 1 min.

ADVANCED

Exercises 1, 3, 5: 20 sec, **Exercises 2, 4:** 15 sec per side *(work on opposite arms and legs)*. Keep the knees, pelvis, and shoulders aligned. Do 3 or 4 sets. Recovery time: 30 sec.

2. Dynamic Core Strengthening

Whether you're in a stable or unstable situation, with or without visual cues, in bare feet or in shoes, the idea here is to connect the marked strengthening of the stabilizing muscles with control over the motor muscles to create synergy during a movement. Squat snatches, stability ball movements, and Bosu ball jumps are very good examples. Similarly, a physical and pedagogical progression should be visualized from the beginning to the advanced level.

You Need to Know

→ This second level of core-strengthening expertise is particularly relevant for judokas and should never be neglected, even when they become experts. Ultra-specific, the progress it creates is actually transferred to their *ne-waza* mobility, attack preparation, counterattacks, creating opportunities, and, in fact, to almost all the athletic movements made in judo.

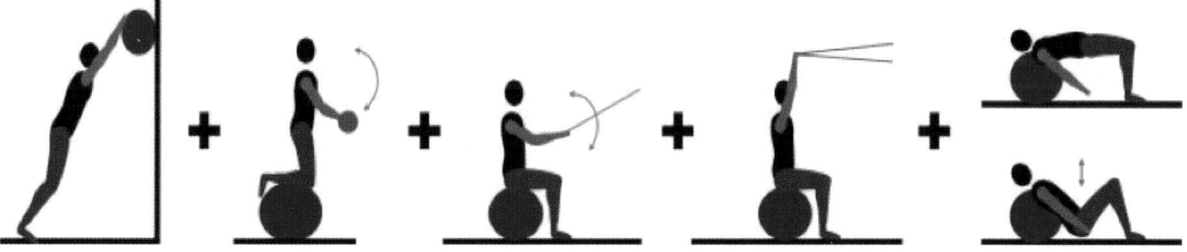

BEGINNER
20 sec per position. Be strict about back positioning. Do 2 or 3 sets. Recovery time: 1 min.

INTERMEDIATE
20 sec per position. Be strict about back positioning. Do 2 or 3 sets. Recovery time: 1 min.

ADVANCED
Exercises 1, 3, 5: 20 sec per position. **Exercises 2, 4:** 5 reps. Comfortable weight.
Do 3 or 4 sets. Recovery time: 1 min to 1 min 30 sec.

3. Core Strengthening Through Jumping

This time, the idea is to position yourself in space and to control your landing after a jump. This type of core strengthening can only be done by seasoned athletes who are already familiar with conventional core strengthening techniques.

Manually disrupted jumps with different landing methods (with or without a balance device) illustrate this approach well. These types of exercises can often be physically grueling, and that's why it is best to work with a training partner; this allows you to incorporate recovery time that is at least equivalent to the working time.

You Need to Know

→ **Once a judoka has reached a level where he or she is able to do these exercises, this final core strengthening stage should also be maintained for the rest of their judo career. Such exercises are useful for setting yourself up, side steps with limited support, throws (throwing your opponent or being thrown), and even spatial awareness. These are the most advanced core movements a judoka is faced with while practicing judo.**

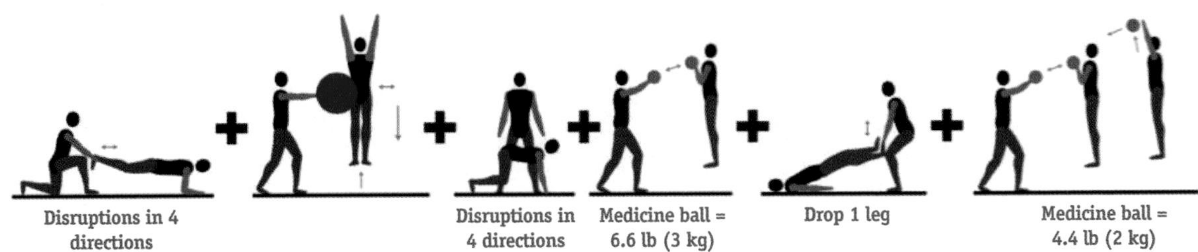

FOR INTERMEDIATE AND ADVANCED LEVELS ONLY

Hold for 20 sec per position. Be strict about back positioning. Do 2 or 3 sets. Recovery time: 1 min.

Judo-Specific Core-Strengthening Workouts

*LIFTING WEIGHTS IS NOT THE ONLY WAY TO INCREASE YOUR STRENGTH.
YOU CAN ALSO BECOME EXTREMELY STRONG
WITH EXERCISES THAT USE ONLY YOUR BODY WEIGHT.*

Judokas, who must constantly alternate between blocks and core movements, get thrown on their backs, or stretch their spines in every direction, can find classic core strengthening exercises—elbow planks, side planks, and so on—a little easy. Judokas strengthen their core naturally through their daily activity, but that is no reason for them not to make progress: All they need to do is adjust the difficulty of the exercises. Here are nine advanced exercises.

ESSENTIAL TECHNIQUE

- → Chest out, head lifted
- → Back flat, not curled
- → Hips in check, avoid back hyperextension, glutes tight
- → Stomach as flat as possible, abdominal muscles contracted
- → Pelvic floor contracted

1 STAR PUSH-UP

POSITION
From the usual push-up position, bend and then extend your arms. Return to the starting position and rotate so that you are balancing on one foot and one hand. Lift your other leg and arm in the air to form a star shape with your body. Repeat the move on the opposite side.

EXERCISE
Start with 3 sets, 3 reps per side. The ultimate goal is to reach 8 sets of 10. Recovery time: 45 sec.

PROGRESSION
Place your supporting hand on a balance disc or a cushion to increase instability. The exercise will be harder, but you will also benefit from preventive shoulder work.

2 INVERTED PLANK

POSITION
With your feet balanced on an exercise ball, grasp the ends of a belt held by your training partner (as strongly as they can with their hands, or with their neck if they put the belt around it for support).

EXERCISE
The judoka tracks the time: He or she must accumulate 1 min and 30 sec in total, in one or several attempts. 1 to 3 sets.

PROGRESSION
Placing your feet on the sides of the exercise ball will increase instability, engage the adductors, which are very important—but often neglected—muscles for judokas (used in leg sweeps, *kouchi-gari*, ground grappling, etc.). Finally, the training partner can also provide instability by moving the belt slightly.

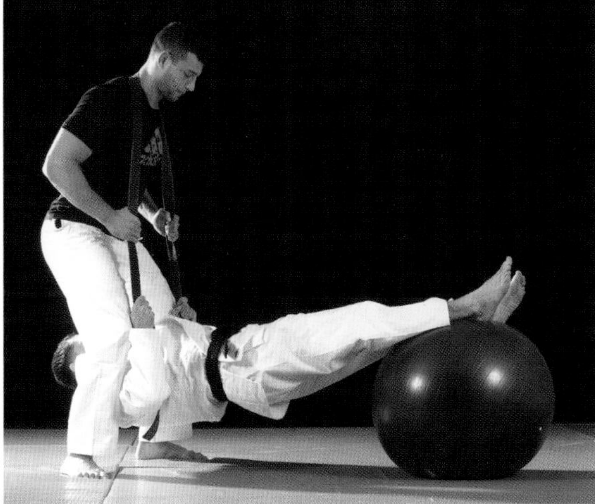

4 ROLL OUT THE STABILITY BALL

POSITION
Begin with your outstretched arms pushing down on the ball, then roll it ahead of you until you reach the plank position, before returning to the starting position.

EXERCISE
5 sets of 3 to 10 reps, depending on your level.

PROGRESSION
Same thing, but with a basketball or medicine ball.

3 CORE BUILDING WITH RANDOM SUPPORT

POSITION
Get into a core-strengthening position with both of your heels in the hands of your training partner. Uke randomly removes one hand, removing Tori's support; despite this, Tori must keep his or her feet aligned.

EXERCISE
Do 3 to 5 sets of 20 to 45 sec of effort. Recovery time: 15 to 30 sec.

PROGRESSION
Perform the same exercise on a Bosu ball, TerraCore balance trainer, or stability ball.

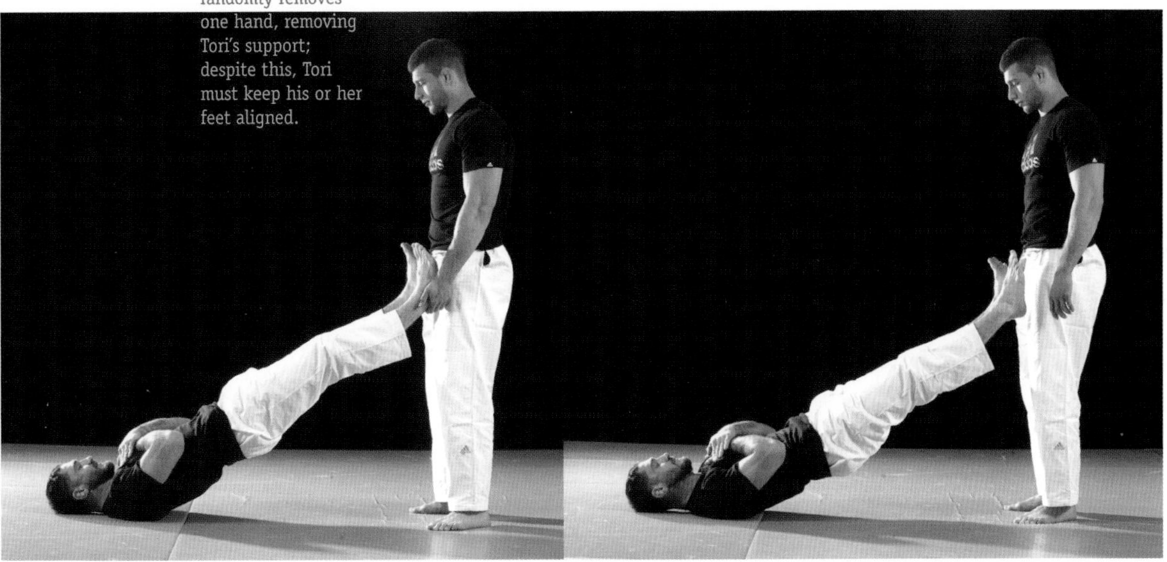

5 BALL BALANCE

POSITION
Place both knees on an exercise ball, with hips completely extended, and then hold a medicine ball above your head and maintain your balance.

EXERCISE
Do 3 to 5 sets of 30 to 45 sec. Recovery time: 30 sec.

PROGRESSION
Ask a training partner to provide instability by moving the exercise ball or medicine ball. If this exercise is too much of a struggle, do not use the medicine ball.

6 CRAWL WITH PULLING AND ROTATION

POSITION
Begin on all fours. Every two steps pull the dumbbells to your ribs and then rotate your body so one arm is in the air.

EXERCISE
Do 3 or 4 sets of 10 reps. Recovery time: 30 sec.

PROGRESSION
Adjust the dumbbell weight or number of repetitions or sets.

7

BRIDGE

POSITION

Intense abdominal, gluteal, and hamstring strengthening can be easily achieved with a bridge exercise, maintaining your hips at maximum extension.

EXERCISE

Do 3 or 4 sets of 30 to 45 sec. Recovery time: 30 sec.

PROGRESSION

If, even after maximum extension of the hips for over 45 seconds, the exercise still feels easy, extending a leg should provide a better challenge.

8

SANTA

POSITION

With a suspension strap or two judo belts tied together, grasp the same end with both hands, pull with a slight rotation of the hips while keeping your spine in good alignment, and rotate completely around the grip.

EXERCISE

Do 3 or 4 sets of 6 to 10 reps (counting both sides). Recovery time: 1 min.

PROGRESSION

Increase the number of repetitions or sets.

9

SUPERMAN

POSITION

With two judo belts tied together or, better still, with suspension straps, begin in a squatting position, with your arms close to your body. Push diagonally upward with your legs until your body is completely stretched out and you are on tiptoe. Hold this position for 3 seconds before lowering your body back down.

EXERCISE

Do 3 or 4 sets of 6 to 10 reps. Recovery time: 30 sec.

PROGRESSION

Adjust the number of sets or repetitions.

Increasing Your Strength

LEARN ABOUT THE MAJOR PRINCIPLES TO DEVELOP THE SACRED ATTRIBUTE OF STRENGTH, AND WHICH TECHNIQUES ARE THE MOST EFFECTIVE FOR JUDOKAS.

The judo community has always been excited about methods that enable us to become more physically strong—sometimes at the risk of forgetting the essence of the sport—while the other half has tended to stick with the trusty inner tube for *uchi-komi* practice. My experience in judo and as a physical trainer encourages me to avoid falling into either of these traps. Yes, of course, strength is a fundamental asset for competitors, but it is no substitute for the art of judo, which is key. Strength does contribute, however, to the expression of the sport during competitions, while increasingly precise methods allow us to practice judo in a better manner.

Conversely, believing that being able to push hard will spare you from having to study closely the balancing act that is judo is just an illusion. This is another dangerous trap, because the transfer of strength you gain from exercises in the weight room is not automatic. It is specific to each type of contraction, movement, angle, and rhythm; being great at pull-ups and squats is not always enough to improve your *hiki-dashi*!

MAJOR RULES FOR JUDO

→ Only use polyarticular movements (those that involve many joints), which require a certain complexity of movement.

→ Only work in training situations that you have mastered perfectly.

→ Only do strength work after you have done a preparatory cycle of physical, psychological, and technical work so that you can gradually increase the weight.

→ Be sure that you recover completely between sets.

→ Always work with a spotter to avoid getting stuck under the weights.

What Are We Trying to Do?

In concrete terms, improving someone's strength involves making them capable of producing greater muscle tension. The choice of method comes down to the use of additional weight that allows us to put the muscle under maximum tension.

All of the suggested methods essentially aim to influence the nervous system: Muscles are made up of fibers that contract when they get a signal from the nervous system. In simpler terms, the idea is to stimulate more muscles, more quickly, and more intensely. This partly explains why hypertrophy (an increase in muscle volume or mass) is not so prevalent. Thus, there should be no concerns about weight management during this period.

What We Most Often Do

Those of you who have done some strength-training exercises in the past will be familiar with the concept of short sets (fewer than 5 repetitions) with a longer recovery period (4-5 minutes), often done in 3 x 3, 4 x 4, or 5 x 5 to develop strength.

For example: Do 4 consecutive sets of 4 reps with the heaviest weight possible (one that you can lift 4 times but not 5). Total recovery time between the sets: 5 min.

The setup is very simple. After a general warm-up of moderate intensity lasting around 10 minutes, featuring an exercise bike, a jump rope, or some judo exercises, you do a specific warm-up to gradually prepare you for lifting heavy weights. This may consist, for example, of 10 reps, then 8 with heavier weights, then 6 with even heavier weights (the idea being that you eventually reach your near limit at 6), with 2 to 3 minutes of rest. It can also be interesting to do some active dynamic stretching (stretch-contract-move) before your warm-ups.

While this approach is very effective (especially for the first few months of training), its limitations quickly become apparent when you try to meet, in a specific manner, the varied demands of judo. Moreover, judokas often find themselves quickly impeded by a strength barrier that they have to get around using other methods. Here are some of my favorites, which can be adapted to a number of situations.

Three-Month Program

Dozens of sequences are feasible, more or less adapted to the level of performance in judo as in strength training. Remember that a balanced program, which should be simple and functional, has three phases.

PHASE 1 Technical learning stage, gradually increasing weight, and controlled muscle hypertrophy. This phase often lasts 4 weeks (note: from 6 weeks onward, the risk of lasting hypertrophy increases) and is characterized by long sets at a slow rhythm that decreases as the weight increases (10 repetitions, then 8, then 6, with increasingly heavier weights). Recovery time is short so as to saturate the muscle.

PHASE 2 Strength building. This stage can last 5 weeks, with a light week in the middle. Any of the exercises that follow can be used.

PHASE 3 Improving explosive strength. This phase, which should be reserved for the run-up to competitions, features short sets (fewer than 6 repetitions), average weight (60 percent of the maximum), and maximum speed. Here, you can use the static-dynamic method.

TRAINING PROGRAM EXAMPLE

1. Hypertrophy-strength endurance with sets of 8 to 10 reps *(4 weeks)*
2. Triangle pyramid *(2 weeks)*
3. Ascending pyramid *(3 weeks)*
4. Static-dynamic *(3 weeks)*

When Should We Do Strength Training?

Strength training can be scheduled at any time during the week, as long as recovery time guidelines are respected: 48 to 72 hours for maximum weight. So, it is possible to fit in up to four strength sessions each week, even though you can obtain excellent results from three. In fact, significant progress can be made from just two sessions—a schedule that may be more manageable.

When Should We Stretch?

Stretching remains a matter of intense debate. I'll come back to it in the section on stretching for judo, but it is worth noting here that stretching is not an effective way to prepare muscles for strength or power work. Clearly, it is not useful, physiologically speaking, to stretch before a strength-training workout. On the other hand, regaining as much mobility as possible (including controlled active flexibility) is, of course, essential. Warm-up stretching is therefore always combined with movement. It is important to remember that, after a set, and right at the end of a workout, the muscles are still contracted. Muscle fibers are composed of microfilaments, which are attached to each other via bridges. These are what produce muscle contractions. Stretching after a set can tear these bridges, creating microscopic lesions that cause muscle soreness. It is best to wait 10 minutes or so after the session before doing any stretching. Finally, it is possible to stretch the antagonist muscle chain (the opposing chain that extends when the primary chain contracts) between sets to calm parasitical muscle contractions and to help during the exercise. Thus, it is important to stretch the pectoral muscles during the recovery period between pull-ups (back and biceps).

At What Age Should We Start Strength Training?

Today we know that a youngster aged 12 to 15 can start working with a reasonable amount of additional weight. Such a technical apprenticeship would enable them to be a step ahead when they reach 16, 17, or 18. However, it is questionable whether spending so much time in the weight room is a sound idea at that age. In fact, the moves available to these youngsters are lacking in complexity compared to those prevalent in judo, in which development is crucial during this period. The judoka who knows how to perform *hiki-dashi* can easily do a bench press. The time spent in the weight room is time lost on the judo mat and is much more difficult to regain later on. Taking all this into consideration, I believe that there is no rush to introduce 12- to 15-year-olds to weights. Judo should come first!

Descending Pyramid

Very suitable if you want to determine your maximum. What's more, this type of workout is particularly relevant to judo because it enables you, once you have achieved your maximum, to extend the work but with decreased intensity and longer sets (maximum strength endurance, which is very important in the middle of a bout). It is possible to work on up to two muscle groups per workout.

Suggested exercise: plank pull or vertical pull

PLANK PULL

VERTICAL PULL

NONJUDO EXAMPLE

→ **1** x **max** *(5 min of recovery time)*
→ **2** x **max** for 2 reps *(5 min of recovery time between each set)*
→ 1-3 sets of **3** x **max** for 3 reps *(5 min of recovery time between each set)*

EXAMPLE (COMBINED WITH JUDO)

→ **1** x **max** *(5 min of recovery time)*
→ **2** x **max** for 2 reps *(5 min of recovery time)*
→ **3** x **max** for 3 reps *(5 min of recovery time)*
→ 2 sets of 5 *nage-komi* with resistance for 5 sec maximum *(3 min of recovery time between each set)*. Ideally, the *nage-komi* should resemble the exercise used, but this is not vital (here we can use *harai-goshi)*.

Triangle Pyramid

More progressive than the previous method, this is more suitable for strength training beginners. However, as we spend more time at an intermediate phase before trying our hand at heavier weights, the maximum for one repetition is often not as high due to fatigue. This approximate maximum is the weak point of the method, which, on the flip side, brings us closer to a maximum strength endurance exercise.

Suggested exercise: squat

SQUAT

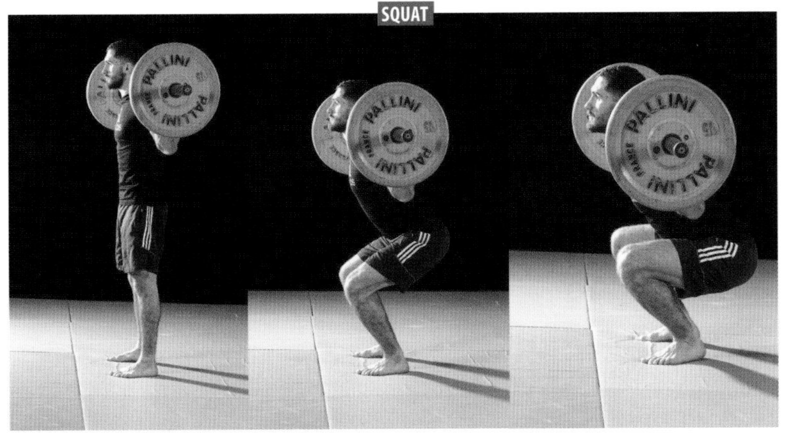

NONJUDO EXAMPLE

→ **3** x **max** for 3 reps *(5 min of recovery time)*
→ **2** x **max** for 2 reps *(5 min of recovery time)*
→ **1** x **max** for 1 rep *(5 min of recovery time)*
→ **1** x **max** for 1 rep *(5 min of recovery time)*
→ **2** x **max** for 2 reps *(5 min of recovery time)*
→ **3** x **max** for 3 reps (You can immediately start another training block, focusing on another muscle chain.)

EXAMPLE (COMBINED WITH JUDO)

→ **2** x **max** for 2 reps + 1 *nage-komi* with resistance for a maximum of 5 sec *(5 min of recovery time) + seoi-nage* throw
→ **2** x **max** for 2 reps *(5 min of recovery time)*
→ **1** x **max** for 1 rep *(5 min of recovery time)*
→ **1** x **max** for 1 rep *(5 min of recovery time)*
→ **2** x **max** for 2 reps *(5 min of recovery time)*
→ **2** x **max** for 2 reps + 1 *nage-komi* with resistance for a maximum of 5 sec.

BENCH PRESS

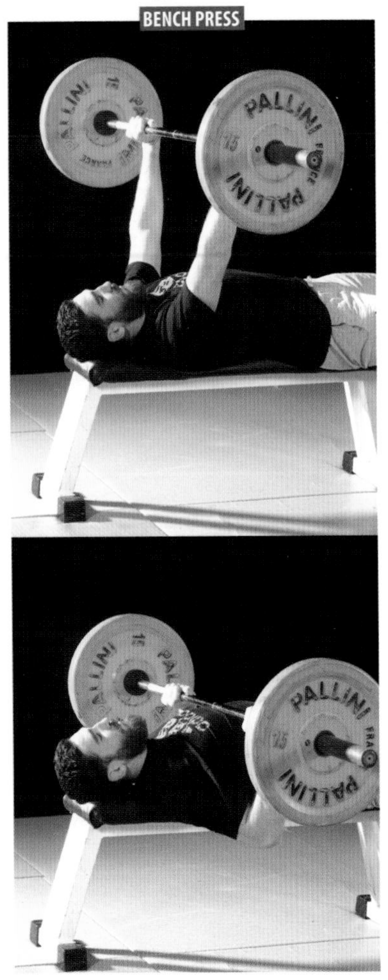

DEADLIFT

SNATCH

PUSH-UPS ON BENCH OR STEP

NONJUDO EXAMPLE

→ 4 **wide-grip bench press, max** for 4 reps *(1 min 30 sec of recovery time)*

→ **Bench push-ups** at maximum speed for 6 reps or **bench press** at 50 percent of maximum weight at maximum speed *(5 min of recovery time)*. Repeat 3 times. *Example:* For a **max for one** at 220 lb (100 kg): 4 x 4 at 198 lb (90 kg) per 6 reps at 110 lb (50 kg) or 6 bench push-ups at maximum speed.

→ 3 **deadlifts** x **max** for 3 reps *(30 sec of recovery time)*

→ 4 **deadlifts** at maximum speed at 130 lb (60 kg). **Other possible exercises:** bench jumps or hurdles for the legs, medicine ball throws or resistance band work for the upper body.

EXAMPLE (COMBINED WITH JUDO)

→ 3 snatches at 40 to 60 percent for 3 reps followed immediately by 4 *nage-komi (harai-goshi)* without resistance and at maximum speed

Alternating Weights

To generate maximum tension in the muscles, you can either opt for a very heavy weight or create as much speed as possible. For power, it's a bit of both. We are interested in maximum strength, so heavy weights are most important. Alternating heavy and light weights from one set to the next, or within the same set, enables you to do the following:

- Increase maximum strength
- Increase power
- Transfer strength gains directly to power
- Overcome the strength barrier that athletes sometimes encounter, suddenly liberating them from the resistance that slows them down, and thereby creating overspeed

Suggested exercises: wide grip bench press + deadlift or snatch

Static-Dynamic Training

What we are doing here is combining a static contraction (no movement), the intensity of which is necessary for strength development, with dynamic weight movement. In this second case, we are looking to accelerate the weight starting from a contracted position, either from a hold (strength tendency) or from a slight countermovement (power tendency). This method offers the dual advantage of maintaining previously acquired strength levels while developing explosive strength or the ability to produce a maximum level of strength in the shortest time possible. It is therefore highly recommended at the end of a preparatory cycle, particularly in the run-up to competitions. It is possible to work on up to two muscle groups per session.

Suggested exercises: horizontal pull or weighted pull-up

HORIZONTAL PULL

WEIGHTED PULL-UP

NONJUDO EXAMPLE

→ 6 x 6 reps at **60 percent of the max** with a 3 sec hold before maximum acceleration *(2 min of recovery time between sets)*. Vary the angles of your holds during the set.

EXAMPLE (COMBINED WITH JUDO)

→ 4 reps at **60 percent of the max** with a 3 sec hold before maximum acceleration. Follow with 2 or 3 *nage-komi* with a 3 sec maximum outside hold before an *uchi-mata* throw (Tori should try to throw Uke throughout the exercise, to the extent that when the resistance lessens, Tori accelerates immediately.) 6 sets *(2 min of recovery time between each set)*.

Repeating Maximum Effort

This final method is typical of an approach to maximum strength endurance. For judokas, the idea is to succeed in keeping their strength levels as high as possible despite fatigue. The principle is to start out with a max for 1, and without completely recovering, start again with a weight that is almost as heavy after 1 minute of rest. It is possible to work on both the upper and lower body in the same workout.

Suggested exercise: leg press

NONJUDO EXAMPLE

→ 2 sets of **5 x max** for 5 reps *(3 min of recovery time)*

→ Then 8 sets of **1 max**, decreasing the weight slightly each time, but always the maximum you can manage *(1 min of recovery time)*

EXAMPLE (COMBINED WITH JUDO)

→ 2 sets of **5 x max** for 5 reps *(3 min of recovery time)*

→ **Max for 1** *(1 min of recovery time)*

→ *Nage-komi (morote-seoi-nage)* with a heavier training partner resisting you *(1 min of recovery time)*. Alternate between **max for 1** and *nage-komi* 4 times, or 8 sets.

Alternating Your Training

*COACHES KNOW THAT TRAINING SHOULD BE VARIED.
A MORE MODERN, SUBTLE APPROACH INVOLVES ALTERNATING WORKOUTS.
HOW DOES IT WORK?*

Do you alternate heavy weights with lighter ones from one month to the next? What about during the same workout? Have you been using different muscle development methods depending on the training period? The cumulative effects of doing them successively in one set may surprise you. That is what alternating means: rotating content that is traditionally used at different periods (during major training phases) within a single session. Fun for the mind and effective for the body, it's a unique way to reproduce the varied conditions prevalent in judo and to move as close as possible toward optimum physical training. Here are four major categories of alternating training options.

Alternating Weight

The principle of combining two weight levels (heavy and light), which is very well known in strength training, is of particular interest in judo when it is applied to *uchi-komi*. Alternating the weight in a workout enables you to replicate the varied resistance encountered during a bout, as well as the consecutive technical adjustments (release, stance, and timing).

Note the following key points:

- Heavy opponent or weight, few repetitions, substantial recovery time: improvement in maximum strength
- Large range in weights used (difference between the heavy weight and the light weight): increase in power (strength and speed)
- High number of repetitions and little recovery time: enhancement of strength endurance
- Average range and resistance: can help the development of energy-related attributes of endurance

Possible Applications

HEAVY OR LIGHT WITH A TRAINING PARTNER slowing down *uchi-komi* (heavy work), or training partner who jumps to help out (light)

Examples

→ 1 set with an opponent slowing you down, and then 1 set with an opponent who jumps

→ 6 reps with an opponent slowing you down, and then 6 reps with an opponent who jumps

→ Alternate with each rep

HEAVY OR LIGHT WITH TWO TRAINING PARTNERS of different builds going back and forth

Variations: distance, training partners' weight

STRENGTH TRAINING/*uchi-komi* 1 set of heavy strength-training exercises (for example, a plank pull), immediately followed by 1 set of *uchi-komi* without resistance (light), while maintaining the same type of movement (pulling or pushing). In addition to developing power parameters, this technique facilitates the transfer of strength gains to competitive action.

Example

→ 8 reps at 70 to 80 percent of the max weight, then 10 *uchi-komi*

Alternating Method

All muscle chains are engaged when practicing judo, whether you are accelerating, slowing your opponent down, holding, or making single or continuous movements using varied levels of strength and frequency of movement. These combinations can be used to pursue a number of different objectives. Performing a long hold (isometric training) followed by a maximum acceleration maintains maximum strength and improves speed and explosive strength. Elastic strength work (plyometric training) is encouraged for enhancing speed and partly influences the effectiveness of launching attacks (action-reaction).

Possible Applications

ALTERNATING MOVEMENT/HOLDING IN *UCHI-KOMI*
(static-dynamic): A third training partner holds Uke by grasping around the waist. You can then alternate the maximum resistance phases (holding), followed by normal relaxation that allows you to do the movement at high speed.

Examples

→ 3 very quick reps. Hold for 3 to 5 sec on the fourth rep. The moment that Uke eases off, try to accelerate the movement as much as possible, ideally without regaining momentum. Repeat the sequence 4 to 6 times with 2 min of recovery time, maintaining your technical position

→ Hold for 3 to 5 sec on the first rep before maximum acceleration as in the previous exercise. Then, immediately repeat the hold-acceleration combo 5 times. Take 2 min to recover, still maintaining your technical position, before repeating the exercise 4 to 6 times

ALTERNATING A PLYOMETRIC EXERCISE AND *UCHI-KOMI*

Example

→ Jumping lunges on a step/*kouchi-gari* entry: 6 forward jumping lunges + 4 *kouchi-gari* entries at maximum speed. Take 2 to 3 min for complete recovery, maintaining your technical position

Variations

→ Vary the height of the jump and the step, work continuously on the same leg or alternate legs
→ Vary the frequency of movement

Alternating Context

To perform effectively, a judoka must constantly create—and deal with—the unpredictability of judo, in other words, the issues of balance and loss of balance. We can, of course, train while alternating between stability and instability. But there is a second alternating possibility, which focuses on the fatigue created in unstable situations. For a judoka who tends to tire more when an opponent unbalances them (indeed, when your level of alertness is elevated, your muscles are intensely engaged), training built on fatigue work is certainly useful. For example, muscles can be engaged before a set of *uchi-komi* (prefatigue) or after the set (postfatigue). The main objective of prefatigue work is strength endurance, and so the focus is on repeating moves that happen during a bout. Postfatigue work boosts balance when the muscles are saturated, improving resistance to your opponent's attacks after you have led a series of intense and demanding attacks yourself.

Whatever the objective, you should always use moves tailored to your level and goals.

Possible Applications

STABLE/ UNSTABLE BALANCE

(the number of repetitions can be varied from one move to the next)

Variations

→ Alternate between stability and instability from one set to the next

→ Move from one supporting leg to the other in one motion (for example, stable right foot, unstable left foot)

PRE- AND POST-FATIGUE

Examples

→ 8 to 10 prefatigue exercises (or 15 to 20 sec), 8 to 10 *uchi-komi*. Take less than a minute's recovery time. 6 to 8 sets.

→ 15-20 *uchi-komi*, then 20 sec of postfatigue. Take less than a minute's recovery time. 6 to 8 sets.

Alternating Speed

Shifting, acceleration, timing, and launch or, on the flip side, holding, slowing down, and containment are the keys to effective judo. Here, more than anywhere else, judo's specific features justify the notion of alternating speed training, which additionally has a lot to offer from an instructional point of view.

Once more, the objectives are different depending on the recovery time, intensity, and amount of work.

→ Complete recovery, maximum speed repeated over several exercises: frequency of movement (velocity) work

→ Complete recovery, several slow repetitions followed by a repetition at absolute speed: speed work for an isolated exercise

→ Incomplete recovery, alternating between near-maximum speed, but repeated, and average speed: speed endurance work

As always, any loss of proper form should signal the end of the set. In fact, as well as being harmful to your judo know-how, it is a sign that you are no longer working on speed but rather on lactic acid endurance. The sets should be short and done with maximum intensity and complete recovery time.

Possible Applications

ALTERNATING SLOW AND FAST MOVEMENTS DURING *UCHI-KOMI*

The idea here is to vary the speed of repeated movements.

1 SLOW SET/1 FAST SET: alternating the types of sets. This method allows for technical corrections.

Examples

→ 15 slow reps, 1 min for adjustments, 15 fast reps, 2 min for adjustments, all done 4 to 6 times.

Start the set slowly but finish it fast: alternating within the same set. Here we're looking to transfer the quality of movement from the start of the set to the speed work.

→ 15 slow reps, 10 reps at maximum speed, 2 min for adjustments, all done 4 to 6 times.

Progressions

→ Pyramid: 1 slow set, 1 quick, 1 slow, allowing you to make new adjustments after the speed phase

Start of slow set, short bursts: speed work arises spontaneously in the middle of a slow exercise. For example, the coach may suddenly order you to accelerate, which recreates the uncertainty of a judo bout, the importance of taking in information, and so on.

Further Progressions

→ Vary the signal: coach's order, sign from training partner (loss of balance, shifting).

→ Vary the exercise: throwing practice, move from *kakari-geiko* to *randori*, from slow *uchi-komi* on the move to maximum-frequency *uchi-komi* on the spot.

DON'T FORGET

→ A poorly mastered technical skill will be jeopardized by intensity and speed. Practicing a skill badly is detrimental to your chances of properly mastering it.

→ The impossibility of exactly calibrating the weights makes this type of work less accurate than a classic strength-training workout. Here too, you have to know when to vary things.

Proprioceptive Bench Press

THERE ARE SOME CLASSIC EXERCISES IN STRENGTH TRAINING. BUT IN TRAINING, THE OLD WAYS ARE NOT ALWAYS THE BEST. IN KEEPING WITH MY OTHER UPDATES, I SUGGEST A SMALL REVOLUTION: THE PROPRIOCEPTIVE BENCH PRESS.

Strength can be temperamental. Depending on the chosen working angles, specific strength transfers will not occur across the entire movement. Because progress depends in part on the exercises performed, you won't feel it in every aspect of your judo skill set. Depending on the direction of the chosen movement, the increased strength will not serve all of your technique. Even beyond this risk of ineffectiveness, repeating a poor exercise with a heavy weight significantly increases the risk of injury. That is why it is so hard to work specifically on this super important muscle quality on a *tatami*. The work carried out in the weight room in this area is often fragmented and inappropriate, or even, at worst, detrimental to the practice of judo.

That is why the bench press maintains its dominant position as a foundational exercise. It is, without a doubt, the most common strength-training move in the gym. Modern, muscular judokas have not been able to resist the temptation to build their muscle capacity to be able to push an opponent away or keep an opponent at a distance. However, the exercise is far from perfect: it lacks specific focus, and also holds the record for causing the most chronic inflammation in the shoulder.

What limits this exercise the most is its setup. It is most often done on a wide bench where the shoulder blades are locked in place by the pressure, and this brings the rotator cuff into play more often than is reasonable. I'd like to help you make your strength training more effective and less risky by putting my own spin on the classic bench press.

BENCH PRESS WITH RESISTANCE BAND

In terms of proprioception, this provides added value. Hands should be shoulder-width apart; bring the bar down to the bottom of your chest as you lower it.

Proprioceptive Bench Press

The problem with strengthening the muscles in the abdominal area is principally anatomical. While looking for a way to make the bench press safer and more specific, I found that using a resistance band as well as a much narrower bench (or even an exercise ball) helped to reduce the effects of the two main drawbacks. I call this exercise the proprioceptive bench press.

→ The shoulder blades, given more freedom on a narrower bench, will decrease conflicting tension in the shoulder.

→ The advantages of using a resistance band are threefold: The instability that it generates brings the bench press closer to the pushing action of a judoka, who must constantly adapt to the unpredictable reactions of their opponent. The backward pulling action generated by the band activates the rotator cuff to help stabilize the shoulders (which is, in fact, its basic role). Finally, this artificial increase in difficulty makes the exercise effective at a lower weight, thereby further reducing your body's risk of injury.

→ Alternating (two arms in the air, bring one down and then the other) and alternative (when one arms drops, the other lifts) bench presses makes the movement more specific by dissociating the left arm from the right arm. In this case, you should use two dumbbells.

→ At the same time, I would recommend a closer grip than usual. This may limit your performance, but it will largely protect your shoulders (by limiting the opening of the joint) and will bring you close to the specific pushing angle in judo.

Bench Press on an Exercise Ball

When we talk about prevention and effectiveness, exercise balls will always be part of the conversation. And for good reason: No other tool engages the deep abdominal muscles and postural muscles as effectively or stresses the neuromuscular structures as much. This is due to precarious balance (if the move is initially mastered in a stable environment), which enables you to increase the effectiveness of the work, as well as its preventive benefits.*

→ Control of the hips by the abdominal muscles, lumbar muscles, and deep muscles is strongly increased during this exercise.
→ The coordination aspect is much more interesting, because you can slightly adjust your posture during the exercise.
→ By varying your posture, you can also change your pushing angle, and consequently diversify the work through countless different angles between an incline press and a classic bench press position.
→ Shoulder blade mobility is not a problem here, because the flexible exercise ball adapts to provide the shoulders with the mobility they require. The same is true for the curve of the spine, which is hugged by the ball.

**The exercise with dumbbells is an alternative that dissociates the work and makes it even more specific.*

BASIC PROGRAM

A. **3 sets of 10 to 20 push-ups**
B. **2 sets of 10 exercise ball presses *(maximum weight for 10 reps)***
C. **2 sets of 5 presses with a band *(maximum weight for 5 reps)***
D. **1 set of 5 presses with a band *(maximum weight for 5 reps)***

→ 1 min 30 sec of rest between each set

Don't forget to switch things up! This program is focused mainly on increasing strength. Within a few weeks, you'll be able to advance to a more intense program with 1 to 3 heavier repetitions.

Mobile bench press on an exercise ball with dumbbells. This is an interesting variation of the bench press with a bar. With your knees bent and shoulder blades in contact with the ball, bridge your body upward with your hips, while extending your weights with a rotation (returning to a collar grip position).

Mobile bench press on an exercise ball with a bar.

Tailored Squats

A MAINSTAY IN WEIGHT ROOMS, THE SQUAT IS A FORMIDABLE WEAPON IN A JUDOKA'S PHYSICAL TRAINING. THIS IS WHY.

One of the maxims you hear in weight rooms goes "if you don't do squats, you're not really doing strength training." This shows the importance of this leg-bending move in the world of physical training.

Of all strength exercises, the squat is the one that engages the highest number of muscles (over 250 of them), including some of the most important ones: as a priority, the quadriceps (rectus femoris, vastus lateralis, vastus medialis, and vastus intermedius) and glutes (gluteus minimus, gluteus medius, gluteus maximus, and tensor fascia latae), as well as the spinal muscles. The hamstrings (semitendinosus, semimembranosus, and biceps femoris) and the calves (gastrocnemius and soleus), which perform a stabilizing role, are also involved.

We shouldn't forget the role of core strengthening in the mid to lower back and abdominal area, because, although the squat is encouraged for strengthening the lower limbs, it is also a wonderful exercise for dynamic core strengthening and for strengthening the pelvic, abdominal, and shoulder regions. This is why it very quickly became part of judokas' training arsenal—this decision is even more judicious when we consider that the exercise is particularly specific to a fighter's muscle-related needs.

Indeed, the squat allows you to work on leg bends and extensions with an additional weight on your back, mirroring, in a simplified fashion, one of the stages of a judo throw. This stylization of movement allows you to increase the exercise's intensity (by increasing the speed or weight, for example), as well as to vary the rhythm and working angles. All of this enables you to refine the exercise and make it more specific to judo.

Furthermore, the legs are intensely involved in this exercise, releasing strength and maintaining balance. This makes the squat a fundamental exercise for strengthening *kumikata*: those who understand judo well know that putting strong pressure on your opponent comes first and foremost from a solid foundation, even when in motion. It could be said that, generally speaking, judo starts with the quality of your stance and with squat work that complements your judo practice.

How Do We Make It Safe While Making It More Specific?

While the joints in the ankle, hips, and knees are anatomically designed to facilitate the squatting position, doing it with twice your own body weight on your shoulders doesn't exactly make sense. The tension in the low back and joints (knees) is such that I would not recommend it at all. What's more, as judo is organized by weight categories, lifting weights that are rather different from your own body weight at such a straight angle is not all that relevant. Finally, the majority of gains in strength are obtained from partial bending of the legs (half squat), which is a move that is very specific to most of *tai-sabaki* (body management).

To make a squat safer, aside from using the right technical positioning, it will not come as a surprise that we aim to avoid placing too much tension on the low back and neck with overly heavy weights, and that we limit the time spent doing complete leg bends. The full squat is ideal when using warm-up bars, but I would advise you to limit yourself to the half squat afterward.

It's worth noting that, while a very heavy half squat may be necessary to increase maximum strength, it is risky for the back and knees to do it for too long, especially since it is not really specific to the needs of a judoka, who has to deal with his or her own body weight.

One solution to the problem of increasing muscle recruitment without upping the weight is to introduce instability or to control posture. Here are some exercises you can use.

Important Pointers

The squat is a very comprehensive move and is therefore extremely technical. I would recommend that you take your time mastering it before adding weight to the bar. Additionally, don't hesitate to strengthen the relevant muscles before throwing yourself into it. An initial cycle of strengthening for the low back and shoulders would be sensible.

For example, you can do the following session for 4 weeks, taking 1 min to 1 min 30 sec to recover between sets.

→ 3 x 12 shoulder press

→ 3 x 12 leg press

→ 3 x 15 crunches on an adjustable workout bench

Basic Squat Technique

→ Keep the back straight throughout the exercise (don't round your back).
→ Focus your eyes on a point above the horizon to keep your head up.
→ Spread your legs.
→ Rest the bar on the back of your shoulders.
→ Stick your chest out, pull your elbows back.
→ Place your feet at an angle resembling the hands of a watch set to 10:10.
→ Your knees should stay in line with your toes but should go beyond them.

Safety

Don't forget to take these precautions:
→ Use pins to lock in the weights.
→ Make sure you have one or two spotters with you in case you need help.
→ Warm up thoroughly beforehand.

Make Progress in Squats in 8 Weeks

1 or 2 sessions per week

BLOCK 1 (2 WEEKS)

→ **Deep squat, empty bar: 2 sets of 10 reps**

→ **Single-leg squat, body weight: 2 sets of 10 reps per leg**

→ **Barbell front squat: 5 sets of 15 slow and controlled reps**

1 min of recovery time

BLOCK 2 (2 WEEKS)

→ **Squat with bar overhead: 2 sets of 10 reps**

→ **Single-leg squat holding a dumbbell in the opposite hand: 2 sets of 10 reps per leg**

→ **Squat at tempo, bar behind your back: 6 sets of 6 reps**

2 min of recovery time

BLOCK 3 (2 WEEKS)

→ **Squat with bar overhead: 2 sets of 6 to 8 reps with an empty bar**

→ **Unbalanced squat: 2 sets of 10 reps**

→ **Normal squat: 4 sets of 4 maximum reps**

5 min of recovery time

BLOCK 4 (2 WEEKS)

→ **Single-leg squat holding a dumbbell in the opposite hand: 2 sets of 10 reps per leg**

→ **Unbalanced squat: 2 sets of 10 reps**

→ **Squat with a hold during the ascent: 4 sets of 6 reps at 50 percent of maximum weight**

2 min of recovery time

→ **Unbalanced squat: 2 sets of 6 reps at 50 percent of maximum weight**

1 min 30 sec of recovery time

Barbell Front Squat

This exercise is especially suited for beginners, forcing them to keep their backs straight throughout the movement so they don't drop the barbell in front of them. Any athlete nursing a back or shoulder injury can use this exercise to replace the traditional squat. It is not appropriate for heavy weights, so I would recommend it if you are looking to increase your strength endurance or gain muscle mass.

EXAMPLE TO GAIN STRENGTH ENDURANCE

→ 5 sets of 15 slow and controlled reps.

EXAMPLE TO GAIN MUSCLE MASS

→ 4 sets of 8 reps (heaviest weight possible for 8 reps). Control the weight as you lower it and accelerate the weight as you lift up.

Squat Press With Dumbbells

One of the specific features of judo is the way in which the muscle chains work: the upper and lower parts of the body always work together. Also, since judokas use their arms asynchronously (one arm pushing while the other pulls) it is appropriate to use dumbbells for this exercise.

EXAMPLE TO GAIN POWER

→ Jump squat with light dumbbells.
6 sets of 6 reps with 2 min of rest.

EXAMPLE TO GAIN STRENGTH ENDURANCE

→ 4 x 8-12 reps with 1 min to 1 min 30 sec of rest.

Unbalanced Squat

By using a rather light weight, it is possible to create an imbalance that makes postural adjustments more difficult for an athlete to execute. Enabling you to assess and—if need be—correct the athlete's side-to-side stability, I would recommend this exercise at the end of the warm-up, with 2 sets of 10 reps on each side, including 1 minute of rest.

Squat With Bar Above Head

This exercise is not directly specific to judo, but is nevertheless worthwhile, particularly for strengthening the core and the shoulders, as well as the muscles in the back. Not suitable for excessive weight, I would recommend it during a warm-up with an empty bar or light weights, in sets of 8 to 10 reps.

TECHNIQUE IS VERY IMPORTANT

- → **Keep your head up (focus on a point above the horizon).**
- → **Stick your chest out.**
- → **Use a wide grip, with the bar slightly behind your head (the chest muscles should be extremely stretched).**

Unstable Squat

Indirectly specific to judo, this exercise remains useful, especially because it helps you to strengthen the core and the shoulders, as well as the back muscles. Not suitable for excessive weight, I would recommend it for a warm-up with an empty bar or with light weights, in sets of 8 to 10 reps.

VARIATIONS

RHYTHM SQUATS

Using rhythm allows you to stimulate muscle contractions differently and thereby improve the quality. Since judo puts your muscles into a wide variety of situations, alternating the rhythm of the squats greatly lends itself to this characteristic.

Strength example
4 sets of 6 reps at a controlled tempo as you descend and then dynamic as you lift up. Rest for 2 minutes between each set.

Strength endurance example
Light weights (30 percent of the maximum) and regular tempo (the same as you descend and as you lift up), 10 sets of 30 sec of effort and 30 sec of recovery.

SQUATS WITH HOLDS

Introducing holds in the middle of a squat or leg extension has many advantages. First of all, gains in strength depend on the working angles and the types of contractions; exploring them successively will only improve your chances of transfer. The hold causes increased recruitment that you can use to wake up your muscles before using them in more dynamic work or saturating them through endurance work.

Dynamic example
Squat with hold on the way up. 4 sets of 6 reps at 50 percent of the maximum weight with 2 minutes of rest. Squat and then hold for 3 sec as you rise up. After the hold, accelerate as much as possible for the remaining part of the ascent.

Strength endurance example
Hold for 5 sec as you squat down. With a weight representing 50 percent of the maximum, descend and hold before you reach the end of your squat. 6 sets of 8 reps will be sufficient to improve the specific strength endurance in the legs and bring about a moderate increase in muscle mass. Do not rest for longer than 1 minute.

Single-Leg Squat

Although judo is one of the few sports that works every muscle group in the body, every athlete always has one side that is stronger than the other. So it is important to rebalance as much as possible so as to

→ avoid injuries related to the weaker side,
→ be able to defend both sides with equal effectiveness, and
→ improve coordination and general mobility.

TECHNIQUE IS VERY IMPORTANT

This exercise is not suitable for maximum weight, so I recommend that you do it at the start of your warm-up by doing 2 sets of 10 reps per leg.

Make sure to always start with your weakest leg because it will tire more quickly than the other leg. This precaution will help prevent the imbalance from getting worse by systematically doing 10 reps for the strong leg and only 8 for the weaker one.

Note: When nursing an injured leg, judokas tend to perform this exercise with their healthy leg so as not to lose any time. This is a mistake that can actually have the opposite effect, slowing progress and creating an imbalance that weakens the leg even further.

Pulling Strength

THE KEY TO IMPROVING YOUR THROWS IS OFTEN TO IMPROVE YOUR ATTACK PREPARATION. BEING ABLE TO COUNT ON SIGNIFICANT PULLING STRENGTH CAN THEREFORE PLAY A DECISIVE ROLE.

People often say that judo is more of a pulling sport than a pushing sport. However, in practice, in *randori*, though pushing away and controlling distance control are essential, there are a number of intense actions that involve pulling.

This is doubtless the reason why advanced judokas often have completely disproportionate strength ratios between pulling and pushing, even though they tend to negate this imbalance by the intensive (and debatable) use of the bench press. Having good pulling strength means that your back muscles (principally the trapezius, rhomboid, teres major, and latissimus dorsi muscles), and arm muscles (biceps, brachialis, brachioradialis, and even the pronator teres muscles) work together effectively.

Strength transfers do not occur automatically from muscle development work to judo, and pull-ups are not always sufficient to enable you to pull more strongly than your opponent during a bout. Bearing in mind that strength transfers have more to do with the way you train, I'd like to give you some pointers to make your pulling-related training more specific and more effective.

1 VARY THE WORKING ANGLES

The first element to consider is the angle used in the exercise. As far as pull-ups are concerned, the angle can be open for a normal pull-up, average in a horizontal pull-up, and closed in an inverted pull-up. Generally, strength transfers are limited to the working angle; when you do traditional pull-ups, you don't necessarily improve your horizontal pulling strength. It is therefore essential to introduce variety.

From an anthropometric point of view, this parameter is also important. Let's take the example of fighters who are very tall for their weight category. They will have fewer open angles to deal with and the specific work they'll need to do will be mainly focused on average- and closed-angle exercises.

OPEN

AVERAGE

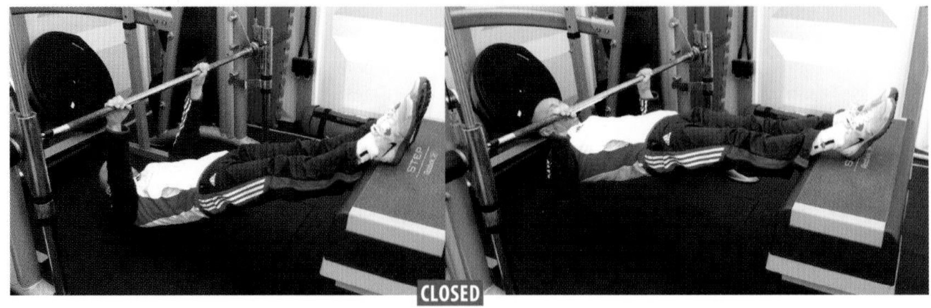

CLOSED

2

VARY THE GRIP

Since pulling strength comes from strength in the back, arms, hands, or all three at the same time, it is possible to manage the involvement of your grip. To do this, you can change the size of the bar from normal (traditional bar, with traditional grip), which enables you to target the back and upper arms, to thick (bar with a large diameter or thickness, like Fat Gripz), with which you can work the muscles in the hands and forearms. A third possibility is to use towels, judo jackets or parts of jackets, or specialized equipment (such as the Dragao Gis grip trainer), to reproduce judo-specific pulling. Since pulling also entails using different arm positions, you should vary your grip on the bar from narrow to wide, whether you are using a pronated or a supinated grip. This way you can focus the work more on the biceps, forearms, or back muscles, depending on your setup.

NARROW

AVERAGE

WIDE

AVERAGE

THICK

SPECIFIC

3

VARY THE COMPLEXITY OF THE WORK

I've already stressed the fact that the more specific the work is, the more difficult it is to control its intensity. This is why there is a continuum between very intense strengthening localized in the muscle chain used for pulling and the type of complex pulling exercises that are more transferable to judo, but less accurate in terms of weight calibration. Pulling focused on the upper body (plank pull or horizontal pull), highly suitable for maximum strength work or power work, will not, therefore, have the same value as a pulling exercise with your feet planted (pulling while leaning forward or pulling vertically), since this can be tailored to any objective but does not have as much intensity as an isolated pull and is not as transferable as a specific pull. The absolute level of complexity can be found in pulling exercises such as the clean-and-jerk, which is particularly well suited to power work, or *hiki-dashi,* suitable for power or strength endurance work.

ISOLATED PULL

PULL WITH FEET PLANTED

COMPLEX PULLS (WEIGHT LIFTING OR JUDO-SPECIFIC)

ELASTIC

INERTIAL

4

VARY THE TYPE OF RESISTANCE

The last element to consider is the type of resistance you'll have to face during a bout. Among the different kinds of resistance, there are two that should be of particular interest to judokas. The first is when an opponent resists being unbalanced as much as possible until they finally give in: this is elastic resistance. The more force we apply, the more the intensity of the resistance amplifies, until a breaking point is reached, such as a throw. It's possible to reproduce this situation with the help of a resistance band. The second type of resistance is usually referred to as inertial. This is the resistance we must overcome in a weight lifting exercise. In this scenario, resistance is high at the beginning of the exercise, but it decreases once the object is moving. In judo, this occurs when you attempt to move your opponent to make him or her lose balance. You feel the resistance lessen and disappear as you throw the opponent. It is, of course, possible—even advisable—to mix these two types of resistance to get as close as possible to the reality of judo.

MIXED EXAMPLE: PERFECT PULL-UP AND PULL-UP WITH A BAND

Suggested 6-Week Program

(once or twice a week after a session or tailored warm-up)

WEEKS 1 AND 2

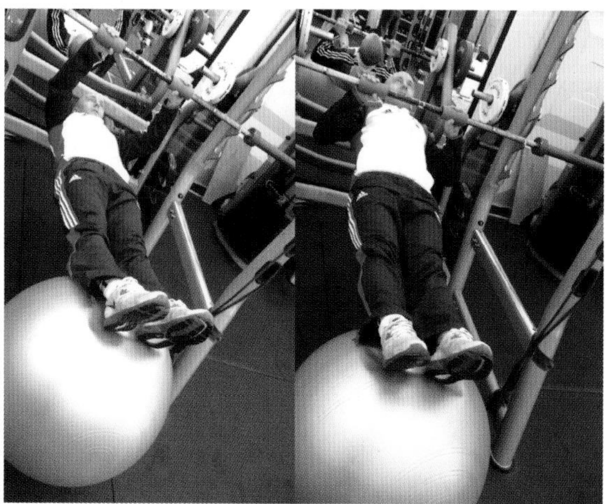

HORIZONTAL PULL WITH FEET ON AN EXERCISE BALL
3 x 8 reps with 1 min of rest

VERTICAL PULL LEANING FORWARD OVER BAR
3 x 4 reps with 3 min of rest

PULL-UPS WITH TOWELS OR GRIP TRAINERS
3 x as many pull-ups as possible

***HIKI-DASHI* WITH A TRAINING PARTNER WHO TRIES TO SLOW YOU DOWN**
3 x 8 reps with 1 min of rest

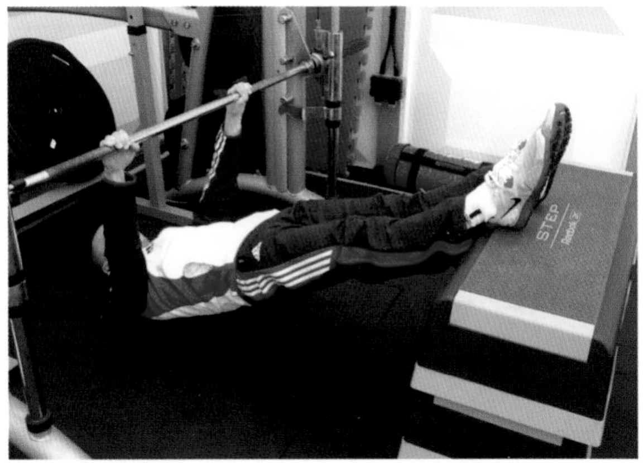

INVERTED PULL-UP
(ideally with thick grips)
2 x 8 reps with 1 min of rest

VERTICAL PULL LEANING FORWARD OVER BAR
3 x 4 reps with 3 min of rest

PLANK PULL
3 x max for 3 with 5 min of rest

***HIKI-DASHI* AND THROWS**
3 x 6 with 1 min of rest

KEY POINTERS FOR MOST PULLING EXERCISES

→ Keep your back straight, maintain your posture throughout the move.

→ Stick out your chest, lift your head, keep your chin up.

→ At the start of the move, pull your shoulders back and squeeze your shoulder blades together.

WEEKS 5 AND 6

PERFECT PULL-UPS
3 x 6 reps

3 PULL-UPS SLOWED DOWN BY A RESISTANCE BAND, 30 SEC RECOVERY TIME, THEN PULL-UPS AT MAXIMUM SPEED
(Clap your hands if possible; use a resistance band if it's too difficult): **3 times with 3 min recovery time**

3 PLANK PULLS AT 80 PERCENT OF THE MAX WEIGHT
30 sec recovery time, then 6 pulls with a resistance band at maximum speed: 3 times with 3 min recovery time

4 *HIKI-DASHI* WITH A TRAINING PARTNER SLOWING YOU DOWN, IMMEDIATELY FOLLOWED BY 4 *HIKI-DASHI* WITH A TRAINING PARTNER WHO JUMPS
3 times with 1 min recovery time

Improving Kumikata

KNOWING HOW TO DEFEND YOURSELF FROM OPPONENTS' GRIPS AND ESTABLISH A DOMINANT GUARD IS ONE OF THE KEYS TO SUCCESS IN COMPETITIVE JUDO. TAKE NOTE OF THREE OF THE CRUCIAL POINTS NECESSARY TO DEVELOP YOUR KUMIKATA EFFECTIVELY.

Part of *randori* (free practice), *kumikata* (gripping methods) has become a key battle in terms of grasping the kimono and performing well during a competitive bout. While improving technical aspects such as approach, speed, and visual coordination (which can be worked on via general or specific speed drills that involve practicing the moves with less aggressive opponents) is essential, establishing your *kumikata* increasingly depends on strength. A strong *kumikata* requires an effective pull chain, which can be achieved by strengthening the forearms, back, and biceps.

Additionally, those who have worked on traditional *kumikata* understand the benefits of strengthening the push chain, both for blocking and for getting your opponent to react. But, even looking through the simplified lens of muscle strengthening, the facts are a little harder to understand.

While rowing exercises, bench press, and other forearm-strengthening drills have been shown to be effective in improving strength quality, modern physical trainers have a number of more comprehensive and more specific exercises in their tool kit to help you tackle *kumikata* in all its complexity. With the idea of sticking as closely as possible to the elaborate *kumikata* moves, I'd like to give you five specific situations that will help enhance your usual exercises.

Push Chain

The suggested exercise has three specific aspects: the association of leg work, the instability of the ball, and support from a nonrigid element (i.e., not a bar or the floor). This is also an excellent way to work on dynamic core strengthening.

Objective

Strengthen the push chain in an unstable situation by mobilizing the entire body.

Pointers

Back straight, pelvis tilted back (pelvic bone is forward), and stomach flat. Push forward with one leg as you lift the other one. Once the leg is bent, bend your arms until your chest touches the ball, and then go back to the start.

Sets and Repetitions

The movement must be slow and controlled. 4 to 6 sets of 20 push-ups will be suitable for most athletes.

Progression

If the exercise becomes too easy, a training partner can slightly disrupt the balance of the ball (but not so much that it interferes with the athlete's posture).

Pull Chain

The pulling exercise here is complemented by balance work, leg engagement at the release point (which is useful for the specific coordination needed by judokas when they must combine a reaction using the upper body and an attack with the legs), and constant engagement of the back muscles. It can be done using a pulley or a resistance band; these allow you to replicate the two types of resistance specific to judo: inertial (pulley) and elastic (resistance band).

Objective

Strengthen the pull chain in an unstable situation by mobilizing your entire body and dissociating your right side and left side, which enables you to rebalance.

Pointers

Always keep your back straight and stomach flat. Lean forward, with your legs and arms tensed, pull the cable or resistance band toward the ribs, or above your shoulder as if you were opening your arms, while your leg lifts to the front and bends at the same time. You can also keep the leg straight.

Sets and Repetitions

4 sets of 15 reps. This can be done at different speeds depending on your goals, as long as your posture is not affected.

Progression

You can increase the load by reducing the number of repetitions during the training program. For athletes who master the exercise perfectly, it is advantageous to replace the pulley grip with a grip trainer or a towel.

Shoulders

More in this exercise than in the others, the movement connects the upper and lower body by engaging the abdominal, lumbar, and pelvic regions. The aim here is to get as close as possible to the work of a judoka, where the body's core is decisive. You can do this exercise with a dumbbell, but with a kettlebell you can benefit from the inertia load—it's more specific to judo, and there are more variations available too.

Objective

Specifically strengthen the posterior chain and hip extension.

Pointers

Keep your back straight, your pelvis tilted forward (slightly arched), and your arms extended throughout the exercise. Bend your legs (no further than 90°) and place your feet more than shoulder-width apart. Straighten and bring your arms up gradually until the dumbbell or kettlebell is level with your forehead.

Sets and Repetitions

4 to 6 sets of 12 to 15 reps. The exercise can be done at different speeds depending on your goals, as long as your posture is not affected.

Progression

Gradually increase the weight.

Grip

This exercise offers core building for Uke and some fun but demanding grip work for Tori.

Objective

Increase the strength of your forearms and the entire pull chain.

Pointers

Uke gets on all fours and cannot lift any arms or legs. Tori must circle around Uke while leaning backward and avoid falling by gripping tight.

Sets and Repetitions

Circle Uke 1 or 2 times per set. 4 to 8 sets.

Progression

Once Uke and Tori are comfortable, Uke can try to move. They must both then try to read the other's movements as best they can to make the correct adjustments.

DON'T FORGET

→ Gripping is not like arm wrestling, which is exclusively about strength. Technical skill, accuracy, the ability to visually process information, and anticipation are all crucial aspects of *kumikata* that are not covered by muscle strengthening alone.

→ Limiting grip work to the upper body alone overlooks the fact that the relevant movement is triggered by synergy in all muscle groups, especially those in the legs and hips.

→ A grip, as rough as it might be, is full of sensory information. Only using an iron bar to train is bound to be restrictive.

→ When the effects of the training start to be felt and the athlete improves, muscular progress must be incorporated into the technical work; otherwise, the athlete may become stronger but less skillful. It's also interesting to incorporate *uchi-komi* and technical grip drills before, during, and after a specific muscle-building session to encourage a transfer of strength gains to movement.

Ropes

Another tool traditionally used in *dojos*, ropes are highly relevant in this *kumikata*-related section. When used well, they are a fantastic exercise for developing coordinated pulling, especially in terms of grip. Ropes are often approached in a very simplistic manner: you go up and then you come down. But this is actually a muscle-strengthening exercise that can be tackled using endurance, strength, and power.

Suggested endurance program using ropes, at the end of a judo session.
1 to 3 sessions per week for 3 or 4 weeks

→ 2 x 1 full rope climb, with 1 min recovery time in between.

→ 1 up-and-down to the middle of the rope, without using your feet: climb to the middle of the rope, come back down, then start again without putting your feet down on the floor or using them to hold on to the rope. 2 min recovery time.

→ 2 x 1 climb and descent with holds: climb a quarter of the way up, hold for 15 sec, then to halfway, hold for 15 sec, come back down to the quarter mark, hold for 15 sec, and return to the floor. 1 min recovery time.

Suggested strength program using ropes, at the end of the warm-up or during a dedicated session.
1 or 2 sessions per week for 3 or 4 weeks

→ 2 x 1 full rope climb, with 1 min recovery time in between.

→ 1 or 2 x 1 fast climbs and descents with holds: climb halfway up the rope, hold for 3 sec, climb to the top, hold for 3 sec, then come back down to halfway, hold for 3 sec, and return to the floor. 1 min 30 sec recovery time.

→ 1 or 2 x 1 eccentric rope exercises (or half-rope): normal climb, try to slow down as much as possible during your descent. 2 min recovery time.

Suggested power program using ropes, at the end of the warm-up or during a dedicated session.
1 or 2 sessions per week for 3 or 4 weeks

→ 2 x 1 full rope climb, with 1 min recovery time in between.

→ 2 x timed power circuit: 4 burpees, 20 m sprint to the rope, climb up and down as quickly as possible. 2 min recovery time.

→ 2 x 1 climb with 2 ropes (or 2 half-ropes): with 2 ropes side by side, grasp one in each hand and climb to the top. If you only have one rope, add a set to each of the preceding exercises. 2 min recovery time.

The Final 15 Minutes

YOU'RE LIKELY VERY FAMILIAR WITH THE ROUTINE OF THE FINAL 15 MINUTES, ONCE PRACTICE IS FINISHED: FOUR SETS OF PUSH-UPS, THE SAME NUMBER OF SIT-UPS, AND SO ON. BUT IS THIS ACTUALLY USEFUL? AND IF SO, WHAT IS THE BEST WAY TO USE THIS TIME?

At the end of the session, when the body is tired, muscle strengthening helps to develop endurance, a decisive attribute in judo, where technical effectiveness is at the mercy of muscle saturation. Another advantage: this exercise helps shape the body. Endurance work has a fast and visible impact on hypertrophy and muscle definition.

What is endurance? It's the ability to extend or repeat a muscle contraction during effort. It involves slow and controlled movements, in long sets (more than 7 repetitions), with a short recovery time (less than a minute in this case) and light weight (often, body weight is enough). The goal is to obtain muscle saturation by the end of the sets, knowing that the number of repetitions will need to be limited for technically perfect execution. If the fighter needs to adjust his or her form, then it's time to stop. Continuing may produce microtraumas that are dangerous in the medium term.

In general, in the dojo, the formula is as follows: sit-ups (for the abdominal muscles), pull-ups (for the pull chain in the upper body), push-ups (for the push chain), leg bends, with or without a training partner holding down your shoulders or arms. Since you have already read the sections of this book dedicated to the abdominal muscles and core-strengthening exercises, you know all about this. As for the rest, let's take a look at each one in turn.

TRAPS TO AVOID

Sunken back or glutes too high in the air, head too low, elbows out too much, shoulder out of alignment so you can get one more repetition. For beginners, I'd recommend that you keep your knees on the floor.

Push-Ups

Judokas regularly find themselves pushing their opponent back, stopping them from getting too close, or forcing the opponent backward with a push. This exercise, which engages the entire push chain (pectoral muscles, triceps, shoulders) is the perfect fit for that final 15 minutes.

How?

→ Since pushing can come from a variety of angles, whether your opponent is close to you or farther away, you should alternate the angle of your push-ups, especially during holds (stop in the bent position).

→ Judokas only rarely use both their arms synchronously: they tend to push more from one side than the other. It is therefore in their best interest not to stick to standard push-ups. I suggest doing staggered-hands push-ups, that is, with one hand farther forward than the other.

→ Fighters don't push in just one direction. Especially when they're on the ground, but also when standing, they may push upward, to the middle (standard push-ups), or downward. This means you should include incline and decline push-ups in your program.

TRAPS TO AVOID

Shoulders out of alignment. Keeping your shoulders in (this restricts the back muscles). For incline or decline pull-ups, avoid breaking the body in half. To do this, you must keep your abdominal and lumbar muscles tight. For beginners, I recommend that you work with a training partner and start with incline pull-ups.

Pull-Ups

Pulling is a dominant feature of judo, entailing an intense engagement of the pull chain (back muscles, biceps, forearms). During a bout, you pull upward, downward, and to the middle. Just as in push-ups, it is worthwhile to explore the full range of pull-ups, be they standard, incline, or decline.

How?

→ Most often, you are trying to pull your opponent, so you should not limit yourself to standard pull-ups, where you pull your body up toward a bar.

→ Grip trainers, kimonos, towels, Fat Gripz, belts, and so on, attached to a bar or to a training partner, are more suitable for specific strengthening.

→ Introducing variety through different angles is also important: alternate the range of pulling actions.

→ The distance between your hands is wider than it is for push-ups. During strength-training exercises, you should try to reproduce the variety of grips, alternating them from one set to the next.

COMBINE WITHIN THE SAME SESSION

In a combined-exercise session, it's tempting to bring together two exercises focusing on the same muscle group. This is a mistake. I'd recommend that you do the opposite: alternate. Using that rationale, you could do the following:

1. Pushing
2. Legs
3. Abs
4. Pulling

SEPARATE THE SESSIONS

At a certain level, doing the four exercises successively with enough sets to attain saturation will take longer than a quarter of an hour. The solution is to divide the work so it remains effective and so you allow enough time for long-term progress to take hold. The following is a reasonable schedule:

SESSION A

1. Pushing
2. Legs
3. Abs I

SESSION B

1. Abs II
2. Pulling
3. Legs

The Lower Limbs

The priority in muscle development is to harmonize the structures where imbalances typically cause injuries. Consequently, strengthening your hamstrings limits the risk of tearing your anterior cruciate ligament, and strengthening the vastus medialis helps limit the external rotation of the tibia, which can put your meniscus and tendons under stress. Strengthening the calf, which is often forgotten, also helps to prevent injury.

Strengthening all of the lower limbs is important because they are used extensively during a bout: angles, extensions, all types of muscle contractions, open or closed chain, legs synchronized or not. But we're talking about the final 15 minutes, not the final hour and a half, so we have to find comprehensive exercises that allow us to reproduce this variety.

How?

→ It's difficult to mirror all the lower-limb dynamics of judo, particularly rotations, but we can try to replicate the balance, maintain posture, and so on. This is why the exercise ball is the perfect support tool, because it's a lot more unstable.

→ Alternative drill: I suggest doing leg bends with one foot on an exercise ball (or on a bench or on a training partner's back if you don't have a ball or a bench), and the other foot flat on the floor.

→ There are many advantages: it's an effective exercise, with or without weight; all of the lower-limb muscles are engaged; and working on one leg enables you to balance the legs out laterally and match the specific features of judo.

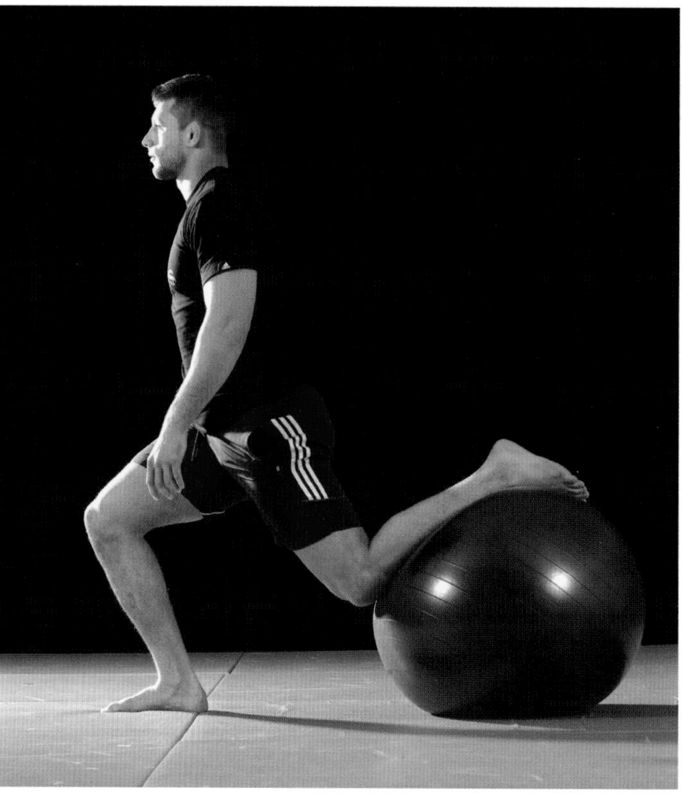

TRAPS TO AVOID

Lower-limb strengthening is often associated with exercises in which the training partner is either in your arms or on your shoulders. This is not a problem unless you always carry your training partner on the same side; in this case you create an imbalance. If you bend your legs beyond 90 degrees (as in a full squat), you risk the integrity of your knees for only marginal gain. If you round your back, the tension in your neck and low back can be catastrophic. I recommend working with no weights or doing one-quarter squats (just the start of the bend).

Using Resistance Bands

I POSITION MYSELF AND I OPEN UP: THE COLLAR OF THE JUDOGI UNIFORM BECOMES TIGHT, YOUR OPPONENT RESISTS YOUR UNBALANCING ATTEMPT MORE AND MORE, UNTIL ABRUPTLY ALL RESISTANCE ENDS. THAT IS A BRIEF INSIGHT INTO WHAT YOU ENCOUNTER IN YOUR BOUTS AND WHAT TRAINING SHOULD ENABLE YOU TO REPLICATE: A FORM OF RESISTANCE THAT HAS SOMETHING ELASTIC ABOUT IT.

In judo, fighters are always battling against two forces: the first, inertial force, is characterized by strong resistance at the start of the move that ebbs away as the fall occurs. It's mainly to confront this that we train with free weights like dumbbells. The second is known as elastic force; it's progressive, and contrary to inertial force, it increases gradually up to a breaking point. It's this type of resistance that we're looking for when we train with resistance bands.

The use of resistance bands in judo training is nothing new. Old instructors still talk about when they would use inner tubes to practice *uchi-komi*. As training techniques advance, equipment adapts, modernizes, and constantly becomes more judo-specific, to such an extent that today we find all types of bands, of varying sizes and resistance, that can be used in a number of different training setups. They can be used, especially in the exercises that I'm suggesting, to pursue three key objectives: muscle strengthening, technical improvement, and cardio work.

RECOGNIZING THE LIMITATIONS

The specific focus of resistance band work is not comprehensive. In fact, in order for the work to get close to 100 percent of the effort put in by a judoka, the resistance band would have to give way suddenly at the end of the move. As this is unsuitable when using a simple resistance band, for obvious safety reasons, it is easier to use *uchi-komi* or *randori*—which also help you to maintain the rate of execution—when trying to replicate this phenomenon.

1. Muscle Strengthening

Two strength attributes can be targeted here: endurance and power. On the whole, in endurance, the movements are slow and controlled, with long sets. For example: 10 to 15 repetitions for 7 sets, with under a minute's recovery time. As for power, there are two possible approaches. We can focus on pure speed, with a weak resistance band and moving at the highest possible speed. It's also possible to work on overspeed through a successive heavy-light routine: the athlete does resistance band exercises with no rest time and then judo-focused work at maximum speed. For example: 4 moves with a strong resistance band immediately followed by 4 *uchi-komi* and 2 minutes of recovery time. This should be repeated 4 to 6 times. The chosen exercises should be biomechanically similar.

2. Technical Improvement

Working with a resistance band, which is more manageable and more patient than a training partner, can help us overcome certain blocks, particularly in the positioning of the pelvis and the spine. It engages proprioception and can, in many cases, be used in technical training, for example, enhancing body positioning with a *kumikata* opening.

3. Cardio Work

Grouped together as circuit training or in stations, the exercises can be used to develop judokas' specific endurance. Here, you should take care to alternate upper body and lower body exercises. Likewise, a judoka can encourage the transfer of the progress made in training to specific skills by combing classic judo exercises and resistance band exercises. For example: 4 exercises (choose from the ones shown on the next few pages), one after the other with no rest time for 15 to 20 sec alternated with *uchi-komi* (8 exercises in total), all done with maximum intensity throughout. Take 4 minutes of recovery time, initially passive, then focusing on technical positioning for the final minute. Repeat 4 or 5 times.

1 COORDINATED RHYTHMIC PULLS

OBJECTIVES

Coordination, cardio training, muscle strengthening (shoulders, back, triceps, biceps, etc.).

POINTERS

Jump with the handle of a resistance band in each hand. Open and close your legs. Stretch your (straight) arms out and then bring them together.

PROGRESSION 1

Alternate forward lunges as you pull the band toward your hips with bent arms.

PROGRESSION 2

Combine 2 x legs apart and 2 x lunges. Same for the arms.

2 THE BEETHOVEN

OBJECTIVES

Cardio training, muscle strengthening (legs).

POINTERS

Held by a resistance band around your waist, alternate between moving forward and to the side.

PROGRESSION

Once you have mastered the exercise, try movements that are specific to judo. Then you can do the exercise two by two.

3 RESTRICTED UCHI-KOMI

OBJECTIVES
Overall muscle strengthening, cardio training.

POINTERS
Held by a resistance band around your waist, move through the technical steps. The band should always be under tension, but not so much that it interferes with your technical execution.

PROGRESSION
Vary the strength of the resistance band, place the band around your ankle, create resistance band combinations.

4 RESISTANCE BAND STRENGTHENING CIRCUIT

OBJECTIVES
Muscle strengthening.

POINTERS
Do these three exercises one after the other without rest in between: upright row, push-up, and squat.

PROGRESSION
Vary the resistance of the band or the number of repetitions.

5

JUMPING JACK

OBJECTIVES

Cardio training, muscle strengthening (legs, shoulders, back).

POINTERS

Grip the band, which is attached to a point some distance away that is higher than your center of gravity, and bend your legs while keeping your back straight and lift your straight arms in front of you until they are horizontal. Jump into the air, spreading your legs and stretching your arms out to the side.

PROGRESSION

You can alternate this with a judo move *(tai-sabaki, hiki-dashi)*.

6

SIT AND JUMP

OBJECTIVES

Cardio training, muscle strengthening (legs, abdominal muscles).

POINTERS

Grip the band, which is attached to a point some distance away that is higher than your center of gravity (ideally higher than your eyes), then sit down and straighten your legs (but not completely). Then, as quickly as possible, pull your legs in as you sit up and then jump to your feet.

PROGRESSION

You can combine this with the jumping jack.

7

THE GORILLA

OBJECTIVES
Cardio training, core strengthening.

POINTERS
Held by a resistance band around your waist, and squatting on your heels, alternate between forward accelerations and controlled backward runs.

PROGRESSION
You can return on your heels and hands rather than running back.

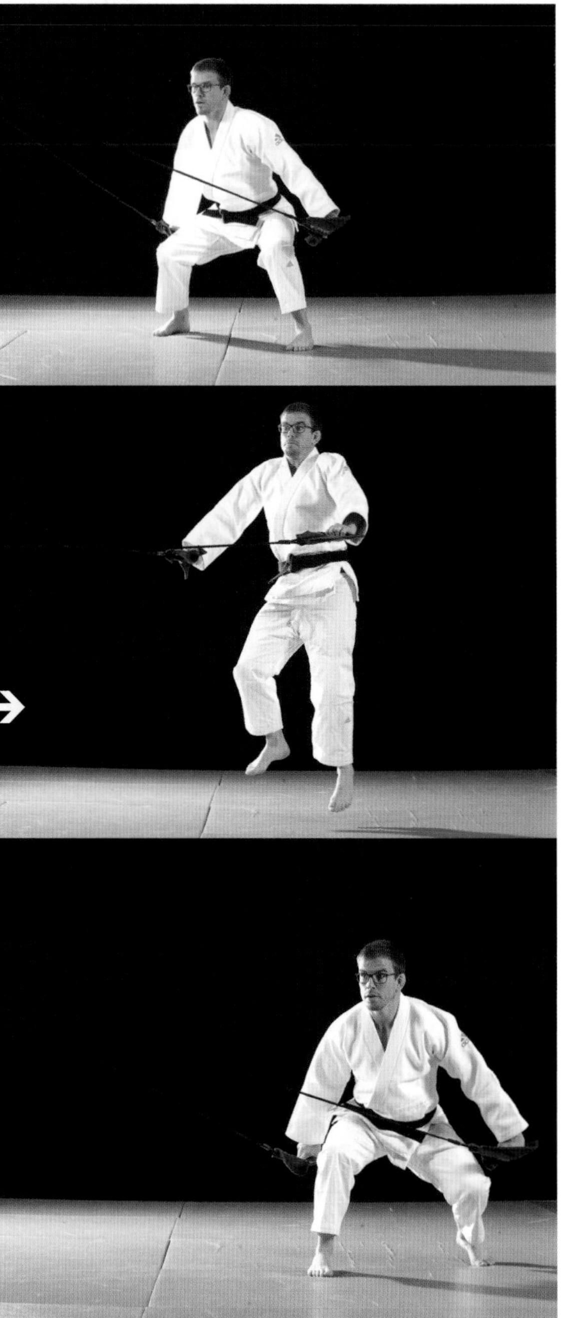

8

LATERAL JUMPS

OBJECTIVES
Cardio training, muscle strengthening (legs, shoulders, back).

POINTERS
Grip the band, attached to a point some distance away higher than your center of gravity, and bend your legs while keeping your back straight. Jump to the side (as far as a side step).

PROGRESSION
You can add a sweep, but you will lose in intensity what you gain in judo-specificity.

9

SINGLE-LEG FRONT JUMPS

OBJECTIVES

Muscle strengthening (legs), preventing injuries to the ankles and knees.

POINTERS

Grip the band, attached to a point some distance away higher than your center of gravity, bend your legs while keeping your back straight, and raise your outstretched arms in front of you until they are horizontal. Jump forward and land on one leg while keeping your balance.

PROGRESSION

As you become comfortable with this exercise, you can let yourself be pulled by the band and jump even higher.

10

TWO-HAND PULL

OBJECTIVES

Cardio training, muscle strengthening (arms, back).

POINTERS

Grip the band, attached to a point at the same level as your center of gravity, bend your legs while keeping your back straight, shoulders back, head up, and chest out, and pull on the band with both hands.

PROGRESSION

If you would rather do an exercise where cardio is the priority, one band should suffice, and you'll need to focus on the frequency of the movement. If you are specifically targeting muscle strengthening, you may need several resistance bands.

SPECIFIC ENDURANCE

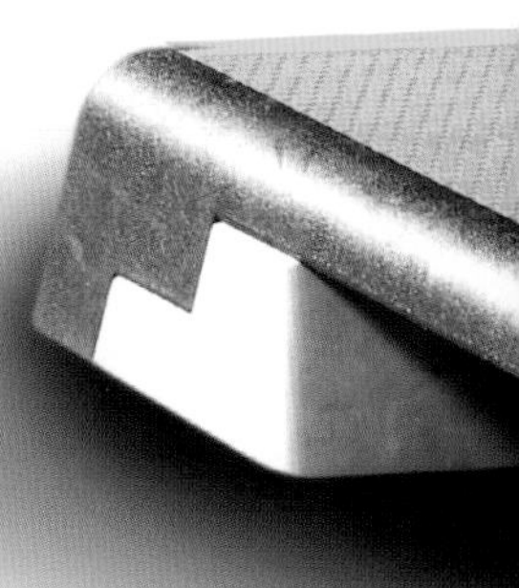

Running-Specific Training

A DESIRE TO LOSE WEIGHT AND A NEED FOR ENDURANCE LEAD A NUMBER OF JUDOKAS TO MAKE JOGGING A KEY PART OF THEIR TRAINING. BUT DO WE ACTUALLY HAVE TO RUN FOR A LONG TIME TO BE ABLE TO FIGHT FOR A LONG TIME?

Endurance is a decisive attribute for the judoka. Participating in five to seven bouts during a typical tournament day, or, more simply, being able to withstand the intensity and length of a training session, falls within the scope of this ability: maintaining effort for a certain amount of time or repeating an effort. Additionally, it is not unusual for judokas, whether they compete in tournaments or not, to maintain their fundamentals—their ability to dig deep when required—by leaving the dojo regularly to do their sacred long run (around 45 minutes). Although this approach is totally dissociated (if running becomes a fighter's main method of movement, we're in trouble), it can nevertheless be effective and specific when we apply sound principles to it.

A Double Dimension

Here we're talking about a system used by the body to produce a long aerobic effort, that is, one in which a muscle contraction occurs with the use of oxygen. This is in contrast to anaerobic effort, which allows for intense but brief effort, and which acidifies the cellular environment, disrupts contractions, and limits performance in the short term. There is commonly a distinction made within the aerobic category between protracted work (referred to by experts as aerobic capacity), and intense work (referred to as aerobic power). Thus, extended effort (45 continuous minutes) in running, cycling, swimming, or other sports falls under the capacity dimension of the aerobic system.

$\dot{V}O_2max$?

The first problem posed by this type of effort is that it is not specific to judo, or to any other sport, in fact. Indeed, when exactly does a judoka produce a continuous effort of weak intensity?

The second argument against this sort of work is related to psychology. Aerobic performance is directly linked to $\dot{V}O_2max$, or the maximum oxygen consumed during a sustained effort. It is the ability to supply oxygen to your muscles. Any progress we hope to make by training the aerobic energy dimension is directly proportional to the time we spend at close to the running speed corresponding to maximum oxygen consumption. But a human being is, in a best-case scenario during continuous effort, capable of maintaining such intensity for just 7 minutes. Worse still, if we look again at our jogging session, which can last from 45 minutes to an hour, the zone of effectiveness (often at the end of the run) rarely exceeds 2 minutes.

Is a Continuous, Prolonged Effort Pointless?

Continuous and prolonged effort is inescapable, but for objectives other than the improvement of a trained athlete's performance. This is especially the case for young people and beginners who are learning about managing effort and running technique. You should make technical progress before improving your physiological parameters. Besides, physiological adjustments are plentiful and of a weak intensity. These are often central system adjustments: blood flow, plasma volume, or the efficiency of the left ventricle. These modifications, which are crucial when you've had no training or are a total beginner, are often already developed when you take part in regular physical activity. Often, simply practicing judo enables you to maintain them. If you're a competitive athlete, add to that some active recovery workouts and jogging to control your body weight, and you will no longer need to go for extra-long runs. It's actually quite simple to find out how you're doing and what you need: if, after a few weeks of intermittent training, you're not making any progress, you should start again on the fundamentals.

AT WHAT INTENSITY?

Sometimes doing as much as you can does more harm than good. Here, the goal is not necessarily to run too fast during intense phases, because you risk changing the type of work you're attempting to do and not achieving the objective of specific endurance.

The first step is to establish a benchmark running speed during a test (see the section of this book that deals with this specifically). This speed is known as maximal aerobic speed (MAS), which is the application of $\dot{V}O_2max$ in the field.

Recent studies have established that the zone of effectiveness of an intermittent exercise must fall between 80 and 110 percent of this MAS for there to be an improvement in performance and endurance. At around 80 percent, you improve what we call the buffering capacity of your body, or the ability to control and use the acidity produced during intense effort (you may recognize it in the desire to vomit during tough bouts). It is, therefore, a question of helping your body handle the lactic load. The closer you get to 100 percent, the more you can target aerobic performance, that is, the ability to repeat moves and last till the end of the match.

Finally, it is increasingly recommended to reduce the range of intensity between work and recovery by remaining very active during the recovery period.

Aerobic capacity also plays a role in controlling your weight, because lipids partly replace the carbohydrates burned during prolonged effort of very weak intensity (from 45 minutes onward for someone with a lot of training, but 1 hour 30 minutes for a sedentary person). Please note that this argument is also increasingly contested, with a number of researchers having demonstrated that intermittent activity can help experienced athletes burn a significant amount of fat as well.

The most essential effect of this kind of work is, without a doubt, that produced by active recovery, which, by increasing blood flow, helps to alleviate the effects of intense effort more quickly, to rebuild muscle, and to replenish energy reserves. In this case, the effort should last for between 15 and 20 minutes, and the intensity should be very moderate so as to not produce further effort, but rather, to maximize recovery.

Intermittent Work as an Effective Alternative*

The solution to spend more time in our $\dot{V}O_2max$ zone is to change our work system. To increase athletes' endurance, modern physical training now favors aerobic power work—in other words, involving a maximum aerobic effort—without straying into anaerobic levels of effort during training sequences, with maximum efficiency obtained through intermittent work. There are two major advantages to dividing the work in this way:

1. **We get closer to the specific effort required in judo (stops ordered by the referee and breaks between bouts).**
2. **We spend more time at an intensity approaching the $\dot{V}O_2max$.**

**What is intermittent work? Simply put, it means alternating your running speed between acceleration phases and active, slow-paced recovery time.*

Suggested Program

1 *DISCOVERING AND MASTERING INTERMITTENT WORK*

DURATION
2 or 3 weeks
2 or 3 sessions per week

After 20 min of jogging (including the warm-up), alternate 5 × 15 sec accelerations and 30 sec of less intense jogging. Recover for 3 min by running at a very weak intensity, then repeat from the start.

HARDER

→ Add a burst of acceleration to each session.
→ Add one full training circuit.
→ Gradually balance out the running time and the recovery time.

EASIER

→ Only do one circuit.
→ Only do 10 sec of acceleration with 20 sec recovery time.

2 *BALANCE OUT THE RUNNING TIME AND THE RECOVERY TIME*

DURATION
3 or 4 weeks
2 sessions per week

After 20 min of jogging (including the warm-up), alternate 6 to 10 × 20 sec accelerations and 20 sec of less intense jogging. Recover for 3 min by running at a very weak intensity, then repeat from the start.

HARDER

→ Add a burst of acceleration to each session.
→ Add one full training circuit.
→ Gradually increase the effort duration to 30 sec.

EASIER

→ Only do one circuit.

3 *FIND YOUR LIMITS*

DURATION
3 weeks
1 or 2 sessions per week

Alternate 4 to 6 × 2 min accelerations with 2 min of less intense jogging. Run for 15 min at 60 to 70 percent of your maximum speed.

HARDER

→ Add a burst of acceleration to each session.

EASIER

→ Only do one circuit.

4 *EXPLORE THE FULL RANGE OF EFFORT*

DURATION
2 or 3 weeks
1 or 2 sessions per week

Combine 15 sec of acceleration and 15 sec of recovery time
then 30 sec/30 sec – 1 min/1 min – 2 min/2 min – 1 min/1 min – 30 sec/30 sec – 15 sec/15 sec.

HARDER

→ Do each step twice.
→ Recover for 5 min then start again (3 times max).

EASIER

→ Stop after the 2 min sets.

5 *INTERMITTENT, HIGH-INTENSITY WORK*

DURATION
3 weeks
1 or 2 sessions per week

Alternate 10 to 12 reps of 15 sec of effort with 15 sec of recovery.
Recover for 3 to 5 min at a trotting pace, then start again.

HARDER

→ Add a burst of acceleration to each session.
→ Add one full training circuit.
→ Run faster.

EASIER

→ Do fewer repetitions.
→ Only do one circuit.

Training on Cardio Machines

FED UP WITH WEARING YOUR JUDOGI? INJURED? NEED A GOOD PHYSICAL WORKOUT? WHY NOT LET OFF A LITTLE STEAM ON A TREADMILL?

Integrated* physical training is obviously not a trainer's only tool, thank goodness. Depending on their mood or on the season, a trainer might prefer dissociated** physical training.

First, there are trainers who like precise effort, illuminated by kilometers, calorie burn, and running speed, among other things. There are also those who prefer a bit of variety, who sometimes push us to leave the dojo for a change of scenery, and then there are the old veterans who care deeply about their oxygen sessions and love their general training cycles. And I obviously can't forget the injured athletes, who don't have a choice. In all these scenarios, the cardio training equipment in a fitness club or the weight room can prove extremely useful. Still, as is often the case, proper instructions are often lacking, and while these machines can be marvelous physical training tools, they can also be a total waste of time if they are used badly. Here, then, are some programs and principles that will allow you to make the most of them.

As I explained in the previous section, intermittent work is now the most effective cardio training method we know of. It enables us to specifically develop athletes' energy production systems in accordance with their individual needs and training and competition requirements. The principle stems from the fact that you can work at an effective intensity for a longer time, for a lower total volume of work, with a level of resulting fatigue that is equal to, or even lower than, the fatigue experienced after continuous work. The supporting activities vary greatly: judo, of course, or, if you want to dissociate the work, running, the rowing machine, the exercise bike, the elliptical trainer, and the stepper. In fact, once the principles are mastered, anything is possible: any supporting activity engaging more than 70 percent of the body will work.

NO TREADMILL?

These programs are suitable for other machines, with the following provisions:

→ **Exercise bike:** reduce the recovery time by 30 percent.

→ **Elliptical trainer:** increase the effort duration by 10 percent.

→ **Rowing machine:** don't change anything.

→ **Running outside:** don't change anything, but run in an area with hills, working hard as you go up and entering the active recovery stage as you go down.

Dissociated but Specific

I tend to repeat myself when I say I don't like general training work, that it's a waste of time, and that we have to try to be as specific as possible. It is tempting to make the leap to my recommending fully integrated training in which there is no place for cardio machines.

But dissociating training content (getting out of the dojo, for example), does not necessarily mean sacrificing the specificity of the work; quite the opposite! You need to identify your targets carefully so that the results are close to what is needed in judo so that they transfer to judo easily. I'd therefore like to suggest a treadmill training program that is judo-specific (but adaptable to other machines; see insert), founded on two energy-related realities:

1. **Training:** intermittent effort lasting between 1 hour and 1 hour 30 min and incorporating numerous levels of intensity.
2. **Competition:** short efforts, interspersed with passive recovery times that last anywhere from a few seconds to several minutes, repeated up to seven times during a tournament.

**Or specific: on a treadmill, using judo-type movements.*

***Away from the treadmill, using other types of movements, like running, cycling, rowing, and weight lifting.*

Your Choice of Two Programs

→ 2-MONTH PROGRAM (2 sessions per week)

	SESSION A	SESSION B
WEEK 1	SESSION 3	SESSION 4
WEEK 2	SESSION 3	SESSION 5
WEEK 3	SESSION 5	SESSION 3
WEEK 4		SESSION 3
WEEK 5	SESSION 7	SESSION 8
WEEK 6	SESSION 4	SESSION 1
WEEK 7		SESSION 2
WEEK 8	SESSION 6	SESSION 5

→ 2-MONTH PROGRAM (3 sessions per week)

	SESSION A	SESSION B	SESSION C
WEEK 1	SESSION 3	SESSION 4	SESSION 3
WEEK 2	SESSION 3	SESSION 5	SESSION 3
WEEK 3	SESSION 4	SESSION 5	SESSION 6
WEEK 4		SESSION 7	
WEEK 5	SESSION 1	SESSION 3	SESSION 6
WEEK 6	SESSION 1	SESSION 4	SESSION 8
WEEK 7	SESSION 4	SESSION 2	
WEEK 8	SESSION 6	SESSION 2	SESSION 5

Practical Advice

Make Progress in 8 Sessions

Heart rate: The target intensity for the so-called lactic sessions (sessions 1 and 2) is between 80 and 90 percent (as close as possible to 90 percent) of the maximum heart rate. For the aerobic sessions (session 3), the target intensity is 75 to 85 percent of the maximum heart rate. Finally, for mixed sessions (sessions 4, 5, and 6), the target intensity will, of course, be more varied: between 75 and 90 percent of the maximum heart rate.* Warm-up and cool-down: Start these sessions after a 10-min warm-up, and then finish with 10 min of gradual cool-down (low-intensity run or walk).

** You often hear that to determine your maximum heart rate, you subtract your age from 220; a 20-year-old athlete would therefore have a heart rate of 200 beats per minute. But individually, genetic and historical variations are such that this calculation may be far from accurate. Some top-of-the-line heart rate monitors do offer a slightly more accurate estimate of maximum heart rate. However, the most effective way to determine maximum heart rate is to do a maximum intensity exercise for 5 minutes (e.g., go as far as possible on the rowing machine within that limited time), and then immediately take note of your maximum heart rate.*

INCREASE THE VOLUME OF WORK

SESSION 1

EFFORT	RECOVERY
3 MIN	3 MIN
3 MIN	2 MIN
3 MIN	1 MIN

→ **RUNNING SPEED:** Between 6 mph (10 km/h) and 11 mph (17 km/h), depending on your abilities
→ **RECOVERY SPEED:** Between 4 mph (7 km/h) and 6 mph (10 km/h)
→ **GRADIENT:** 0%
→ **TOTAL VOLUME:** Do the set 2 or 3 times, with 3 min of recovery time between sets

SESSION 2

EFFORT	RECOVERY
3 MIN	3 MIN
2 MIN	2 MIN
1 MIN	1 MIN

→ **RUNNING SPEED:** Between 6 mph (10 km/h) and 11 mph (17 km/h), depending on your abilities
→ **RECOVERY SPEED:** Between 4 mph (7 km/h) and 6 mph (10 km/h)
→ **GRADIENT:** 0%
→ **TOTAL VOLUME:** Do the set 2 or 3 times, with 3 min of recovery time between sets

REPLICATE THE INTENSITY OF A BOUT

SESSION 3

EFFORT	RECOVERY
1 MIN	3 MIN
40 SEC	2 MIN
30 SEC	1.5 MIN
20 SEC	1 MIN
10 SEC	30 SEC

→ **RUNNING SPEED:** Between 10 mph (16 km/h) and the treadmill's maximum possible speed
→ **RECOVERY SPEED:** Between 4 mph (7 km/h) and 6 mph (10 km/h)
→ **GRADIENT:** 0.5%
→ **TOTAL VOLUME:** Do the set 4 times, with 2 min of recovery time between sets

SESSION 4

EFFORT	RECOVERY
3 MIN	3 MIN
2 MIN	2 MIN
1 MIN	1 MIN

→ **RUNNING SPEED:** Between 6 mph (10 km/h) and 11 mph (17 km/h), depending on your abilities
→ **RECOVERY SPEED:** Between 4 mph (7 km/h) and 6 mph (10 km/h)
→ **GRADIENT:** 0%
→ **TOTAL VOLUME:** Do the set 2 or 3 times, with 3 min of recovery time between sets

TRAINING EFFECTIVELY

SESSION 5

EFFORT	RECOVERY
1 MIN	1 MIN
40 SEC	40 SEC
30 SEC	30 SEC
20 SEC	20 SEC
10 SEC	10 SEC

→ **RUNNING SPEED:** Between 9 mph (14 km/h) and 12 mph (20 km/h)
→ **RECOVERY SPEED:** Between 4 mph (7 km/h) and 6 mph (10 km/h)
→ **GRADIENT:** 0.5%
→ **TOTAL VOLUME:** Do the set 4 to 6 times, with 2 min of recovery time between sets

FIGHTING IN MULTIPLE BOUTS

SESSION 6

EFFORT	RECOVERY
1 MIN	3 MIN
40 SEC	2 MIN
30 SEC	1.5 MIN
20 SEC	1 MIN
10 SEC	30 SEC

→ **RUNNING SPEED:** Between 9 mph (14km/h) and 14 mph (22 km/h)
→ **RECOVERY SPEED:** Between 4 mph (7 km/h) and 6 mph (10 km/h)
→ **GRADIENT:** Increase the gradient by 1% for each set, or 0%, 1%, 2%, 3%, 4%, 5%, and decrease the speed by .5 mph (1 km/h) for each gradient increase
→ **TOTAL VOLUME:** Do the set 4 to 6 times, with 2 min of recovery time between sets

INCREASE THE VOLUME OF WORK

SESSION 7

EFFORT	RECOVERY
2 MIN*	3 MIN
1 MIN*	1.5 MIN
30 SEC**	1 MIN
20 SEC**	20 SEC
10 SEC**	10 SEC

→ **RUNNING SPEED:** Between 9 mph (14km/h) and 14 mph (22 km/h)
→ **RECOVERY SPEED:** Between 4 mph (7 km/h) and 6 mph (10 km/h)
→ **GRADIENT:** 0.5%
→ **TOTAL VOLUME:** Do the set 4 times, with 2 min of recovery time between sets

SESSION 8

EFFORT	RECOVERY
2 MIN*	3 MIN
1 MIN*	1.5 MIN
30 SEC**	30 SEC
1 MIN*	1.5 MIN
2 MIN*	3 MIN

→ **RUNNING SPEED:** Between 9 mph (14km/h) and 14 mph (22 km/h)
→ **RECOVERY SPEED:** Between 4 mph (7 km/h) and 6 mph (10 km/h)
→ **GRADIENT:** Increase the gradient by 1% for each set, or 0%, 1%, 2%, 3%, 4%, and reduce the speed by .5 mph (1 km/h) for each gradient increase
→ **TOTAL VOLUME:** Do the set 4 to 6 times, with 2 min of recovery time between sets

Average speed/Fast speed*

Tread(mill) Lightly

FROM TIME TO TIME, I TALK ABOUT TREADMILLS FOR INJURED ATHLETES OR THOSE WHO NEED TO LOSE A BIT OF WEIGHT. WHAT I HAVEN'T TOLD YOU YET IS THAT A TREADMILL CAN IN FACT BE JUDO-SPECIFIC.

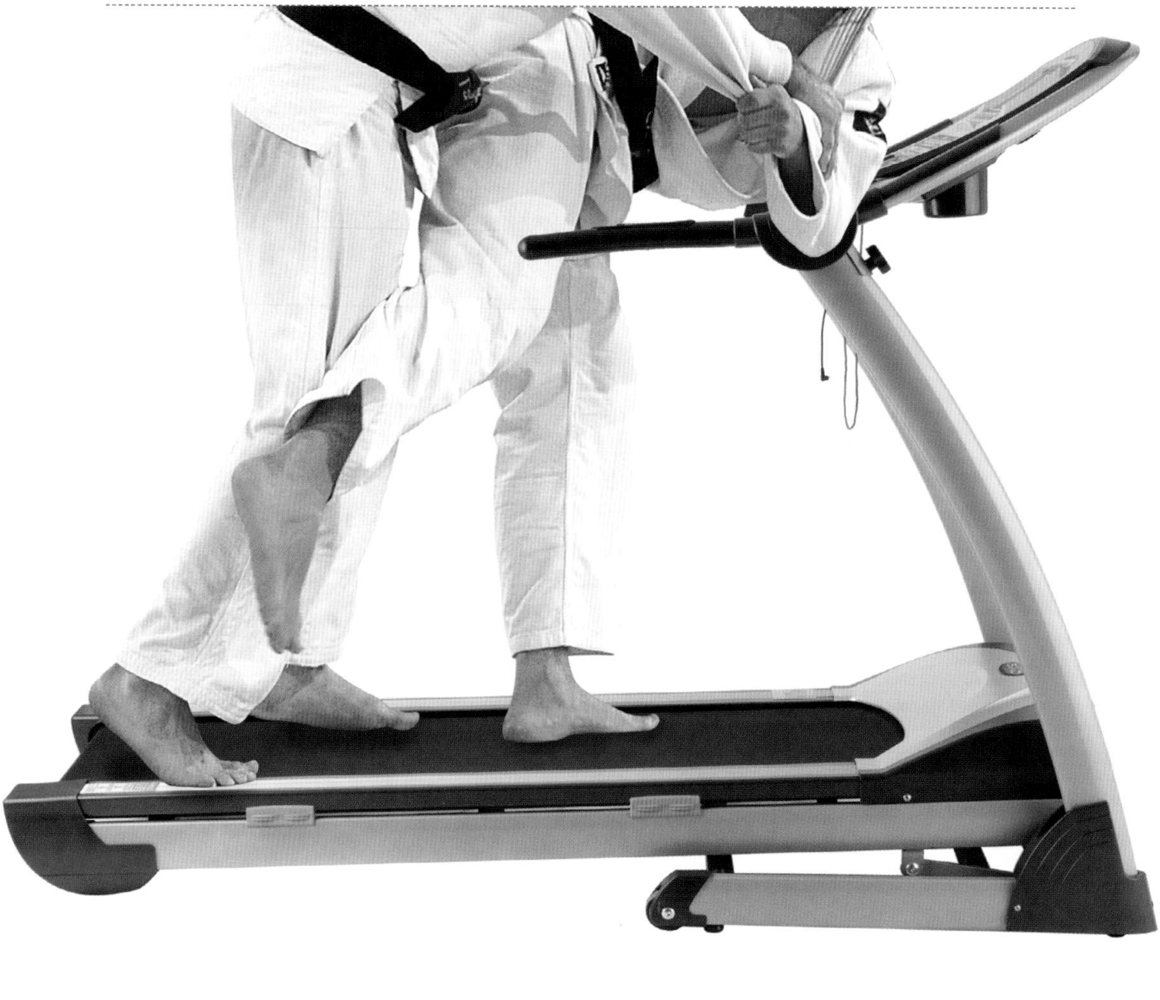

A treadmill is very simple: You get on, you settle into a percentage of your maximum, and you run through your session, which will be intense if you want to improve your endurance, or long if you want to lose weight. These days, you can even watch a movie at the same time. Once you're comfortable, the only thing left to do is run. But yours truly has never-ending creativity and is never at a loss for ideas about how to adapt an exercise to make it more relevant to judo. Let's leave proper running to Olympians; as for the real fighters like you, you can pick from the following exercises instead.

1 IMPROVE YOUR LATERAL SUPPORT

It won't have escaped your notice that treadmills often have small steps on each side. Most people use them for resting between runs so that they don't have to stop the machine. We're going to use them to improve coordination and frequency of movement. The way in which your feet contact the floor is key in judo—moving them, reversing them, and changing their direction—must become a reflex if you want to break the rhythm or create space. And without ever losing your balance, of course. The following exercise should enable you to improve both your stride rate and your stability.

POINTERS

While running, instead of putting the foot you just lifted in the air back onto the belt, place it on the closest step. Then lift your other foot, complete a stride as usual, and touch the belt with the same foot. Now the first foot takes back over: it should hit the belt and then you can change sides.

EASIER

Reduce the running speed and increase the number of times your foot hits the belt between each move out onto the step. Hold onto the machine's handles.

HARDER

Increase the speed of treadmill, let go of any bars or rails, bring in knee lifts or butt kicks, and stop looking at your feet!

2 SIDE STEPS

Side steps, which are essential preparation for all types of judo-style leg sweeps, require no introduction. The treadmill is the ideal training aid for this because it imposes a tempo. As soon as you feel ready, pivot to the side, and step to the side for lateral movement.

EASIER

Reduce the running speed and hold onto the side rail.

HARDER

Step up the pace, increase the gradient, or let go of any bars or rails.

Alternate between two side steps with legs bent and two with legs straight. You can also incorporate crossovers, knee lifts, and butt kicks. And stop looking at your feet!

3 BACKWARD RUN

Ostensibly the least specific of the different routines I've recommended, this exercise is actually indirectly useful for judo. In fact, your stance in judo often has you positioned slightly on the front of your foot, toes mobilized, with the receptors on the sole of your feet in an active state. Running backward prevents you from rolling your foot from the heel, favoring the front of the foot instead. Consider the positioning of the feet, this exercise is therefore more specific than it first appears. What's more, the posterior chain of the lower body (glutes, hamstrings, calves) is often insufficiently strengthened in judo, perpetuating an imbalance with the quadriceps that can lead to injuries such as cruciate ligament tears. The posterior chain is also severely tested during ground grappling (bridges, movement) and upright moves *(o-soto-gari, uchimata,* etc.). Running backward brings the posterior chain to the fore, as far as motor function is concerned, making this exercise enormously useful for judokas.

EASIER

Doing this at walking pace is already quite tricky. Hold onto the side bars. Start running backward from the outset (you thereby avoid the transition from running forward or doing side steps, which can often be complicated).

HARDER

Let go of any bars or rails, include knee lifts or butt kicks, and look straight ahead.

4

TURN AROUND

This exercise combines all three previous exercises and can be done in the same or the reverse order.

EASIER

Spend longer on each individual exercise, hitting the belt more often.

HARDER

Do them all in a row, one foot in contact with the belt at any given moment.

How to Use These Exercises

These exercises can be used during your warm-up (in preparation for a treadmill session, but not exclusively). You can do them one after the other (from the simplest variants to the more complex and intense ones) for 10 to 15 minutes before any session. You can also use them for a treadmill endurance session.

Here are some examples (the exercises just described are referred to as complex runs):

→ **Session 1: Endurance**

10 min standard warm-up run, then immediately do the following 4 times:
5 min complex run, 5 min normal run

→ **Session 2: Power endurance**

15 min standard warm-up run, 30 sec fast run, 20 sec complex run, 10 sec recovery time (stop or low-intensity effort)

→ **Session 3: Recovery potential**

10 min standard warm-up run, 30 sec forward run with step onto treadmill ledge, 30 sec right-facing side steps, 30 sec backward run, 30 sec left-facing side steps, 1 min low-intensity normal run. Repeat 4 to 8 times, depending on your level

Step Training

DO FITNESS ACTIVITIES INSPIRE YOU TO IMPROVE YOUR PHYSICAL CONDITION? ARE YOU NOT REALLY A JANE FONDA FAN? AND YET, THERE ARE THINGS TO LEARN HERE, ESPECIALLY WHEN USING A SIMPLE AND VERY BENEFICIAL TOOL: THE STEP. HERE ARE SOME IDEAS FOR ENHANCING SPECIFIC SPEED, POWER, COORDINATION, AND ENDURANCE ON THIS USEFUL PIECE OF EQUIPMENT.

The step, the star attraction of a fitness discipline that exploded during the 1990s, is now so widespread that it's not that unusual to find one close to the *tatami*. If you are thinking of buying one, you'll find that they are relatively inexpensive. It's important to approach this type of tool, which has quietly risen in popularity, with the seriousness it deserves. I'd like to suggest a few exercises that will enable you to simultaneously improve your balance, cardio, and power via this magic object.

Take Your Sense of Balance to the Next Level

Let's recall that proprioception is an athlete's ability to position different parts of the body, and their movement in space, without the need for a visual stimulus. This parameter greatly influences judokas' balance. Changing your elevation or orientation in space, at different tempos and speeds, engages sensory receptors located in the arches of the feet, the muscles, and the tendons, and connects them with the visual information available, enabling judokas to adjust their posture and movement.

Improve Your Elastic Strength

A judoka's effectiveness depends not only on strength and the ability to maintain that strength; it also entails being able to alternate mini-accelerations with holds constantly, to quickly reverse the movement of your own body weight so you can better accelerate, feint, produce actions and reactions, and so on. Plyometrics are widely used in judo, since these types of muscle contractions are found in many technical moves. Additionally, the similarities with the step are very simple to understand: each step produces an elastic contraction that allows you to slow down or accelerate your own body speed, which is an essential element in judo.

Increase Your Endurance

The commercial success of the step clearly stems from its ability to make people sweat. A remarkable cardiovascular training tool, it helps to increase the calorie burn of any basic movement. Side steps, forward lunges, walking, jumping, and even *tandoku-renshu* (*uchi-komi* without a partner): any move done without intensity on the floor takes on a new dimension when done on a step. A few tailored exercises will make it a fantastic piece of equipment to improve your endurance.

THE STEP

Step training was invented by Gin Miller in 1986. The apparatus obviously takes its name from the activity it is used in. A little low bench made from rigid plastic, it enables you to do a large number of exercises to improve and maintain your physical condition.

Power: plyometrics + *tandoku-renshu*

Each drill can be done up to 4 times with a short recovery time (1 to 2 min) and up to 8 times with a more substantial recovery time (5 min) every 4 sets: **2 complete drills → 5 min break → 2 new complete drills. Of course you can also alternate the drills in a circuit.**

→ 4 to 6 lateral jumps

1

→ 4 to 6 forward lunges

2

→ 4 forward jumps or backward jumps

3

→ 4 to 6 jumping push-ups (knee push-ups are also possible) from one side to the other

4

→ 4 to 6 lateral sweeps

PLEASE NOTE
It's possible to raise the step or to stack several steps to make an exercise harder or to adjust it for different builds.

→ 4 to 6 *tsugi-ashi*

→ 4 to 6 *tai-sabaki*

→ 4 attempts at pushing away a training partner who tries to hold on to you

Speed of Movement

Each set can be done with different goals in mind.

SPEED OBJECTIVE
Do the exercise at maximum speed for up to 8 sec, with a recovery time of 2 to 3 min (up to 8 sets)

RESISTANCE OBJECTIVE
Do the exercise at maximum speed for 45 sec with a recovery time of 4 to 5 min (up to 8 sets)

ENDURANCE OBJECTIVE
Do these exercises as circuit training: 20 sec of effort for 20 sec active recovery time (hopping or jogging). Alternate between upper and lower body exercises.

Specific Endurance and Balance Exercises

Here too, when using these as additional training sessions, you can organize the sets differently.

SPEED OBJECTIVE
Do the exercise at maximum speed or height (for the jumps) 6 times with 30 sec recovery time between exercises. Take 2 min to rest before starting again.

ENDURANCE OBJECTIVE
Do 20 jumping lunges, 20 squat jumps, and 10 diagonal squats in a circuit without stopping for a rest.

→ Jumping lunges

→ Squat jumps

→ Diagonal squats

→ *Seoi-nage*

Focused and Integrated Physical Training

IN COLLABORATION WITH PATRICK ROUX

WE DON'T DO PHYSICAL TRAINING TO BECOME MORE ATTRACTIVE, OR STRONGER, FASTER, OR MORE RESISTANT. PHYSICAL TRAINING HAS JUST ONE GOAL: TO MAKE YOU A BETTER JUDOKA. FROM THAT POINT ON, THE KEY ISSUE AT EACH STAGE OF TRAINING IS HOW TO TRANSFER WHAT IS BEING LEARNED, OR HOW TO FOCUS, AND EVEN INCORPORATE, THE EXERCISES AS MUCH AS POSSIBLE SO THAT ANY BENEFITS GAINED ARE IMMEDIATELY FELT ON THE JUDO MAT. WITH THAT IN MIND, HERE ARE A FEW THINGS WORTH PONDERING.

What Is Integrated Training?

We commonly distinguish between two major training models. The first, more traditional, is dissociated training. On the one hand, you do judo sessions, and, on the other, you work on each athletic attribute according to models borrowed from track and field and bodybuilding. Strength comes from lifting weights, and cardio comes from running on a track.

The second model is known as integrated training. The idea is to replicate what usually happens outside the dojo inside the dojo. And so we integrate circuits—in which we work on power, speed, and endurance—via discipline-specific moves as much as possible, which are integrated into judo practice. While there's no doubt that all methods have their limits, and it is possible to train athletes well in different ways—the dissociated method has certainly been proven to work—we believe that the integrated method offers many advantages, especially because you can do a lot in a short amount of time.

The Advantages of Integrated Circuits

One of the essential problems in physical training stems what from we call transfer. This is the notion that your new potential, acquired in training, is transferred to your technical skills and becomes a source of performance. However, there is something of a gray area in dissociated training. Some athletes are capable of bench pressing 355 lb (160 kg), which is supposed to help them become better at *seoi-nage*, for example. But studies have shown that during a successful *seoi-nage*, the strength exerted is around 55 lb (25 kg) to 77 lb (35 kg). The difficulty of pulling off such a move in competition obviously lies elsewhere, and the effectiveness of a transfer of gained strength is very random, as countless examples have shown. There are multiple benefits to integrated circuits: You constantly remain centered on judo, working on moves that are close to those used in competition, and this obviously saves a lot of time since you can simultaneously accumulate technical experience by varying the movements and the difficulty. Another advantage? While the intensity is not as specific as when you're under a barbell calibrated to the nearest 3.5 oz (100 grams), it is so much closer to the complexity of a judo move that the transfer is much more successful. You can target several factors at the same time, both technical and physical, and all of this combines to produce an experience that approaches that of a bout, where you don't choose what kind of effort you put in, and where the entire body—in other words, every muscle chain—is engaged. Finally, you can work in a very successful manner, both locally and overall, by doing, for example, some lactic training through drills involving the hands and forearms with which no 400 m run will be able to compete. As far as injury prevention goes, this work is also more advantageous because it is more balanced and adapted to judo. Please note that there is nothing stopping you from combining this with dissociated work, such as when you're working on maximum strength, where additional weight is still necessary. To help you enter the world of integrated circuits, we'd like to suggest these examples of circuits used at the very highest level, which target different objectives. They should serve you well.

Power Endurance Circuit

GOAL: REMAIN STRONG FOR THE DURATION OF THE BOUT. THIS IS A CIRCUIT THAT SHOULD ENABLE YOU TO MAINTAIN AN AMPLE LEVEL OF STRENGTH FOR YOUR ENTIRE FIGHT.

Alternate Three Types of Exercises:
→ A general unstable exercise
→ A stable exercise with a heavier load
→ A judo transfer exercise

Intensity
→ Between 50 and 70 percent of your maximum

Speed
→ Maximum for judo moves

Number of Reps
→ 8 to 10 per exercise, 3 times per muscle chain, before moving on to the next one. You can repeat the circuit two more times.

Recovery Time
→ None between the exercises, 2 min between each muscle chain set

Push Chain Work

1

UNSTABLE EXERCISE

→ Two-person push-up

→ For further instability, place one of your feet on a traditional medicine ball or on an exercise ball

SUBSTITUTION
Alternating push-ups with one hand on an unstable surface, then the other (move through the unstable hand position as you switch hands)

2

STABLE EXERCISE

→ Bench press

3

JUDO TRANSFER EXERCISE

→ Push your partner away (always on the same side)

Pull Chain Work

1

UNSTABLE EXERCISE

→ Rope pull with feet balanced on an exercise ball

→ You can do the same exercise using a fixed bar

STABLE EXERCISE

→ Pulling exercise using a low pulley or a resistance band

JUDO TRANSFER EXERCISE

→ *Hiki-dashi* (simple opening with maximum pull)

Lower Body Work

1

UNSTABLE EXERCISE

→ Leg bend while leaning back on an exercise ball

2

STABLE EXERCISE

→ Squat or squat using a resistance band

3

JUDO TRANSFER EXERCISE

→ *Seoi-nage* with a catch

MAP Circuit

GOAL: BE ABLE TO TAKE PART IN SEVERAL CONSECUTIVE BOUTS. THIS IS A MAXIMUM AEROBIC POWER (MAP) CIRCUIT THAT WILL GIVE YOU THE MEANS TO SUSTAIN, OVER THE COURSE OF A DAY, AN ELEVATED LEVEL OF EFFORT DURING A SERIES OF SUCCESSIVE FIGHTS AS WELL AS RECOVER MORE QUICKLY FROM THOSE FIGHTS.

WHAT IS MAP?

MAP stands for maximum aerobic power, or the maximum intense effort (often intermittent) produced while consuming oxygen. Contrast this with anaerobic effort, for which the body does not need oxygen to produce energy (speed, for example), and aerobic capacity effort, where the intensity is moderate (we often call it endurance or basic endurance).

The 30/30 Model

→ Choose 6 exercises—you can go up to 10—that are likely to engage at least 70 percent of your body mass (otherwise they become localized strength endurance exercises) to do with a partner, 30 sec for each one. Intensity: Sustained

Number of Reps

→ Minimum of 3

Recovery

→ 30 sec, alternating with your partner, no rest between exercises, no rest between sets

Practice the Technique, Work on the Sequences

→ This simple aerobic circuit is a fantastic base that can help you progress, not just in MAP, but also in your technical moves. You can use all variations to reinforce combined coordination work. You can start with simple and work your way up to complex moves by introducing more elaborate sequences, openings, combined moves, and specific feints. It's a remarkable way to reach the total number of moves you need to work on. Of course, it goes without saying that your form and technique must be excellent.

My Advice

→ Film yourself regularly so that you can note and correct your weaknesses.

EXERCISE 1

Japan test (side steps; crouch down by bending your knees as if you were picking something up off the floor)

EXERCISE 2

Back-and-forth *tsugi-ashi* (move your body in and out of your training partner's guard)

EXERCISE 3

Tsugi-ashi/tai-sabaki (*ippon-ko* type; alternate between opening in your partner's guard and rotating to get into position)

EXERCISE 4

Hiki-dashi (opening with maximum pull)

EXERCISE 5

Wheelbarrow

EXERCISE 6

Uchi-komi without a partner

EXERCISE 7

Uchi-mata or another judo-specific move

Making Your Body's pH Buffer Work for You

THE GREATEST PERFORMANCES ARE THOSE THAT LAST. TRUE, BUT ALSO DIFFICULT! HERE'S A FORMULA TO ENSURE THAT LENGTH DOESN'T EQUAL PAIN.

Although the duration of bouts may have been reduced, over the past few years new rules have forced judokas to keep fighting the same amount of time or even extend their efforts. The duration of effort has barely changed: it's about 7 minutes, for attacks lasting from 10 sec to 1 minute, with less than 30 sec of recovery time during *matte*. When you consider that the best fighters compete in 5 to 7 bouts to secure a gold medal (OK, so the majority won't win one, but if you don't aim for gold, you may as well stay home!), you get a sport in which endurance is still one of the more important factors in performance. And in training, this is even more true. When the mats are busy, there can be waves of judokas doing long series of *randori,* with a duration of effort that is equal to the recovery time. When there are fewer people involved, the stages of work are naturally more intense. If we add in exercises with different intensities like *uchi-komi, tate,* and *yaku-soku-geiko,* and do all that in 1.5 to 2 hours, we see, once more, that judokas with serious endurance can outlast others. In a competitive environment, as well as in training, here is what you need to know to improve your endurance.

Aerobics and Lactates

It's important not to forget that humans are aerobic creatures. Our predatory nature, and our tradition of hunting on foot, predisposes us to put in prolonged efforts of moderate intensity, rather than brief, dynamic effort. In the animal kingdom, there's no doubt that humans resemble a migrating bird more than a leopard. In this way, our energy system, often presented in terms of the most powerful pathway (the anaerobic alactic system in a dynamic athlete), should actually be approached via the aerobic system (in an athlete with high endurance). People have different types of muscle fibers available to produce muscular effort: slow-twitch and fast-twitch fibers. When the human machine switches on, the slow-twitch fibers are the first to get to work: they use the primary fuel, glycogen (the stored form of glucose), to produce pyruvate, a key element in the production of energy within the muscle energy system: the mitochondria. This system, in the presence of oxygen, is where the precious energy necessary for muscle contraction forms. But when the intensity increases, the fast-twitch fibers, producing the most intense contractions, start to work. But their mitochondria, which are significantly less efficient, are quickly overtaken by the production of pyruvate, which, instead of being immediately converted into energy, builds up at the entrance to the mitochondrion and becomes lactate.

What You Need to Know About the Physiology of Endurance:

Without getting into the obscure (and arduous) physiology of effort, let's still try to understand what makes some athletes more effective than others at maintaining or repeating effort. Why does a particular athlete possess endurance? You've likely heard talk of different energy systems, which are different ways the body processes energy to produce muscle contractions. Most often, you hear about three of these energy systems: the speed system, which doesn't require oxygen to function (explosiveness), the lactic system, which can also function without oxygen (resistance), and the enduring system, which allows you to produce effort in the presence of oxygen (athletes with stamina). These energy systems are often presented "in a row," one taking over from the other, depending on the type of effort. The reality is more nuanced than that: like a hybrid engine, the human body uses all of its systems to produce energy, right from the start. Depending on the intensity and duration of effort, each of the three systems participates more or less in total energy production.

EXERCISES

CIRCUIT 1

No rest between exercises. 20 sec per exercise. Repeat 6 times with 1 min of rest.

EXERCISE 1 Side steps

EXERCISE 2 Run in place

EXERCISE 3 *Yaku-soku-geiko*

EXERCISE 4 Lobster move

EXERCISE 5 Drop down on all fours and jump back up

EXERCISE 6 *Yaku-soku-geiko*

Duration
3 weeks, 1 or 2 circuit(s) per week during your judo session

CIRCUIT 2

No rest between exercises. 15 sec per exercise. Repeat 8 times with 1 min of rest.

EXERCISE 1 Side steps with sweep

EXERCISE 2 Lobster move

EXERCISE 3 *Kouchi-gari*

EXERCISE 4 Square exercise

EXERCISE 5 *Tsugi-ashi*

EXERCISE 6 Hurdles

EXERCISE 7 *Tai-sabaki*

EXERCISE 8 Bridges

Duration
3 weeks, 1 or 2 circuit(s) per week during your judo session

CIRCUIT 3

No rest between exercises. 12 sec per exercise. Repeat 6 times with 1 min of rest.

EXERCISE 1 Side steps with sweep

EXERCISE 2 Lobster move

EXERCISE 3 *Ko-uchi-gari*

EXERCISE 4 Square exercise

EXERCISE 5 Burpees

EXERCISE 6 *Tsugi-ashi*

EXERCISE 7 Hurdles

EXERCISE 8 Run in place

EXERCISE 9 *Tai-sabaki*

EXERCISE 10 Bridges

Duration
2 weeks, 1 circuit per week during your judo session

pH Buffering, a Key Performance Factor for Judokas

But lactate doesn't stop there: It is redirected to the slow-twitch fibers to take its own turn at producing energy. This means lactate is not the counterproductive performance factor as is often claimed; quite the contrary, in fact! It helps produce energy. Furthermore, the production of lactate helps accelerate the use of glucose by liberating it from H+ ions during transportation. So, the better we are at producing lactate, the better we perform. In fact, it's the increase in the H+ ions in the blood that causes problems and short-term disruptions in muscle contractions. These ions increase the acidity of the environment (incorrectly attributed to lactic acid) and should be taken care of by the body's buffer system, which is responsible for regulating acidity. The way in which the intracellular buffer system performs, therefore, plays an essential role in the way you perform in judo: as intensity rises, a well-trained judoka can generate a spectacular level of power during a fight, which means a huge amount of lactate and lots of H+ ions. This is when effort becomes rather difficult—you feel you might vomit, you become less lucid, your movements are less accurate and slower, you get cramps in your forearms, and so forth. This is a specific endurance parameter; it is therefore essential that judokas develop their buffering capacity to make progress.

Improve your Buffering Capacity

Numerous studies have been carried out with the goal of determining the best type of work to improve the body's buffering capacity. The most recent research agrees on a protocol of 2 minutes of effort at around 80 or 90 percent of the athlete's $\dot{V}O_2$max (the maximum amount of oxygen consumed during a drill; an intensity index), with one minute of recovery time. I have designed an eight-week program for you that guarantees you will reach the maximum possible intensity for the entire duration of the circuits. In other words, if you aren't able to finish the following circuits or if the intensity plummets, preventing you from finishing, it means you went too fast. During the next set or session, slow down. The exercises have been selected to provide a minimum level of intensity. This means you cannot hide in these circuits. Get ready, because you're going to sweat!

SEOI-NAGE

DROP DOWN ON ALL FOURS AND JUMP BACK UP

YAKU-SOKU-GEIKO

SWEEP

SQUARE EXERCISE

BRIDGES

HURDLES

LOBSTER MOVE

DON'T FORGET THE REST!

The body's buffering capacity is a major component of a judoka's endurance, but it's not the only one! Don't forget to take a look at the other sections of this book that explain how to increase your aerobic power or lactic endurance.

TAI-SABAKI

SIDEWAYS *TAI-SABAKI*

KO-UCHI

SIDE STEPS

BURPEES

RUN IN PLACE

LACTIC ACID DOESN'T EXIST!

This is a misnomer, used to describe what we formerly believed was responsible for acidity during heavy, lactate-producing effort. In fact, as you've no doubt understood, lactate is not as responsible for disrupting effort as H+ ions are. The pH necessary for us to talk about lactic acid is 3.5. But, within muscle, pH never surpasses 6.5. In fact, it's the breakdown of water molecules during energy production that liberates an H+ ion. For as long as the process takes place within the mitochondrion, the H+ ions are immediately recycled. But when intensity increases, mitochondrial saturation leads to energy being produced outside the mitochondrion, and the H+ ions are then not recycled, actually making your blood more acidic!

Lactic Circuit

HEAVY LEGS, FOREARM CRAMPS, NAUSEA, AND MORE AFTER 2 MINUTES; JUDO CAN BE PRETTY HARD WORK! HERE ARE MY TECHNIQUES FOR MAINTAINING TOP PERFORMANCE THROUGHOUT YOUR BOUTS.

You've likely experienced the sensation of nausea and fatigue in the first *randori* when you haven't warmed up sufficiently, or during the first bout of a competition. This unpleasant effect is linked to a specific function of an energy production system that makes muscle contraction possible: anaerobic glycolysis, more commonly known as the lactate system or resistance. After a few seconds of very intense effort, the reserves of explosive energy in the muscles run out, and you then have to draw on the sugar reserves in the muscles, liver, and blood to keep going. This causes a problem because, to produce muscle contractions, this process is accompanied by secondary effects that are very annoying for judokas, such as reduced coordination and accuracy of movement, a loss of lucidity, and nausea. These effects last until either your effort stops or you decrease your intensity, which changes how energy is produced by calling on more oxygen (aerobic system) to continue the exercise.

Since judo involves producing movements of continual quality and effectiveness for 5 minutes interspersed with *matte,* it's clear that the lactic dimension plays a significant part. The intensity of a judo bout requires constant use of this system.

It's crucial for judokas to practice the following:

→ Unleashing, if necessary, all the power they possess, by working at near-maximum intensity very quickly in the fight

→ Improving their ability to recover from these specific efforts, especially through oxygenation of the body

→ Increasing their physical and mental tolerance of this kind of effort

→ Maintaining accuracy of movement despite losing coordination and lucidity

The rules for effective lactic work are simple:

→ Long and passive recovery periods (4 to 6 min in the following examples)

→ Short and very intense sets (intermittent and under 3 min)

→ Near-maximum intensity, repeated several times during a set by dividing the effort

CIRCUIT 1

Adjustable

The goal here is to maintain a dizzying tempo throughout the bout. The circuit helps you work on your ability to push the boundaries of extreme physical effort and to renew this effort numerous times during a fight. You can modify the exercise to focus either on lactic capacity (i.e., keeping up a vigorous level of exertion for as long as possible) or on lactic power (i.e., pushing your effort to the maximum).

THE 45/15 MODEL

Alternate a long exercise (45 sec) with a need for coordination and a short judo drill (15 sec). With 8 exercises in a row, the intensity is at its maximum. Repeat the lactic capacity circuit 3 times and the lactic power circuit 2 times. Recovery occurs during the lactic capacity circuit; do the first exercise ball part without stopping, then take 4 to 5 min to recover. The recovery protocol is identical for the resistance band part. In the lactic power circuit, do all the exercises in a row without stopping, and then take 8 min to recover.

INTENSITY

Maximum intensity. 3 reps for the lactic capacity circuit, 2 reps for the lactic power circuit.

RECOVERY

In the lactic capacity circuit, do the exercise ball part without stopping (so 2 min of effort should be broken into 45 sec, 15 sec, 45 sec, 15 sec); then take 4 to 5 min to recover before doing the same thing for the resistance band part. In the lactic power circuit, you should do the exercises without stopping, and then take 8 min to recover.

→ Side steps while rolling the ball in a figure 8 around cones (45 sec)

→ Sweeps without a partner (15 sec)

→ Two training partners; each one should grip the ball with two hands (north-south and east-west) and fight for control of it (45 sec)

→ *Hiki-dashi* (simple opening with maximum pull), stressing the opening, or *kumikata* with a training partner (15 sec)

→ Coordination work with a band (45 sec)

→ *Uchi-komi* (15 sec)

→ Sideways movements via side steps with a resistance band, keeping the forearms at 90 degrees (45 sec)

→ Movement in a pair (15 sec)

CIRCUIT 2

The Three 15s

An athlete's resistance may emerge in several ways in judo. After roughly 15 seconds of effort, you have to be able to keep producing high levels of muscle power. As bouts are broken up by *matte*, this initial endurance phase entails the use of full power for up to 1 minute. This particular circuit will help improve this stage of effort.

→ 15 sec of running in place; try to do the highest possible number of steps

→ 15 sec of tuck jumps; jump as much as you can in 15 sec

→ 15 sec of *uchi-komi;* irrespective of the move, try to do as many as you can within the time allotted while maintaining accuracy

→ Finish with 5 *nage-komi* at top speed. After a cardio and judo-specific warm-up, I'd recommend you do 4 to 6 sets, with 4 to 5 min of recovery time between sets

---

CIRCUIT 3

The Longest 90 Seconds

Another form of resistance occurs at 1.5 min or at 2 min, when you are repeating intense actions and struggling against a loss of intensity. A very useful exercise, then, is to set up a simple circuit that we try to repeat as many times as possible during a given amount of time. As an example, I suggest the following routine, based on *ne-waza*.

→ 10 lobster moves

→ Move forward about 4 yd (4 m) on all fours

→ Combine forward movement on all fours/jumps

→ Move forward about 4 yd (4 m) on all fours

→ 10 square moves

→ Repeat in the other direction

→ Take 5 min to recover and do 3 to 6 sets in a row, after a specific warm-up

CIRCUIT 4

Stop and Go

Lactic endurance also manifests itself in the ability to renew your intensity after a phase of extreme fatigue. This is why longer circuits, where effort is divided up, make a lot of sense. Here's an example of a judo-integrated circuit to be done without any recovery time between exercises. Each exercise should be done at maximum intensity.

- → Side steps in a square for 30 sec
- → 10 sprints in place, 2 tuck jumps: repeat for 15 sec
- → 3 x 15 sec of *uchi-komi* with a throw at the 15 sec mark
- → 5 *nage-komi* with two training partners and 5 sec of resistance
- → 5 *nage-komi* at maximum speed
- → Do 4 sets with 5 min of recovery time

CIRCUIT 5

Infernal Sprints

Finally, it is crucial to recover properly between bouts so that you are ready to perform in the next fights. The quality of recovery is linked to the judoka's ability to use oxygen. Additionally, the circuit's intensity should be slightly lower and the length of recovery time a little bit shorter to prevent the athlete from recovering completely.

I suggest the following drill: Face a training partner who is at the other end of the dojo, and sprint back and forth between your partner and your starting position. While you're working, your partner rests and vice versa. Do 8 sets of 30 sec of effort with 30 sec of rest.

→ 6 *tai-sabaki*

→ Sprint to your partner at the other end of the mat

→ *Uchi-komi*

→ Sprint to your starting point

→ Repeat until the end of the 30 sec, when Uke switches roles with Tori

→ It's important to try to stick to the same number of sprints back and forth during each 30-second set

→ 10-WEEK PROGRAM EXAMPLE

2 WEEKS	INFERNAL SPRINTS
2 WEEKS	THE LONGEST 90 SECONDS
1 WEEK	INFERNAL SPRINTS
2 WEEKS	STOP AND GO
1 WEEK	INFERNAL SPRINTS
2 WEEKS	THE THREE 15s

IMPORTANT INFORMATION

How Should You Determine Load?

For any exercise involving a load percentage, you have to know how much you can lift, push, or pull, depending on the exercise, and your single-rep maximum. From there, it's easy to calculate the load percentage. A good tip: you can generally lift 75 percent of your single-rep max 10 times.

What Is an Unstable Support?

One of the most versatile unstable supports is, without a doubt, the Bosu ball, but what I use most often is the TerraCore balance trainer (see photo opposite), which is wider and more suitable to judo movements. On the other hand, this new piece of equipment is expensive and may be hard to find. As for the exercise ball, an essential tool for physical training, it is available in various sizes for a reasonable price. If necessary, a medicine ball lying around in the dojo should fit the bill.

How Can You Maintain the Accuracy of Your Skill Moves?

Be aware that a side effect of lactic work is a disruption of technical skills. You have to strive, even during physical and nervous fatigue, to maintain your move and its intention perfectly. Note that the transfer to judo will depend on how much you demand of yourself when doing the work.

Pointer

During warm-up and rest periods, work on technical moves used in the exercise so that you do them correctly during the exercise.

How Can You Work on Speed?

Without making any major changes, it's possible to convert the lactic circuit into a speed circuit. To do that, do each of the 15 sec exercises but try to do the maximum number of moves within that time. Take 2 to 3 minutes to recover between exercises.

When Should You Do These Circuits?

The speed and lactic power circuits require you to be fresh, so you should do those immediately after your warm-up. Lactic capacity can be worked on at any time, so long as you're not exhausted from a previous training session. Speed can be worked on all the time. Traditionally, we start the year by making lactic capacity a priority, but we can just as easily do lactic power circuits. Don't ever get stuck in a routine!

The amount of rest you should take between two identical circuits is as follows:

- → **72 hours for lactic circuits**
- → **24 to 48 hours for speed work**
- → **There's no reason not to do an aerobic circuit regularly. Why not make it a regular thing at the end of your training?**

Strength and Endurance: A Winning Combination

IS THERE ANYTHING MORE TRADITIONAL OR NATURAL THAN ALTERNATING SPRINTS AND PUSH-UPS IN A PHYSICAL CONDITIONING SESSION? BUT IT DOESN'T ALWAYS WORK. IN THIS SECTION, I'LL EXPLAIN HOW TO BALANCE OUT YOUR TRAINING WITH A BLEND OF MUSCLE STRENGTHENING AND ENDURANCE THAT WILL MAKE IT MORE EFFECTIVE.

Old methods are tried and true, and we need to keep some of them handy so we can go back to them and update them for today's needs. In fact, although sessions that combine muscle development and cardio have come back into fashion in the world of physical training, it's not necessarily in the same way as it was done in the past. The idea of mixing running with squats in the same training drill is not really all that novel, and it was always a fairly natural thing for an athlete and coach to do, up until the emergence of more specialized models. During the 2000s, a pair of researchers, Docherty and Sporer, were the first to brush the dust off this old concept. Why? Saving time by working on two physical attributes instead of one, during a single session, and getting as close as possible to competitive athletic effort.

Watch Out for Interference!

In the area of strength and endurance, judokas have always been rather intuitive, applying their method, consistently, for preserving the spirit of judo in training by participating in what we might call a crazy session.

Unfortunately, in the wake of Docherty and Sporer, it has become clear that "crazy" can be more, or less, effective. This appears to be due to interference, for example when two training components become contradictory and conflict with each other. It turns out that the maximum zone of interference between strength training and endurance training is reached during a situation that we might tend to fall into accidentally: combining high-intensity aerobic effort (e.g., a set of back-and-forth sprints) with strength work involving sets of 10 to 12 repetitions. That precise mix imposes incompatible physiological pressure on the body and renders one component or both ineffective. To be clear, it just doesn't work. But there are lots of other blends that do work, from which I've selected the two I'm suggesting for you here, via four exercises. These can be used for a combined training that is effective.

COMBINATION 1

Maximum Strength and MAP

Aerobic power and high-intensity strength appear to combine well within the same session. Please note that if the supporting activity during training is judo itself (*uchi-komi, nage-komi, randori,* etc.), then we can hope for an immediate strength transfer.

AFTER A FULL WARM-UP

[A] 3 x 3 plank pulls at 90 percent of your max (the heaviest weight you can manage with maximum effort in a single repetition); *5 min of recovery between sets*
[B] 10-15 x 15 sec of *uchi-komi* with *15 sec of recovery* between sets*
[C] 5 min to recover
[D] 3 x 3 squats at 90 percent of your max; *5 min of recovery between sets*
[E] 10 x 30 sec of kumikata work in motion; *30 sec of recovery**

**Low-intensity recovery during which the athlete remains active.*

COMBINATION 2 CIRCUIT 1

Strength and Endurance 1

The muscles will adapt to the suggested strength training without any negative reactions to the physiological adaptations of the cardiopulmonary mechanisms (hypertrophy work: average weight for 8 to 10 repetitions).

CONTINUOUS EFFORT FOLLOWED BY A STRENGTH CIRCUIT

→ **Continuous effort:** Run for 20 to 40 min at variable speeds

→ **Strength:** Body weight muscle-strengthening circuit with no rest time.
Combine:
[A] 8 push-ups
[B] 8 forward lunges per leg
[C] 8 pull-ups
[D] 8 leg bends on one leg, then 8 on the other

→ Recover for a maximum of 1 min, and then repeat the entire strength circuit 4 to 7 times

COMBINATION 2 CIRCUIT 2

Strength and Endurance 2

Within a circuit, without any recovery time, alternate between muscle-strengthening and cardio exercise. There are two options, depending on your inspiration and resources: dissociated (i.e., without judo) or associated (working with a partner for certain exercises).

DISSOCIATED

[A] Shuffle the feet, 30 sec

[B] 8 bench presses *(with max weight for 10 reps)*

[C] Jumping lunges on a bench, 30 sec

[D] 8 pull-ups on a bar *(assisted or weighted if necessary)*

[E] Back-and-forth sprints, 30 sec

[F] 8 squats *(with max weight for 10 repetitions)*

[G] Japan test *(side steps, with bent legs, as if you were picking up an object)*, 30 sec

[H] 8 high pulls with a resistance band attached to your feet or a bar

[I] Knee lifts, 30 sec

[J] 8 deadlifts

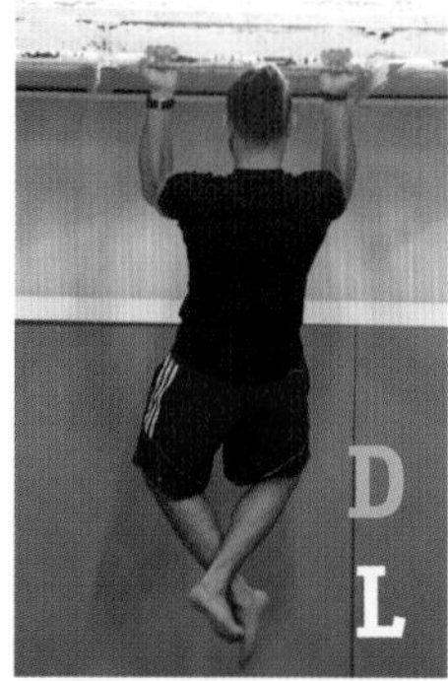

ASSOCIATED

→ ***Uchi-komi* in motion,** 30 sec

[K] 8 bench presses

→ ***Uchi-komi* in the mirror** (each take a turn), 30 sec

[L] 8 pull-ups (assisted, if need be)

[M] Move in a square, 30 sec

[N] 8 squats

→ **Alternate *nage-komi*,** 30 sec

[O] 8 high pulls with a resistance band attached to your feet or a bar

[P] Lobster move, 30 sec

[Q] 8 deadlifts

Recovery: 2 to 3 min between circuits so you can rehydrate.

COMBINATION 3

Strength and Endurance 3

In combination: It's possible to use strength and cardio hybrid exercises. They should be simple enough that they can be done when you are very tired, but sufficiently complex that they activate the cardiorespiratory process. This model has the advantage of being the most specific work you can do without a partner.

EACH EXERCISE LASTS 20 SEC WITH 10 SEC OF RECOVERY TIME

[A] Presses

[B] Sideways step up onto bench + front lift with dumbbells

[C] Jumping pull-ups (with rope or bar)

[D] Step up onto the step with one leg, then back down, with a dumbbell press

[E] Push-up followed by a vertical jump

[F] Deadlift + high pulls

[G] Cleans

[H] Alternating jumping lunges

Recovery: 2 to 3 min after each full circuit so you can rehydrate.

Repeat the circuit 3 to 5 times.

A

C

B

E

H

D

F

Battle Ropes

*ROPES CAN BE USED IN A THOUSAND DIFFERENT WAYS.
THE TIMES WHERE WE ONLY USED THEM FOR CLIMBING HAVE CHANGED.
TODAY, ROPES ARE ALSO USED ON THE GROUND.*

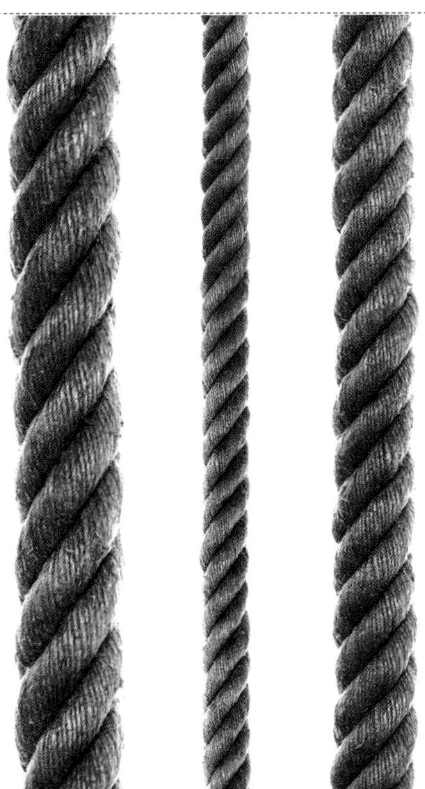

Ropes have been detached from the ceiling. We're talking about the battle ropes, part of modern retro sports training ideas. Cross-training, CrossFit, fitness boot camps, and Strongman competitions have specialized in taking these tools out of the attic. Ropes are gradually moving from a pure muscle strengthening tool toward a collection of more mixed exercises, in which the dominant feature can range from strength to cardio. Because it is ultra-specific to judokas, I felt obliged to come back to this tool since it simultaneously develops grip strength, the rotator cuff, the back muscles, the scapular stabilizers, and even, if you really apply yourself, the lower limbs. Abdominal muscles, biceps, triceps, and forearms are also significantly engaged.

It is therefore an incredible tool: A major cardiovascular and preventive dimension is added to the intense muscle engagement already present when climbing the rope. It is becoming increasingly popular and can now be found at a number of sources.

Installing the Rope

To achieve maximum intensity, you need a strong anchoring point. If you're outdoors, a tree or a pole will do the trick. In the middle of a *tatami*, you could use a kettlebell or dumbbell (but these must be heavy enough for the anchorage, and by extension, the length of the rope, to remain fixed). Once it's attached, uncoil the rope completely, taking care to keep two parts that are equal in length.

Choose Your Rope

There are two parameters to consider when choosing a rope, based on your goals: the diameter (and thus, its weight) and the length (and thus, the strength required for the undulating waves to reach the end of the rope). The thicker the rope, the greater the emphasis on grip, strength, and lactic aspects as you work. The longer the rope, the more your power ranges (and power boosts in the case of prolonged effort) are engaged. The thinner the rope, the more suitable it is for aerobic circuits and elevated heart rate workouts.

As a guide, these ropes often weigh between 29 lb (13 kg) and 33 lb (15 kg) and have a diameter of 1.5 in (40 mm) and a length of 17 yd (15 m). They can, however, be a lot lighter, much heavier (you can even equip yourself with the kind of rope used for boats), or longer, up to 27 yd (25 m) or even 33 yd (30 m). Judokas have widely varied objectives and can therefore benefit, for different reasons, from distinct types of rope.

EXAMPLES OF FULL CIRCUITS

→ Improve the start of your fight.
Do the following sequence as quickly as possible (time yourself):
20 *uchi-komi*
10 rope slams
5 *nage-komi*
10 x 1 rope slam + 1 burpee
5 *nage-komi*
4 to 6 sets
5 min of recovery time

→ Ramp things up in the second part of the fight.
Do all of the following sequence while avoiding a drop in intensity:
20 sec of undulating waves, varying the amplitude
10 sec rest
20 sec maximum intensity, low amplitude
10 sec rest
20 sec slams
10 sec rest
20 sec spent alternating 2 slams and 2 tuck jumps
20 sec *uchi-komi*
5 *nage-komi*
3 to 5 sets
4 to 6 min of recovery time

→ Improve your ability to compete in successive bouts during *randori* or tournaments.
10 exercises or stations:
Station 1: Low amplitude work
Station 2: High amplitude work
Station 3: *Uchi-komi*
Station 4: Slams
Station 5: Side slams
Station 6: *Nage-komi*
Station 7: Crossovers
Station 8: Low amplitude
Station 9: *Uchi komi*
Station 10: *Nage komi*
Repeat this circuit 3 times by working for 30 sec and recovering for 20 sec between the exercises in the first circuit, for 10 sec in the second circuit, and for 15 sec in the last circuit.

EXERCISE 1

Low-Amplitude Work

Keep your back straight and knees bent throughout the exercise. Lean slightly forward, pulling in your stomach and keeping your core tight. You can intensify the cardio aspect by either putting one knee on the floor, walking slowly backward, bouncing, or opening and closing your legs, and so forth. Aim to keep the undulating waves going along the entire length of the rope.

CARDIO ★ ★ ★	STRENGTH ★ ★	COORDINATION ★ ★	CORE STRENGTH ★

DEVELOPING FREQUENCY OF MOVEMENT

→ Produce as many waves as possible in 8 sec, take 2 min to recover, and repeat 3 to 6 times.

DEVELOPING LACTIC ENDURANCE

→ Keep up the highest tempo you can manage (ideally with a large-diameter rope) for 4 x 20 sec, with 5 to 10 sec of recovery time. Then rest for 4 min and repeat 3 to 6 times.

DEVELOPING AEROBIC ENDURANCE

→ By slightly reducing the intensity (but still maintaining enough speed to keep the waves constant), do 10 x 15 sec of effort with 15 sec of recovery time. Stop for 1 min to rehydrate and repeat up to 3 times.

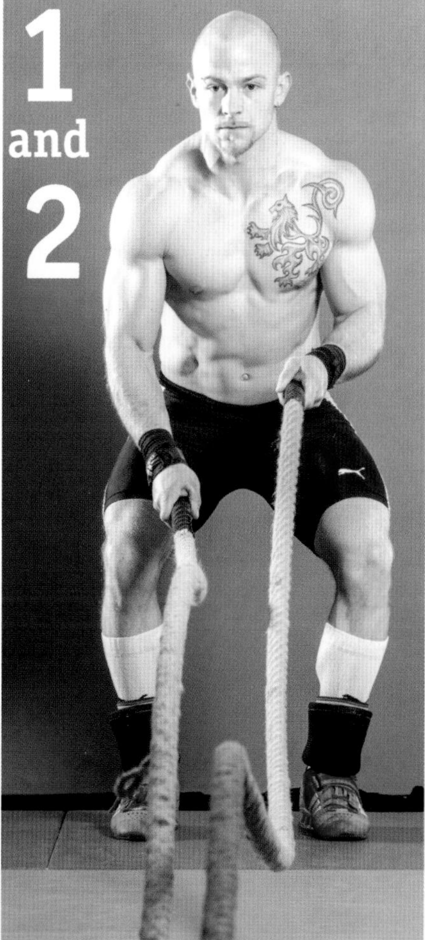

EXERCISE 2

High-Amplitude Work

Tempo is key in this exercise, where you'll produce a large range of motion. Compared to your position in the previous exercise, you'll need to straighten up to maximize the amplitude and the engagement of the rotator cuff. Keep your back straight and stick out your chest.

CARDIO ★ ★	STRENGTH ★ ★	COORDINATION ★ ★	CORE STRENGTH ★ ★

DEVELOPING POWER ENDURANCE

→ Do 16 undulating waves of maximum amplitude as fast as you can. Recover for 2 min, and then repeat 2 to 5 times.

DEVELOPING LACTIC ENDURANCE

→ Keep up the highest tempo you can manage while maintaining maximum amplitude (ideally with a large-diameter rope) for 40 sec. Take 3 to 4 min to recover and repeat 4 to 6 times.

DEVELOPING AEROBIC ENDURANCE

→ Slightly reduce the intensity, perhaps with a small-diameter rope (still keeping up sufficient speed to constantly maintain the waves) and do 8 to 10 x 20 sec of effort with 15 sec of recovery time. Stop for 1 min to rehydrate and repeat up to 3 times.

EXERCISE 3

The Slam

The goal here is to generate maximum power by accelerating the rope as much as possible before dropping it to the ground. Your position should not change relative to the two previous exercises.

CARDIO ★	STRENGTH ★ ★ ★	COORDINATION ★	CORE STRENGTH ★ ★

DEVELOPING CORE STRENGTH

→ Do 8 slams at maximum amplitude and speed. 2 min of recovery time, and a total of 4 to 6 sets.

DEVELOPING LACTIC POWER

→ Do the maximum number of slams (ideally with a large-diameter rope) for 45 sec to 1 min. Take 5 min of recovery time and repeat 4 to 6 times.

EXERCISE 4

Lateral Slams

This exercise adds a torso rotation to the arm- and back-strengthening aspects, as well as the cardiovascular stimulation, making it a formidable, dynamic, core-strengthening drill. The work is much more intense for the obliques and the comprehensive muscle synergy makes this exercise particularly good for judokas. The starting position is identical to that used in the previous exercise, with a straight upper body; however, the grip is reversed. The waves are created by swinging the two parts of the rope from right to left while keeping the waves going along the entire length of the rope.

CARDIO ★	STRENGTH ★ ★	COORDINATION ★ ★	CORE STRENGTH ★ ★ ★

DEVELOPING CORE STRENGTH

→ Do 20 waves (10 per side). Recover for 1 min 30 sec. Do a total of 4 sets.

DEVELOPING LACTIC ENDURANCE

→ Do 5 x 20 waves (10 per side), taking 5 sec of recovery time. Keep up the highest tempo you can manage while maintaining maximum amplitude (ideally with a large-diameter rope). Take 3 to 4 min to recover and repeat 4 to 6 times.

DEVELOPING AEROBIC ENDURANCE

→ Slightly reduce the intensity, perhaps by using a small-diameter rope (still keeping up a sufficient level of speed to constantly maintain the waves) and do 8 to 10 x 30 sec of effort with 20 sec of recovery time. Stop for 1 min to rehydrate and repeat up to 3 times.

EXERCISE 5

Crossovers

Maintain your very straight posture, with or without lower-body movement. Now the wave is horizontal instead of vertical. The lateral raise of the arms changes how the shoulder and upper arm muscles are engaged, rounding out the judoka's training.

CARDIO ★	STRENGTH ★	COORDINATION ★ ★ ★	CORE STRENGTH ★ ★

DEVELOPING STRENGTH ENDURANCE

→ Do 20 waves every 30 sec. The faster you do this, the more recovery time you should take, so if you take 15 sec to perform 20 waves, rest for 15 extra sec and begin the next set of 20 waves. Do 10 to 15 sets.

DEVELOPING LACTIC ENDURANCE

→ Keep up the highest tempo you can manage while maintaining maximum amplitude (ideally with a medium-diameter rope) for 20 sec. After 10 sec of recovery time, repeat twice. After you've done it 3 times, take 3 to 4 min of passive recovery time and then repeat 4 times.

DEVELOPING AEROBIC ENDURANCE

→ 12 x 15 sec of effort with 15 sec of recovery time. Stop for 1 min to rehydrate, and then repeat up to 3 times.

Uchi-Komi: The Ultimate Weapon?

LET'S CONTINUE THE DEBATE ABOUT THE BEST WAY TO MAXIMIZE A JUDOKA'S ENDURANCE BY LOOKING AT THE HOW USEFUL UCHI-KOMI *IS AS A TRAINING TOOL.*

STAY ON COURSE!

Let's not forget this recurring theme:

Uchi-komi is an exercise that involves repeated practice of throwing motions, a fundamental element of judo.

This move can only become a supporting activity in training if it is correctly integrated and constantly done in a way that mirrors a real throwing situation, including the correct intensity and speed.

A poorly executed move will cost you technically, and with less engagement and poor positioning, it will become a less effective training support. Fatigue or a desire to move quickly should never prevent you from achieving the best possible technique. Only judokas with excellent technique (and a good partner) will be able to use more complex exercises like *nage-komi* and *yaku-soku-geiko* during training.

MY ADVICE

→ Work regularly on technical aspects in specific sessions to improve your abilities.

→ The goal is to throw an opponent. To make your placement more realistic and to maintain the logical end of the movement, it is wise to insert some *nage-komi* at the end of your sets.

The question that springs to mind most often when we talk about cardio training for judo is one that I continue to ask myself quite often: What is the ultimate supporting activity? By that I mean an activity that allows judokas to increase their endurance, become more resistant, and enhance their performances. It's the Holy Grail for any physical trainer.

I've already talked about the vast range of options trainers have available now: running, treadmills, elliptical trainers, rowing machines, punching bags, jump ropes, team sports—but these rarely incorporate judo. However, the philosophy of cardio training as part of physical training is very easy to sum up: It's a way of simplifying the athlete's usual activity to increase the intensity. In other words, we limit the complexity of the setup to favor physical density. For example, a soccer or rugby player will run a lot in training, because it's their principal method of movement. However, without a ball or opponents, they end up doing it at a much higher intensity than during a game. In rowing, the activity is often simplified by using a rowing machine, which reduces the difficulty of coordinating the movement so that rowers can focus more on the effort.

Given the variety involved in their sport, judokas have even more training aids available to them: *uchi-komi, nage-komi,* and even *yaku-soku-geiko* are simplifications of judo's complex throwing move. But, for the most part, they are essentially used for technical purposes; they're simplified so that you can perfect the right movement, the right positioning, the right pace, and the right sequence. These exercises are not used very often to achieve physical training goals, especially *uchi-komi*. I suggest using it in several types of routines to achieve different physical targets.

The 15/15: Endurance-focused *uchi-komi,* renewable energy

When?

This type of routine can be used at the start of the season and continued throughout. This endurance applies to other qualities and is often called basic. It enables you to

→ be more effective in training,

→ recover more quickly between sets, sessions, and competitions, and

→ finish bouts more easily and build momentum during a tournament.

Example of a Specific Endurance Routine

Effort duration = recovery time

15 sec *uchi-komi,* 15 sec of recovery time while your training partner works

Set duration: between 8 and 12 min

1 to 3 times within the same session

3 min of recovery time between sets

Intensity

Regulates itself automatically throughout the exercise.

The Pyramid: Resistance-focused *uchi-komi*, a diesel engine

When?

This type of session comes a bit later in the season for nonelite athletes. In fact, the required intensity calls for a sufficient level of physical and technical training so that the exercise is still judo despite the intensity the judoka has to face. If you practice this exercise regularly, you'll be able to accelerate more easily and repeat these accelerations after 1 min of your bout.

Example of a Specific Resistance Routine

Effort pyramid (to represent the different durations of judo bouts): 15 sec, 20 sec, 30 sec, 20 sec, 15 sec.

Recovery 10 sec without doing anything between sets. This routine can be repeated 3 to 6 times in a session, with 4 to 5 min of recovery time in between.

Intensity Maximum, regulated by the need to sustain it throughout the exercise. Tori does the entire routine before switching places and becoming Uke.

The Descent: Power-focused *uchi-komi*, a 16-valve engine

When?

The athlete must also be well-prepared for this type of effort. It is, therefore, possible to start it after a few weeks of regular training. This time, the goal is to set a very intense pace right from the outset of the fight, from the opening few seconds up to the 1-minute mark.

Example of a Specific Power Routine

Decreasing duration: 30 sec, 20 sec, 15 sec.

Recovery 5 sec of recovery time between sets.

Repeat up to 6 times during the session. After each routine, take 5 min of recovery time.

Intensity As soon as you are no longer able to work at the highest intensity, it's time to stop! The goal is to maintain maximum intensity to the end.

Using Judo to Train for Judo

IT'S A FACT THAT JAPAN IS, TECHNICALLY SPEAKING, THE TOP NATION IN THE WORLD. BUT ITS NATIONAL TEAM IS RARELY OUTMUSCLED, EVEN THOUGH THE ATHLETES PRIMARILY FOCUS ONLY ON JUDO. THEY ARE A FANTASTIC EXAMPLE OF HOW JUDO CAN SERVE AS A SUPPORTING ACTIVITY FOR PHYSICAL TRAINING.

The technical and tactical complexity of judo has no equal when it comes to the variety of physical skills that are developed. Judokas must simultaneously be powerful and have great endurance, as well as be fast and very strong, in all planes of motion and in all muscle groups. With that in mind, it seems pertinent to use judo for physical training. While the Japanese have always shown how effective this can be, it has only become obvious to the rest of us over the past couple of years. Although our judo culture and our Western training methods do not necessarily lend themselves to its exclusive use in training, it can, nevertheless, be very useful to think about calibrating the load to achieve our goals.

In fact, this strategy, which is particularly good for competitions, can also serve as an alternative for young athletes who often don't have time for dissociated physical training. Here are a few key exercises to help you focus on specific physical training.

Increase Your Endurance by Combining *Randori, Uchi-Komi,* and *Yaku*

A judoka's effective endurance comes with intensity and not just length of time. A judo session is actually a succession of a many *hajime-matte* in a series of intense phases. So, the key to a consistent training routine lies in dividing phases of intense effort and alternating with active recovery periods. Moreover, this strategy will increase the fighter's exposure to a near-$\dot{V}O_2$max level of intensity, where we consume the maximum amount of oxygen and see a marked improvement in our endurance.

3 SESSIONS: BUILD YOURSELF AN ENGINE FOR JUDO-SPECIFIC INTERMITTENT EFFORT

The first step is to get used to intermittent effort, especially if it's specific to judo. With an attack during a bout ranging from 5 sec to 2 min in the worst-case scenario, you will need to explore all of these situations. Remember that the more active you are in the recovery period, the more beneficial the work is for specific endurance. Ideally, then, you should favor training situations where you recover while your partner works.

I suggest a pyramid-like setup of themed work: When Tori attacks, Uke defends while recovering (you can give each other pointers), before switching roles. In this way, if you start as Tori, you'll attack for 5 sec and then do 5 sec of active defense.

10-10 / 15-15
30-30 / 45-45
60-60 / 120-120
60-60 / 45-45
30-30 / 15-15
10-10 / 5-5

During the session, you can repeat the exercises 2 or 3 times, taking 2 min to rest.

3 SESSIONS: VARY THE INTENSITY OF THE SESSION

Long- and middle-distance runners use a technique known as fartlek, where variations in speed or grade enable them to alternate very high-intensity work with active recovery. The goal is to participate in a session in which you spend as much time as possible at an effective intensity level and you consume a lot of oxygen. This type of method is largely transferable to judo, where we can use *uchi-komi* for pushing the intensity to the maximum, *randori* for medium to high intensity, and *yaku-soku-geiko* for active recovery.

Try, for example, the following circuit:

→ *Randori* for 140 sec

→ After a very short *matte* (like what happens during a bout), high-intensity *uchi-komi* (Uke and Tori attack constantly)

→ Short, maximum-intensity *randori*: you have 40 sec to throw your partner

→ High-intensity *uchi-komi* for 20 sec

→ Active recovery then *yaku* for 60 sec

Here you have a 5-min aerobic power (intense endurance) sequence, which is as specific to intermittent effort as it is to the supporting activity, which is judo. Depending on your level or your group's level, you can repeat this exercise 3 to 5 times in one session without any breaks.

3 SESSIONS: SHORT-SHORT

In physical training, we usually end an endurance training cycle with a particularly intense short-short effort, repeated several times. Static *uchi-komi* and *uchi-komi* in motion lend themselves very well to this type of work.

Judoka 1:
30 sec static *uchi-komi*

Judoka 2:
30 sec *uchi-komi* in motion

Judoka 1:
15 sec static *uchi-komi*

Judoka 2:
15 sec *uchi-komi* in motion 3 times without recovery time. Recover for 2 min and then switch roles. Do 2 to 4 times during the session.

Accelerate Your Throws With Contrasting Loads

Explosive strength development enthusiasts in the weights room will be familiar with the heavy-light workout where you incorporate both loads into your routine. As long as you have perfectly mastered the technical moves, you can transfer this principle to judo. Here is an example of a progression over nine sessions (at a rate of 1 or 2 sessions per week).

3 SESSIONS: EXPLOSIVE-STRENGTH-FOCUSED *UCHI-KOMI* AND *NAGE-KOMI*

The more the work is focused on strength, the bigger should be the gap between the heavy and light load. To be precise, you should become acquainted with these contrasting techniques as you develop your explosive strength.

Use the following circuits:

→ 6 *uchi-komi* with resistance. Lift your training partner onto your back (3 sec for each repetition) while a third person holds him or her back by the belt, then lowers him or her back down

→ 50 sec of recovery time

→ 3 *nage-komi* at maximum speed, with minimal resistance from your partner. To go faster still, you can even throw a much lighter partner

→ 2 min of recovery time (to give you time to switch roles and take your turn at holding Uke)

Do up to 6 sets.

3 SESSIONS: OVERSPEED AND TRANSFER-FOCUSED *UCHI-KOMI*

This time, the light stage follows the heavy stage immediately, causing overspeed during the technical execution. This transition also optimizes the transfer of the intense muscle contraction during the heavy stage to rapid movement.

→ 6 *hiki-dashi* with a training partner deliberately slowing you down followed by 6 *hiki-dashi* with a partner who jumps while moving so that he or she feels lighter

→ 1 min of recovery time after each set. 2 min every 3 sets. Repeat this exercise 6 to 9 times. You can also change the supporting activity.

3 SESSIONS: SPEED *UCHI-KOMI* AND *NAGE-KOMI*

This exercise is about speed, so the time between the heavy and light exercises is reduced to initiate the transfer effects (this is more pronounced in the third section of exercises).

→ 6 *hiki-dashi* (major opening using the arms) with a training partner deliberately slowing you down

→ 30 sec of recovery

→ 6 *nage-komi* at maximum speed

→ 2 min of recovery time (during which you act as the partner and then take a turn holding back Uke)

Do up to 6 sets.

→ *Uchi-komi* while being held back by a partner.

Use *Nage-Komi* to Increase Your Power

Speed and strength attributes combine to help your technique by generating the specific throwing power you need in judo. Whether we're talking about explosive strength (the ability to exert maximal force in minimal time), speed-focused power (medium to light loads at maximum speed), strength-focused power (heavy to medium loads at maximum speed), or even a repetition of a certain level of power, judo itself is all you need to generate watts in training. Here's how!

3 SESSIONS: EXPLOSIVE STRENGTH

Static-dynamic training is very effective at developing explosive strength and sustaining maximum strength. In judo, this takes the form of a *nage-komi* held in place; this creates an intense static contraction, which is suddenly released by the throw, generating maximum acceleration.

Tori attempts to throw Uke while a third person holds Uke back by the belt. Tori, at maximum intensity, tries to throw both partners within 5 sec. After 5 sec, Uke is released by the third person in order to be thrown. 6-throw set, up to a 5 sec hold each time.

Take a 2 min rest before repeating 3 to 6 times.

3 SESSIONS: POWER ENDURANCE

In judo, maximum strength or maximum power are rarely part of the equation since the goal is not to produce a "killer" muscle contraction of absolute intensity. Renewing your optimum levels of power throughout the bout, session, or competition so you can perform effectively can, however, be decisive, and you should always be in a position to produce and reproduce high-intensity actions despite your fatigue.

3 sets of 8 *nage-komi* with 1 min of rest at the end of the session have proven very effective in achieving this goal.

3 SESSIONS: SUSTAINING POWER

Once you are comfortable with throwing at maximum intensity, even when you're extremely tired, you have to be able to maintain that level of power, throw after throw. With this in mind, a formidable exercise is to repeat a maximum number of throws in a set time frame, with 2 or 3 training partners who take turns being thrown and getting back up again as quickly as possible.

Try this exercise for 30 sec, then take 15 sec to recover. Do it again for 30 sec and recover for 15 sec.

Do it one last time for 20 sec and then recover for 6 min. This will give your three training partners—if you're in a group of four—time to take their turn.

Repeat 3 to 5 times.

Uchi-Komi and Rhythm: A Winning Blend?

TECHNICAL WORK AND PHYSICAL CONDITIONING: THESE ARE THE GOALS OF JUDOKAS' FUNDAMENTAL EXERCISE, UCHI-KOMI. *HOWEVER, IF DONE TOO QUICKLY, THIS EXERCISE CAN END UP BEING COUNTERPRODUCTIVE. BUT WHAT IF EVERYTHING WERE A QUESTION OF RHYTHM?*

Uchi-komi is an absolutely key component of judo training. We ascribe to it great benefits related to learning and technical development, as well as to the improvement of physical attributes (speed and endurance in particular). However, even focusing solely on the technical dimension, there's still no escaping the eternal battle between speed and accuracy. And when we add the element of physical work, fatigue can ultimately hamper your efforts.

Sometimes, this is where you see a bit of everything: A superb *tsugi-ashi* that impacts your opponent can quickly be transformed into a sad-looking side step that looks more like Zumba than judo.

But can we reconcile the technical and physical dimensions? Can we become fast and accurate and improve our endurance through *uchi-komi*? Since we are great fans of integrated physical training, we like to think so! Let's take a little detour and look at the concept of *uchi-komi* rhythm.

SPEED

The *uchi-komi* sequences should be short (20 sec max) and the rhythm must be optimal (i.e., 10 sec for 10 *uchi-komi*). There may be an additional rep in one or two sets. The quality of movement must be the priority, otherwise your motor pattern may become affected. It is best to stop work once you cannot maintain the optimal rhythm in two consecutive sets (-2 repetitions compared to the optimal rhythm).

ENDURANCE

The sequences are long (minimum of 30 sec) and the rhythm is slower than for speed circuits (e.g., 40 reps in 45 sec). The rhythm must be maintained; you can be more lenient with the number of repetitions, but not with the quality of execution. Beyond 45 sec, the quality drops significantly. We do not recommend going longer than 60 sec.

LACTIC

Sequences are an average length. The optimal rhythm should be maintained for as long as possible, and a decrease in the number of repetitions likely indicates that fatigue is setting in.

Uchi-Komi Rhythm

By *uchi-komi* rhythm, we mean the number of repetitions within an allotted time, for example, 25 *uchi-komi* in 30 sec. The rhythm depends on the technique used, the capabilities of each judoka, and the degree of resistance offered by Uke. We talk about optimum rhythm when the judoka cannot manage another repetition without the technical execution being impaired. With fatigue, the optimum rhythm may decrease.

Be wary of extrapolating: Being able to do 10 *uchi-komi* in 10 seconds does not necessarily mean that it's possible to do 60 *uchi-komi* in 1 minute. It is better to assess the rhythm using different timings, providing you with specific benchmarks for each movement and each number of repetitions.

Finally, it's worth noting that the subrhythm is not without interest: It can be beneficial for active recovery, as well as for tiny technical adjustments. As you vary your *uchi-komi* rhythm, you'll become aware of the physical and technical effectiveness of the method, and you may find yourself going so far as to vary the rhythm within the same set (slow-fast-slow, fast-slow-fast, for example).

What Does It Do?

This allows you to personalize your *uchi-komi* training. Instead of imposing a fixed number of repetitions for everyone, we establish a time frame (30 sec, for example) and each judoka knows the number of *uchi-komi* that he or she needs to perform according to the chosen technique.

In this way, everyone has a clear indicator of their training intensity, but also of his or her progress. Always remember that the quality of execution must remain the priority. If your technique deteriorates, you should stop the set.

Is It Relevant?

Yes, to the extent that the physiological adaptations are specific to the muscle actions used (Hather et al. 1991), the speed of movement (Kanehisa and Miyashita 1983), and the energy systems involved (Mac Dougall et al. 1998). Consequently, the concept of optimum rhythm can be a versatile tool, falling somewhere between technical and physical development.

How Can You Use It?

Step 1: Find Out Your Optimum Rhythm

All you have to do for this is count the number of (correctly executed) repetitions for a technique within a given time frame. Do an assessment for each exercise duration and for each technique that is part of your attack plan. We recommend you use the following 5 standard durations: 10, 20, 30, 45 sec, and 1 min.

Step 2: Develop Your Physical Condition

Then you can plan a routine depending on the desired goal: speed, endurance, or lactic. The benefit of a rhythm is that it gives you a tempo and a goal while helping you to see how you are working, whether too slow or too fast. As for the trainer or coach, it helps them assess the work the judoka puts in and how invested he or she is.

THROWING IS THE GOAL!

Remember that *uchi-komi* helps you adjust your positioning in readiness for a throw. That's why the advice we give to all our judokas is as qualitative as it's always been: Plan your throw. We like to push this philosophy to its rightful conclusion by releasing the movement at the end of the set with a *nage-komi* as the very last repetition.

Examples

FORWARD-MOTION TECHNIQUES (with a half turn, as in *seoi-nage* or *tai-otoshi*)

→ **FAST:** 7 sec, 1 min of recovery. The number of repetitions depends on the judoka's skill and rotation capacity when performing these techniques; we generally include 6 to 10 reps

→ **FAST-SLOW-FAST:** 5 sec at high speed, immediately followed by 4 sec of slow recovery time and adjustments (about 2 movements), and then 5 sec at high speed

→ **SLOW-FAST-SLOW:** 5 sec of slow physical and rhythmic preparation, then 10 sec at full speed, and then 5 sec returning to a slower pace

BACKWARD-MOTION TECHNIQUES (such as *o-soto-gari* or *tsugi-ashi* basics)

→ **FAST:** 15 sec, 1 min of recovery time. The number of repetitions depends on the judoka's stride rate and skill level when performing these techniques; we generally include 10 to 20 reps

→ **FAST-SLOW-FAST:** 7 sec at high speed, immediately followed by 5 sec slow recovery time and adjustments (about 2 movements), and then 7 sec at high speed

→ **SLOW-FAST-SLOW:** 6 sec of slow physical and rhythmic preparation, then 15 sec at full speed, and then 5 sec returning to a slower pace

ALL MOVEMENTS

→ **SESSION 1:** 10 × 30 sec of effort with 20 sec of recovery time, 1 min of recovery time, 10 × 30 sec of effort with 10 sec of recovery time, 1 min of recovery time, 10 × 30 sec of effort for 15 sec of recovery time

→ **SESSION 2:** 15-15/20-20/30-30/40-40/30-30/20-20/15-15 pyramid 1 to 3 times, depending on your training level, with 2 min to recover between sets

→ **SESSION 3:** 3 to 6 × (6 × 30–30) at maximum intensity with 4 min of recovery time between sets

→ **SESSION 4:** 20 sec at maximum rhythm, 10 sec of passive recovery, 15 sec at maximum rhythm, 5 sec of passive recovery, 10 sec at maximum rhythm, 4 min of rest before the next set (2 to 6 sets in total)

SPECIFIC ATHLETES

What to Work On, and When, With Young Judokas

THE MAJORITY OF COACHES WORK WITH CHILDREN AND TEENAGERS MOST OF THE TIME. THIS IS AS GOOD A REASON AS ANY TO REVIEW A FEW PHYSICAL TRAINING PRINCIPLES FOR THIS SPECIFIC AGE CATEGORY.

Growth rate of young male judokas.

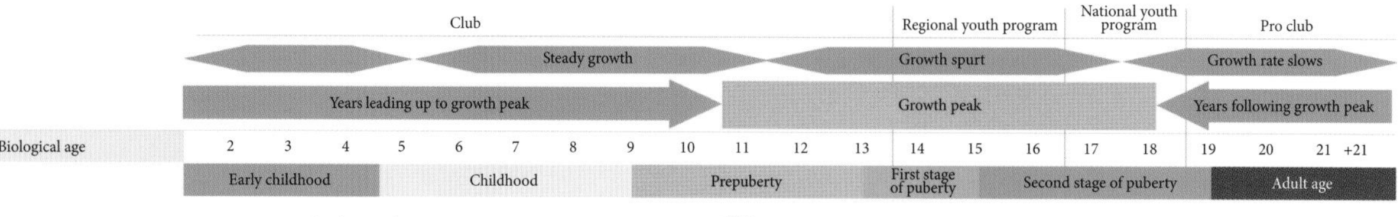

Growth rate of young female judokas.

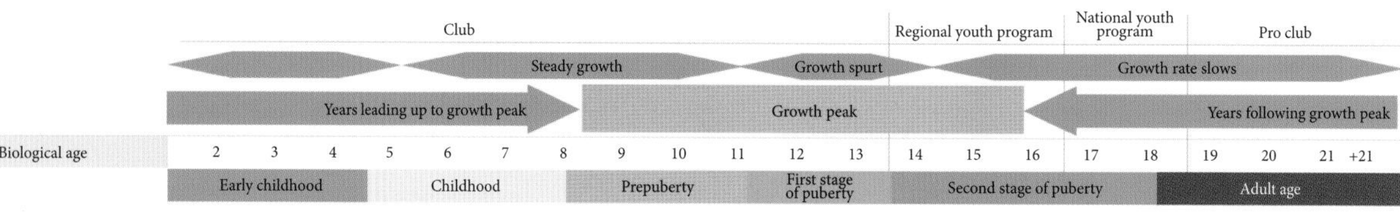

When talking about physical training with young athletes, I am often met with a barrage of questions, and this has made me realize how much coaches need specific guidelines for this age category. We often just train youth using a simplified version of our adult programs. Let's cover what we can and can't do with young athletes.

From Chronological Age to Biological Age

From birth onward, age is often looked at through the lens of chronology. Academic, social, and athletic progress are, in fact, systematically expressed through chronological age. However, I'm sure we can all think of great Russian or Greek champions whose physical and psychological maturity was at a more advanced stage of development than their chronological age. Two judokas with the same chronological age of 17 can therefore have very distinct levels of physical development: In this scenario, we would say that they don't have the same biological age. As an example, the researcher Faigenbaum, in 2008, talked about differences in the height and weight of 14-year-olds of 9 in. (23 cm) and 40 lb (18 kg) respectively. It is essential to take these variations into account in physical and educational training progression: An 11-year-old girl might, therefore, easily beat an 11-year-old boy if her biological development allowed it. And this is all the more likely since girls often reach puberty a little ahead of boys. Here, the physical aspect sometimes spills over into the teaching side of things; you may have to preserve the egos of some of the less developed young boys who could, to put it bluntly, find themselves destroyed by some of the more mature young girls!

Stages of Development

PREPUBERTY STAGE (girls: 8 to 11; boys: 9 to 13)

Motor and metabolic stability. This is a particularly comfortable period for varied improvements in motor skills. It's the point when all of the fundamental skills are developed, such as technical range, mobility basics, stability, and safety, and a variety of techniques become automatic reflexes. The physical training content is very general and similar to gymnastics.

FIRST STAGE OF PUBERTY (girls: 11 to 13; boys: 13 to 15)

Athletes will exhibit desynchronized growth of their different body sections, and an elevation in basal metabolic rate and hormonal activity that could limit or disrupt their ability to initiate effort. Motor precision is disrupted. You have to be patient, because the judoka can regress technically. It's important to reinforce the skills previously learned and to show great patience if it takes time for the athletes to master new moves. Physical training content should be focused on motor control and an introduction to situations that will be explored in greater detail during the next stage.

SECOND STAGE OF PUBERTY (girls: 13 to 18; boys: 15 to 19)

Decrease in all growth and development parameters. Increases in width and density are replaced by an increase in length. Body proportions start to match up and facilitate an improvement in coordination. The gradual enhancement of physical and mental abilities enables athletes to handle larger training workloads. This is the time where integrated and dissociated physical training should be developed more intensely.

Training Age

Along with biological age, which accounts for the fact a 15-year-old judoka could be ready to begin strength exercises while a 17-year-old might not yet be physically prepared, we also have to consider the training age. The consequences of the training age—the number of years that a young fighter has spent training seriously—are more difficult to anticipate. Nevertheless, the talent-spotting problems encountered by regional or national youth development programs compel us to carefully consider this issue. Judo is a very particular case, as it is one of the rare sports in which children can start participating at the age of 4. By the age of 10, when the serious work begins, they have already built up 6 years of experience. It is imperative, therefore, that we take this element into account from a developmental standpoint and make changes to the training content for the body and the mind. The long-term approach to fighters' development should incorporate their chronological, biological, and training ages to alter the general, specific, and competitive content so as to meet the real needs of the moment. The young judoka will not, then, immediately train to win, but will go through some more basic stages, first and foremost learning to train.

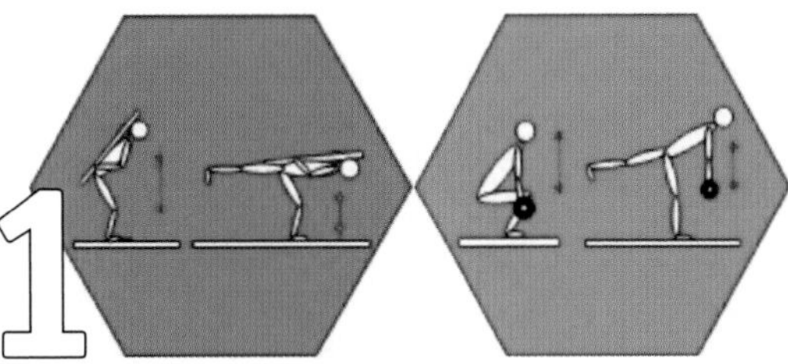

STAGE 1 TECHNICAL TRAINING

Without the athlete using any weights, and just holding a stick, the first stage consists simply of understanding the movements in their entirety and the positioning they require. The empty bar is then introduced, with the goal of teaching positional precision and a mono-rhythmic tempo. Trainers should give feedback about the pelvis position as well as the sensation of extension, the respect of natural body curves, and the trajectory of the knees.

STAGE 2 INTEGRATION OF BALANCE WORK

The work is focused on achieving control of posture and movement, in spite of destabilization. Load levels should remain low. The load intensity, in terms of weight or speed, is not something we could be concerned about at this stage. Above all, the point is to work on the complexity, with an increasing amount of psychomotor control.

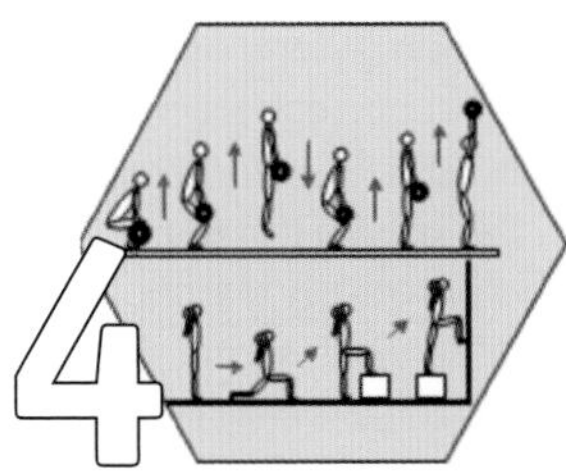

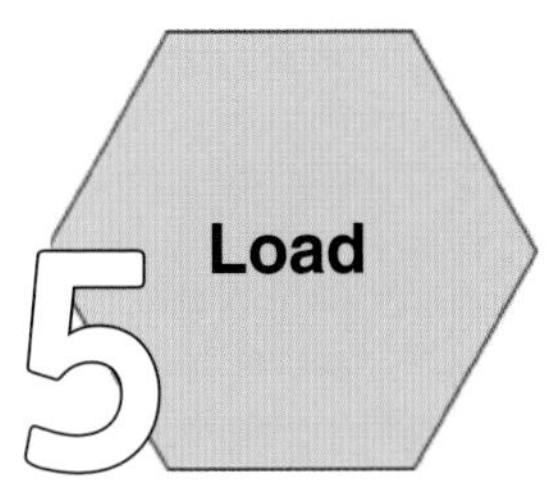

STAGE 3 TOWARD MORE SOPHISTEICATED MOVEMENT

Engagement becomes more complex and comprehensive. This is when the concept of acceleration is incorporated, and dynamic core building is integrated into young athletes' motor experience.

STAGE 4 MOVEMENT AND RHYTHM

This stage involves a combination of several movements with a strong notion of acceleration and deceleration and changes in rhythm. It is the one that most favors a transfer to physical and sporting activities. This is the final stage before a significant addition of load.

STAGE 5 LOAD VARATION

During the four previous stages, young fighters have had the time to build their physical fundamentals (mobility, motor control and balance, static and dynamic core building), and to understand the notion of rhythm. Now it is time to add load and make the most of those motor gains.

Dissociated Muscle Development

There has been a lot of concern about the role of muscle development in youth training. The core of the controversy stems partly from unreasonable approaches taken by certain coaches and parents, partly from the bad press associated with bodybuilding, and, finally, due to seemingly contradictory studies. The first research published on this topic failed to show any benefits for preadolescents. The studies carried out by Docherty in 1987 and Hetherington in 1976 are still, to this day, regularly used to argue against strength development training for young people.But there are several examples of bias in those studies, which reduces their relevance, especially in regard to the overly short duration and unsuitable volume of work. What the studies do show is that the effects of short, low-volume training are practically indistinguishable from those resulting from normal growth. Taking a progressive, technical, reasonable, and sensible approach, other studies have shown strength improvements in children independent of their normal growth (Pfeiffer and his team took a good look at the subject in the 1980s, prior to Ramsey and Lillegard doing the same in the 1990s. Faigenbaum published three new studies on the topic at the beginning of the 2000s). Additionally, no scientific proof exists that strength training tailored to young, healthy athletes either delays or speeds up growth (Bailey 1994, Malina 1994, Falk 2003). Some research, such as that carried out by Vicente-Rodriguez in 2006, has even established that physical activity, and more specifically activities that involve weights and dumbbells, generate a compressive force that is essential for bone development and growth. In fact, compared to other physical and sporting activities, muscle development exercises have actually been proven to be rather safe (Hamill 1994). Incidentally, we should not limit this reasoning just to increasing strength attributes; some studies (Falk 1996, Lillegard 1997, Nielsen 1980, Weltman 1986) have also demonstrated these connections with other sports.

Remember: It seems that strength in adolescents and preadolescents is just as trainable—if not more so—than it is in adults. It's their ability to improve their absolute maximum strength that limits them, with some authors pointing out that adults' ability to increase maximum strength can be twice as high. Maximum strength programs are therefore not the most suitable option for young fighters.

A PLACE FOR CORE STRENGTHENING?

Core strengthening is, without a doubt, when there is the most connection between various joints. The more it is addressed when athletes are young and with a varied approach, the more strength development through complex exercises will happen naturally. Remember that core strengthening for judokas is not static but dynamic, and that young athletes (and less young ones) hate spending hours in the plank position. Those two reasons should encourage a move toward dynamic core building (exercise ball activities while moving in pairs, etc.) as soon as possible (once judokas are capable of maintaining their natural body curves in an unstable situation).

Be aware that the core-strengthening technique must be flawless, otherwise you could do more harm than good. Often, we neglect the importance of limiting the lower back curve, which is the main cause of injuries among adolescents participating in sports. If, despite the advice, the pelvis does not remain in the backward tilt position, flattening the curve in the lower back, then this area of the back must be strengthened first (sit-ups, etc.).

Training Seniors

SORE ALL OVER? DO YOUNG FIGHTERS PUSH YOU RIGHT TO THE EDGE, CLOSER AND CLOSER TO JOINING THE OLD TIMERS? USE MY POINTERS TO MAKE JUDO YOUR TRUMP CARD AS YOU ENTER A MORE MATURE STAGE OF LIFE, AND YOU'LL HAVE THE LAST LAUGH!

Time is not on our side. First, because we become more fragile, but also because we gradually lose our ability to adapt (loss of sensitivity in our proprioceptive receptors, decline in reflexes). Some might say that this is the price of wisdom. But judokas, who are clearly even wiser than their sedentary peers, pay a double price because the more they become aware of the decrease in their abilities, the more they are susceptible to being thrown. While some manage to adapt judo to their growing limitations, others simply stop judo altogether. And yet, judo can actually be a great friend to you in later life if you anticipate and lay the groundwork early enough.*

Avoid Deconditioning

Sometimes we get old too fast. When other obligations arise and your level of motivation drops, you train less. You might go from one training session per day to three per week, and then one per week, or maybe even less. Each session can then seem like you're starting from scratch. You lack endurance, overall strength, core strength, and general judo-related senses. This probably has nothing to do with physical aging; it most likely comes from deconditioning.

My first piece of advice is, therefore, quite straightforward: Don't give up! On the other hand, try to be realistic and careful, and take things gradually. There's no need to do all the *randori* with the young guys like a crazy person.

Make Your Warm-Up an Individual Exercise

Young judokas with a lot of training under their belts are happy with a warm-up that lasts 15 to 20 minutes. But, as we get older, the warm-up is more important, even crucial. I'd advise you to always take an extra 10 minutes to warm-up before "leaping" into a set of *randori* on the floor or some dynamic technical exercises.

Here are the key points for a senior's warm-up:

→ Make it longer, about 20 to 30 min: You can't allow yourself to only be half warmed up.

→ Focus more on fragile and exposed areas: neck, ankles, hips, and lower back.

→ Include light and controlled stretching. While this approach can put a young athlete's muscles to sleep a little bit, the older, recreational athlete will find a way to activate the receptors in the muscles and tendons.

→ A word to the wise: There's no rush.

Fight Excess Weight

Although obviously not all seniors have weight issues, the natural order of things generally causes us to move up a weight category every decade. The result? There is more pressure on the joints, which grow weaker over time. This is the most common explanation for back, ankle, and knee pain.

It is obviously no longer possible to do what you did in the 66 kg or less category once you're a well-fed 81 kg or less competitor. The potential increase in strength levels is largely offset by a drastic drop in speed, mobility, and footwork. Cardiopulmonary effectiveness is also negatively impacted by excess weight.

Muscle Loss

It doesn't really matter whether you're exercising less because of muscle loss or you're experiencing muscle loss because you're training less: You have to prepare

** Further reading: Thierry Paillard, Vieillissement et Condition Physique, Ellipses 2009.*

for it in advance. You can do some very simple exercises that focus on the most exposed areas, providing you with a useful framework for judo and everyday life.

Anticipate the Loss of Proprioception

The biggest mistake we make is thinking that we're too young to start preparing. Even though judokas tend to be spared because they practice judo regularly, in bare feet and moving in all planes of motion, as human beings age, we lose sensitivity in the proprioceptive receptors in our tendons, muscles, and joints.

Foreseeing this enables you to greatly limit these losses, which is not that easy—not by a long shot—once the effects have taken hold, because they are accompanied by postural restructuring. The most damaging loss is, without a doubt, proprioception in the arch of the foot, restricting athletes' ability to balance and plant the feet using their ankles. These gradually stiffen, forcing the hips to pick up the slack, initially causing back pain. Subsequently, muscle loss sets in until you can no longer stand up straight, which is so important for mechanical comfort. At the end of the process, you need a cane to walk—but all this could have been mitigated 20 years earlier!

To avoid all this, *tachi-waza* is the ultimate weapon.

Once again, don't give up! When practiced well, judo is excellent for your twilight years. You should, however, add the following proprioceptive exercises to your program:

→ Balance on one leg, with your legs apart or together, while shifting your weight to the front, back and outside of your foot. Do the same thing on a soft mat.

→ Do balance work on a wobble cushion.

→ Move on a wobble cushion: On this unstable tool, move from front to back or left to right with a side step. You can also do judo-inspired movements, such as sweeps or *tai-sabaki*, on one or several balls.

SHOULDERS | SCAPULAR STABILIZERS | CORE STRENGTHENING

EFFECTIVE BELT USE

Other than the judo belt, the best option is still to use a suspension strap jammed in a door or attached to a horizontal bar. Keep your body straight with your pelvis tilted backward, and contract your abdominal and gluteal muscles throughout the exercise.

Lean back with your arms extended and open up. Examples of positions: arms extended (*I* position), arms apart (*T* position), then arms bent (wrists curled, *W* position). Be careful not to arch your back. Stick your chest out and focus on squeezing your shoulder blades together.

→ 4 sets of 6, then 9, and then 12 repetitions (i.e., 4 x ITW)

BASIC POSITION

I POSITION

T POSITION

W POSITION

PULL CHAIN | BALANCE | CORE STRENGHTENING | GLUTES/HAMSTRINGS

ARABESQUE RESISTANCE BAND PULL

The resistance band should be jammed in a door or held by a training partner. Keep your back straight. Lift your back leg as you lean forward; your extended arm and leg should remain roughly parallel throughout the exercise. Don't arch your back or open up your hips. Keep your head in a neutral position.

→ 4 sets of 6 to 12 repetitions per leg, starting with the weaker leg and doing the same number of repetitions on each side

CORE STRENGTHENING | SHOULDER PROPRIOCEPTION | PUSH CHAIN

ELBOW TO HAND PLANK ON AN EXERCISE BALL

With a free-moving exercise ball, held in place by a training partner or jammed in a corner of the dojo, start with your elbows supporting your weight on the ball, your pelvis tilted backward, your feet on the floor, your body stretched out, and your abdominal and gluteal muscles contracted. Bring your hands up one after the other so that they now support your weight, then drop back down to your elbows. Don't arch your back. Try to avoid swaying with your hips.

→ 4 sets of 6 to 12 repetitions, alternating the starting arm

LOWER LIMBS | NECK STRENGTHENING

SQUAT WITH AN EXERCISE BALL

Start with the shoulder blades against an exercise ball pinned against a wall, and your feet just in front of your center of gravity, at an angle resembling the hands of a watch set to 10:10. Descend and ascend again over your full range of motion, controlling the ball with your back and head.

→ 4 sets of 6 to 12 repetitions

CORE STRENGTHENNG | HAMSTRINGS | CALVES

BRIDGE ON AN EXERCISE BALL

LOWER BACK MUSCLES | DEEP SPINAL MUSCLES

BACK EXTENSIONS

On an adjustable workout bench, keep your back straight and lower your torso as much as possible. Slowly and completely unroll your back. Come back up gradually until your back is straight and then lift your torso. Keep your chin up throughout the exercise.

→ 4 sets of 6 to 10 repetitions

Training Plan for the Week

MONDAY

- → **Balance on a wobble cushion (3 × 30 sec per leg)**
- → **Lower limbs and neck strengthening: squat with an exercise ball (4 × 10 repetitions)**
- → **Lower back muscles and deep spinal muscles: back extensions (4 × 8 repetitions)**

WEDNESDAY

- → **Shoulders, scapular stabilizers, and core strengthening: *ITW* position (4 × 6 repetitions)**
- → **Pull chain, balance, core strengthening, glutes and hamstrings: arabesque resistance band pull (4 × 8 repetitions)**
- → **Core strengthening, hamstrings, calves: bridge on an exercise ball (4 × 8 repetitions)**

FRIDAY

- → **Core strengthening, shoulder proprioception, pull chain: elbow to hand plank on an exercise ball (4 × 6 repetitions)**
- → **Judo move on a wobble cushion (4 × 8 *ko-uchi*)**
- → **Judo move on a wobble cushion (4 × 8 *seoi-nage*)**

Wobble cushion

Should You Adapt Your Judo Training as You Get Older?

You often hear it said that as you advance in years, it's sensible to reduce the duration of your bouts a little. Indeed, in senior tournaments, the length of bouts is often cut back to 3 minutes. However, here's the rub: For some older judokas, a shorter bout often means a more intense fight!

In this case, the reduction in bout duration brings about exactly the opposite effect of the one we're looking for. You end up with a more intense clash, requiring a range of endurance that is less comfortable for seniors and that exposes them to more potentially harmful situations. My advice is to opt for a more relaxed *randori*, closer to *yaku-soku-geiko*, but one of a traditional duration, provided it's not too long. *Ne-waza* is ideal for what we need here.

How Intense Should Your Effort Be?

The aerobic potential of a sedentary person reduces by 0.8 percent every year. However, it can be maintained—and even improved—at any age through training. As far as the judoka is concerned, I'd recommend an intensity greater than 60 percent of the maximum, to obtain an adaptation of effort, but lower than 90 percent, to avoid the production of adrenaline, which can be bad for the heart.

Endurance in Female Judo Athletes

SO, JUDO'S NOT A WOMEN'S SPORT. REALLY? HERE ARE SOME ANSWERS ABOUT SPECIFIC ASPECTS OF FEMALE EFFORT IN JUDO.

At the dawn of 2014, the International Judo Federation decided to reduce senior women's bouts by 1 minute (they dropped from 5 minutes to 4 minutes, as has been the case for men as well since 2017), despite female athletes having dealt perfectly well up to that point with fights that were as long as men's. This inevitably led to debate about differences between the sexes, when the international regulations had, up to that point, opted for a lack of differentiation, or, to put it in more precise terms, had recognized both the ability of female judokas to cope with the same workload as men and, looking at it from a gender equality point of view, the right of women not to be considered weak and needing protection.

As all of the major sports with significant media coverage have shown, the international performances of women, who are now trained just like men, are quite remarkable in most sports, and sometimes even get close to the men's performances.

Nevertheless, physiological differences do exist, even though some athletes are heading in a direction that might eventually erase them. My intention here is not to delve greatly into theory, which has already been done by others, but rather to raise specific points that can optimize your training and make it easier to lose weight (or maintain your figure). Having a better understanding of these differences will improve your effectiveness.

5 HEALTH RULES FOR THE FEMALE ATHLETE

[1] Aerobic activities and muscle strengthening to maintain body weight
[2] Strength training for all parts of the body, with polyarticular movement and stable footing
[3] Development of balance and proprioception—associated with core strengthening—while on an unstable surface
[4] A nutrition regimen that includes appropriate quantities of calcium and vitamins
[5] A balanced diet with an energy intake equal to what is expended during exercise

How Do You Train (Hard) for Judo?

Judo is a (very) high-intensity sport. Recent studies agree that we should differentiate the behavior and perception of each sex in terms of coping with intense cardio training sessions. For example, if conditioned female athletes choose their own intensity of effort, even if recovery time decreases, they can maintain that intensity for longer, attaining maximum heart rate values (Laurent et al. 2014).

However, women, because of their lower muscle mass (for average individuals), generate lower power peaks. In other words, women are statistically less comfortable with short and intense effort, and more at ease with prolonged effort, probably making use of a more aerobic method of energy production.

What You Need to Do

Physical training for women should be mainly (but not exclusively, of course) focused on intense aerobic effort. Intermittent exercises with limited recovery time (and therefore limited intensity in the first few sets) seem particularly relevant. More specifically, for judo—a discipline with a high lactic acid production—female athletes should consider a strategy to limit weaknesses by gradually introducing workouts just at the edge of a lactic workout, and then fully lactic, without losing sight of the basic aerobic objective. The best results are obtained by 2 to 4 maximum- to high-intensity sessions per week. Whether it's for the improvement of health, performance, or body composition, slightly longer intervals and high-intensity—but not maximum-intensity—exercises appear to be the most effective.

→ **My advice:** Start with, for example, sequences of one minute at 80 percent followed by 30 sec of recovery time.

When you repeat this sequence a dozen times, play around with the intensity, the volume, and the recovery time, within the following framework:

randori duration **1 to 2 min** / *randori* intensity **80 to 90 percent**
number of bouts **5 to 20** / recovery time: **2/1 or 3/1**

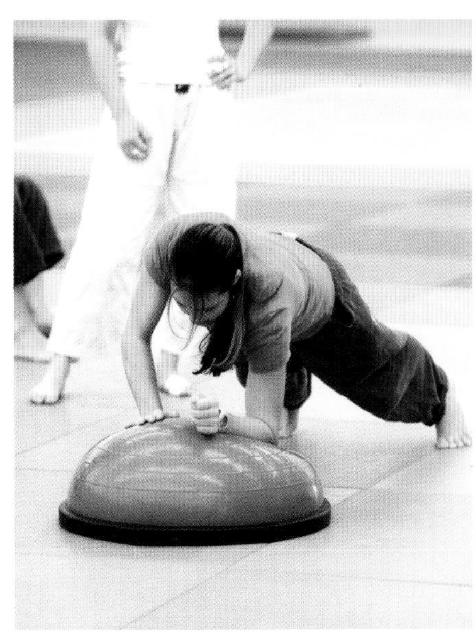

How to Manage Energy Stores

It is recognized that women store fat specifically and use it differently than men (Blaak 2001). During effort, women burn more lipids than men. It would make sense, then, if they were able to lose fat more easily through training, but that discounts lipid burning during exercise as a proportion of what is used during all daily activities. In fact, the main reason women have trouble losing weight is their resting metabolism. They have a natural tendency to store dietary fats and to use glucose (and not lipids) as the primary fuel when resting.

What You Need to Do

Women's specific use of fuels therefore calls for a significant adjustment of nutritional and training strategies, which have, up to this point, been mainly inspired by studies done in men. Since they burn more lipids during training, women also use fewer carbohydrates than men (around 25 percent). We should, then, reduce women's carbohydrate intake (adjusted on an individual basis) to optimize the use of fats, and avoid overloading their bodies with sugar. What's more, it is in women's best interest to train regularly to optimize the use of fats in their metabolism.

How to Lose Weight

As far as this particular goal is concerned, women who are not exercising regularly seem to be fighting a losing battle when compared to men, who tend to rid themselves of fat more quickly and more easily via aerobic workouts coupled with a sensible diet. And yet aerobic workouts are generally what is recommended in weight loss programs aimed at women. In fact, these disappointing results stem from women's response to the excess stress brought on by aerobic training and dieting: This combination causes progesterone, the precursor of testosterone and estrogen hormones, to be used for the production of the stress hormone cortisol, and this hormonal imbalance results in an inhibition of lipid use in poorly conditioned female judokas.

What You Need to Do

Conversely, recent studies on combined training (e.g., Sanal, Ardic, and Kirac 2013), recommend combining short but intense anaerobic efforts (such as sprinting) with an intermittent strength training program.

This combination has recently been shown to be effective for athletes looking to lose weight, particularly with regard to the lower limbs (traditionally the stubborn spots targeted by diets).

In concrete terms, women must actually do the opposite of what is typically recommended, by distancing themselves from male-focused models. To lose weight, women need intense anaerobic effort, combined with a progressive strength training program. Additional intermittent training (watch out for interference!) can also be included to stimulate lipid metabolism. Regular training is essential to optimize the use of lipids by the body. Women who follow this program must also be as active as possible throughout the day, to encourage their bodies to use lipids instead of carbohydrates. Finally, special attention should be paid to your diet: Changes should be gradual, to limit stress on the body. A drastic reduction in calories runs the risk of increasing cortisol and blocking the use of fats. Although it is not exhaustive, the following table gives you a framework you can use for intense training with the goal of maximizing weight loss in women. It's inspired by the Wingate protocol, which has been proven effective in a number of studies.

MAXIMIZING WEIGHT LOSS

	INTERVAL INTENSITY	INTERVAL DURATION	NUMBER OF SETS	RECOVERY TIME
PHASE 1	80-90%	3-4 min	6-12	2-4 min
PHASE 2	100%	8 sec	10-30	12 sec
PHASE 3	90-100%	15-30 sec	6-20	15-30 sec
PHASE 4	100%	under 15 sec	6-20	2-4 min

How Can We Avoid Physiological Damage?

The side effects of excessive sports practice can impact women in a particular way. The most well-known syndrome is known as the female athlete triad (Devienne 2006). Sometimes affecting female judo players, it manifests itself in one or more of these three undesirable conditions: eating disorders, amenorrhea (lack of periods), and osteoporosis. Concerns relating to performance and health are obvious. Female adolescents are particularly susceptible, and they must be supported early and throughout their career so that they are not affected by this phenomenon.

Sometimes resulting from an overly high training volume, intensity, or frequency over a prolonged length of time, amenorrhea may set in gradually and become a serious problem. A total absence of periods in young girls, or missed periods for 3 months in a row, are clear warning signs that should not be ignored under any circumstances.

Under optimum conditions, the body stores calcium and other minerals that are essential for producing physical effort and maintaining osteoarticular solidity. When the human machine slows down due to a shortage of calcium and minerals, as in women with amenorrhea, specific cells dig directly into the bone tissue. The immediate risks are stress fractures and even osteoporosis.

What You Need to Do

The athlete's coach and family must take amenorrhea very seriously and not just think of it as a typical condition from which female athletes tend to suffer. To prevent it from occurring, it is essential to control the training workload (including its progressive nature, volume, intensity, and frequency). Once the problem has been detected, and if it recurs over three consecutive months, the athlete should visit the doctor. It is also essential to monitor diet so that output and intake are balanced and to be vigilant about any sign of an eating disorder.

Physical activity helps combat the weakening of women's bones: By strengthening bone and joint structures (via gradual tension exercises and postural muscle-strengthening exercises), by adapting nutritional intake (in particular, calcium, iron, vitamin D, and minerals), and possibly by turning to pharmacological assistance, physical activity can reduce bone tissue loss or facilitate an increase in the minerals found in the bone. Needless to say, muscle-strengthening exercises, combined with balance work, help fight these deficits and their effects.

Weight Categories: Lightweights

THE HOLY GRAIL OF THE HEAVYWEIGHT TITLE TENDS TO TEMPT BEGINNERS MORE THAN EXPERTS, WHO UNDERSTAND THE APPEAL OF ATTENDING COMPETITIONS WITH SMALLER WEIGHT CATEGORIES. SPEED, MOVEMENT, RHYTHM: EVERYTHING COMES TOGETHER FOR QUITE A SHOW. BUT WHAT ABOUT THEIR TRAINING?

As we know, a judo bout differs depending on the weight category, and this applies both to men and to women. While the lightweights seem to move in every direction, representatives of the heavier categories seem fixed in place so they can make better use of their arm strength. We could even go so far as to say that the 60 kg or less (men) and the 48 kg or less (women) and, to a certain extent, the 52 kg or less division (for women) categories could be considered disciplines in their own right. Consequently, one might wonder if it is sensible to train them in the same way as the rest of our judokas. Training should be tailored, yes, but how can we do this with 15, 20, 40, or more judokas on the mat?

EXERCISES

[1] *Hiki-dashi* in overspeed. For each movement, your training partner (select the lightest partner available) will follow the movement and jump, so that required strength is reduced as much as possible in favor of speed.
→ 4 to 6 sets of 6 to 8 repetitions, repeated every minute.

[2] *Nage-komi* in overspeed. The initial setup is a three-person *nage-komi*, with a second partner holding back Tori. Tori starts to move against the resistance, and the second partner lets go as soon as Uke is positioned correctly (careful: no longer than 1 to 2 sec since it's not a strength exercise). Uke should try to produce as much speed as possible, taking advantage of the sudden release by the second partner to move into overspeed.
→ 4 or 5 sets of 4 or 5 repetitions, repeated every minute.

What Do We Know About the Particulars of Lightweight Judokas?

During a fight, these athletes are often especially dynamic, exhibiting great movement, *kumikata* battles, attacks, swerves, combination moves, *ne-waza*—all with significant speed and few breaks. As you know, lightweight judokas are hyperactive. Consequently, their training and preparation should take this high frequency of activity into consideration.

Training is, after all, about making choices, so we define primary and secondary physical attributes. The major physical attributes of lightweight athletes are specific endurance (lactic, MAP, maintaining speed) and speed (maximum speed, frequency of movement, agility, coordination). Their secondary physical attributes are maximum strength aspects (and anything related to strength or power).

Let's keep in mind a judoka's fundamental attributes, which cut across all disciplines: balance (proprioception and dynamic core strength) and mobility (flexibility and motor control).

Speed of Movement

Recommendations

Lightweight judokas move a lot and extremely fast. The principle of increasing the speed of movement is based not only on doing a movement more quickly but also on deciding more quickly to make that movement. We can, therefore, play around with just the execution of the move, then with the selection of moves, and finally with performing the move quickly.

To improve judokas' decision-making ability, they must be given signals they can see, hear, or feel. They can then build a motor pattern: A certain piece of information will be met with a certain reaction. For example, when two right-handed athletes face each other, Uke almost always puts the right foot forward first. But, occasionally, when the opposite happens, Tori must spot it and take advantage by opting for *o-uchi-gari*. This type of work is especially good for sweeps.

Since improvements in speed depend specifically on the movement, you should opt for judo-related moves. Still, if the judoka hits a slump despite doing speed training, it is a good idea to use nonjudo-specific drills, such as sprints, rope ladders, and the like.

The problem with speed is that it's very difficult to work on by completely removing the strength aspect. Much as maximum strength with no speed is easy to develop (for example, a squat held for a few seconds with a maximum load increases pure strength without involving speed), pure speed is always affected by gravity and therefore by body weight, always involving significant strength levels. The trick, then, is to find ways of working in overspeed, a preferred tool of lightweight judokas.

Specific Endurance

Recommendations

The way we approach endurance is necessarily specific (otherwise we're wasting our time). So, it is a question of being able to repeat *randori*, *shiai*, and all of their included movements. For a lightweight, if you've been paying attention, this means repeating judo actions of high or even maximum intensity at an elevated frequency. The high-intensity lactic and aerobic ranges (which regular readers of my writings are familiar with), are obviously a priority, and repeated explosive actions should be incorporated throughout the circuit with minimal energy loss.

Special Lightweight MAP Circuit

3 rounds of 27 sec per exercise, with 27 sec of recovery between them.
Recovery time between circuits is 2 min.
EXERCISE 1 Maximum-frequency ladder drills
EXERCISE 2 Clap push-ups
EXERCISE 3 Maximum-frequency *uchi-komi*
EXERCISE 4 Hurdles
EXERCISE 5 Maximum-frequency elbow to hand planks
EXERCISE 6 Maximum-frequency *uchi-komi*
EXERCISE 7 Burpees
EXERCISE 8 Thrusters with sandbags, medicine ball, or dumbbells
EXERCISE 9 Maximum-frequency *uchi-komi*
EXERCISE 10 *Nage-komi*

Special Lightweight Lactic Circuit Example

Maximum intensity throughout the exercise.

30 sec of burpees with maximum jump, 4 maximum-speed *nage-komi*, 20 sec tuck jumps, 4 maximum-speed *nage-komi*, 5 clean and jerks, *kumikata* movement, 5 min of recovery time, 4 to 6 rounds.

Strength

Recommendations

This is probably the most innovative part of our approach. Over the years, we have become certain that lightweight judokas, if they have developed the aforementioned attributes sufficiently, do not need to go through as large a strength filter as other weight categories. Elite-level judokas like Sophie Cox (two-time silver medalist in the 52kg or less women's category at the European Judo Championships) or Walide Khyar (European champion in the 60 kg or less men's category) use very little strength, if any. Things vary widely within speed-focused power ranges, with medium or light loads still handled at maximum speed. Such an experiment could even go so far as to remove strength training from the program entirely.

Exercises

Example of power-speed for lightweights
4 sets at 50 percent of the max, 5 at 40 percent, and 8 at 30 percent. 1 min of recovery time.
Up to 6 exercises per session.

WHAT IF YOU HIT A PLATEAU?

Even if they engage in regular and precise training workouts in line with some of the simple suggestions presented above, lighter athletes, like all judokas, can still be subject to plateaus. Sometimes long and frustrating, despite intense training, there are, thankfully, ways to escape this unpleasant phase.

→ You can still make progress in physical terms. If the recommended training isn't working, then maybe some basic aspects are missing or have regressed. Or maybe, despite your weight category, you in particular have additional requirements. This could be the point where you start a traditional maximum strength or basic endurance development cycle.

→ You can still make progress in technical and tactical terms. Special moves can be altered, and you will end up broadening your technical range. Remember that the physical side of things only serves your technique. If the technique isn't there, you're basically making physical progress for nothing.

→ You can still change weight categories. Lightweight judokas still have to maintain their weight. As they age, they naturally tend to drift into a higher weight category. Repeated diets also promote tolerance in the body; the proliferation of different diets always makes them more difficult.

Weight Categories: Heavyweights

WHILE LIGHTWEIGHT JUDO IS A VISUAL TREAT THAT IS FAST, ATTRACTIVE, AND SOMETIMES EVEN ACROBATIC, HEAVYWEIGHT JUDO MIGHT SEEM LIKE IT'S HAPPENING IN SLOW MOTION. IN REALITY, THE APPEAL OF THESE CONFRONTATIONS LIES ELSEWHERE. LIGHT JUDOKAS MIGHT BE QUICK, BUT HEAVY JUDOKAS ARE JUST INCREDIBLY STRONG!

An over 100 kg (men) or over 78 kg (women) bout is different from other weight categories. In fact, judokas in these categories seem to attack less frequently and more slowly. For all that, is their fight more economical? Not at all. The battle is done differently: Through *kumikata* and other, slower attacks, and phases with no movement, a duel of strength rages on. When national team coaches are asked (Krstulovic 2012) about specific features of the heavyweight categories, they pinpoint strength and specific endurance as their major attributes, relegating speed to a secondary consideration.

Strength

Recommendations

A constant work in progress, the development of maximum strength will enable you to improve your explosive strength (factors related to the nervous system), joint stability (prophylactic role), and coordinated movement and will help to support improvements in specific endurance. A heavyweight training plan must contain at least the following two essential phases:

- **Nervous system adaptations:** Gains are made quickly and involve little muscle mass variation. Everything comes down to the fine coordination between muscle fibers and the muscles. Put plainly, the idea is to produce even more intense muscle contractions.
- **Hypertrophy:** This is the medical term for an increase in muscle mass. This is more long-term work and should be considered at the beginning of the season, although it will continue, of course, for the rest of the judoka's life, especially in the case of heavyweights, who are not limited by weight categories. You should be careful, however, always to limit the time frame of these phases; since they can be destabilizing, they can make a judoka a bit clumsy out on the mat. You should therefore alternate them with nervous system work and judo moves, above all.

Because judo is a complete sport, we use all of the muscles in the body to stop, hold, and accelerate. We shouldn't forget, then, to do concentric (contractions as the muscle shortens) as well as eccentric (contractions as the muscle lengthens) exercises and to incorporate an isometric phase (holds) within a dynamic exercise (static-dynamic). Please note that working with heavy weights requires you to have sufficient core strength (it's a prerequisite) and to increase the weight gradually.

Exercises

→ Strength-development program for the nervous system

Prioritize strength exercises: plank pulls, bench presses, squats, or deadlifts. You should use your max weight for the number of repetitions suggested.

WEEKS 1 TO 3 5 sets of (6 strength moves, 90 sec of rest, 3 *nage-komi*, 5 min of rest). Do up to 3 different exercises per session (2 upper body exercises + 1 lower body exercise per session, or the opposite).

WEEKS 5 TO 8 4 sets of (4 strength moves, 40 sec of rest, 4 *nage-komi*, 4 min of rest).

WEEK 9 **Rest.**

WEEKS 5 TO 12 4 sets of (2 to 3 strength moves, 30 sec of rest, 5 *nage-komi*, 4 min of rest).

→ Hypertrophy program

Prioritize strength exercises: plank pulls, bench presses, squats, or deadlifts. You should use your max weight for the number of repetitions suggested.

WEEKS 1 TO 3 5 sets of (8 strength moves, 2 *nage-komi*, 1 min 30 sec rest). Do up to 4 different exercises per session (2 upper body exercises + 2 lower body exercises per session).

WEEK 4 **Rest.**

WEEKS 5 TO 8 4 sets of (6 strength moves, 2 *uchi-komi*, 2 *nage-komi*, 1 min 30 sec rest).

WEEK 9 **Rest.**

WEEKS 10 TO 12 5 sets of (4 strength moves, 2 *nage-komi*, 4 strength moves, 2 min rest).

WHAT IF YOU HIT A PLATEAU?

While the physique of heavyweight judokas can help them stand out positively in training, it can turn out to be limiting in competition. What are the problems encountered and how can we fix them?

→ A wide variety of morphologies: size, weight, muscles, and reach. Through muscle-building drills for muscles and *kumikata* exercises for reach, it's possible to level the playing field.

→ So heavyweights don't have a weight management problem? We think they do. Although they are not restricted by the rules in this respect, there is still a fitness weight or optimum weight that they need to try to reach. Additionally, these judokas are not limited by the search for functional hypertrophy.

→ Precautions for improving basic endurance: running and the shocks it can cause to the body can result in physical injury, so unloaded sports (cycling, swimming) are preferred.

→ Heavyweight judokas sometimes lack a little core strength, which can restrict strength development and increase the risk of injury. It's important, then, to provide sufficient core-strengthening exercises for these judokas.

Specific Endurance

Recommendations

Heavyweights' specific endurance is not exactly the same as other judokas' endurance. Let's talk about strength endurance and aerobic endurance. The intensity and frequency of movement are much lower, relegating lactic work (resistance) to a secondary role, even though it's a reality that needs to be worked on. So we have to develop specific endurance parameters, but don't forget that these fighters need to use a lot more energy to move, and what may seem like an easy training circuit for someone who weighs 60 kg (132 lb) can end up being insurmountable when you weigh 100 kg (220 lb). Consequently, to reach the desired intensity, we need to lighten the load for these athletes and, just this once, you'll hear us say that the best specific cardio training for heavyweight judokas is cycling.

Exercises

WEEKS 1 TO 3 20 min cycling, 5 min of *ne-waza* from a standing start, 20 min cycling, 5 min of *ne-waza* from a standing start.

WEEK 4 10 min cycling, 5 min of *ne-waza* from a standing start, 10 min cycling, 5 min of *ne-waza* from a standing start, 10 min cycling, 5 min of *ne-waza* from a standing start.

WEEKS 5 AND 6 10 min cycling, 3 min cycling, 3 min rest, 3 min of *ne-waza*, 2 min of rest, 3 min cycling, 1 min rest, 5 min cycling.

WEEKS 5 TO 7 10 min cycling, 2 sets of (3 min cycling, 3 min rest, 3 min of *ne-waza*, 2 min rest, 3 min cycling, 1 min rest), 5 min cycling.

WEEKS 8 AND 9 10 min cycling, 3 sets of (3 min cycling, 3 min rest, 2 min of *ne-waza*, 2 min rest, 1 min cycling, 1 min rest), 5 min cycling.

WEEKS 10 TO 12 5 × (1 min fast cycling, 1 min slow cycling), 5 min of *ne-waza* from a standing start, 5 × (1 min fast cycling, 1 min slow cycling), 5 min of *ne-waza* from a standing start.

PLANNING

RECOVERY AND PREVENTION

Testing the Judoka

HERE ARE SOME PROTOCOLS TO ASSESS A JUDOKA'S PHYSICAL POTENTIAL SIMPLY AND EFFECTIVELY.

The test accurately establishes a starting point for training and the direction that it should take. Several series of tests are then scheduled throughout the season, like tracking markers punctuating the annual schedule, allowing you to confirm the quality of work that has been done, and justifying, if necessary, any adjustments to the schedule. The test therefore has a dual assessment and monitoring function, making it absolutely essential.

We have only provided the simplest tests to implement; these require a minimum of equipment and theoretical knowledge, but they are still relevant to judo. The following list attempts to include all of a judoka's physical attributes, even though the complexity of judo renders any supposed completeness illusionary. For each test, we provide a goal, possible prerequisites, information regarding functional operation, and a simple and helpful reference (e.g., senior male judoka, 73 kg or less). You know your potential as a judo athlete, be it technical or competitive. But where do things really stand as far as your physical condition is concerned? Are you faster or do you have more endurance? Are you quicker or more resistant? Are you very strong or just dynamic?

Test Your Capacity for Effort

SPECIFIC ENDURANCE IN JUDO BOUTS

The lactic energy production system dominates in a judo bout. It's what allows you to repeat intense muscle contractions (and, by extension, throws), particularly between 30 seconds and 3 to 4 minutes into the fight.

EQUIPMENT

→ Cones, a flat surface measuring at least 30 m, a stopwatch, and a tape measure.

OBJECTIVES

→ Ascertain the lactic performance index.

→ Define a level of performance in power and lactic capacity.

→ Track the athlete's lactic performance.

→ Determine lactic changes over time.

→ Establish the athlete's ability to recover from lactic effort.

PREREQUISITE

→ Previous experience with lactic intensity.

SETUP

→ Place a cone every 5 m over a 30 m area. Over 6 attempts lasting 30 sec (interspersed with 30 sec of passive recovery), the athlete should try to set a personal distance record.

ADAPTATION OF THE AUSTRALIAN SHUTTLE TEST BY FRED ROUALEN

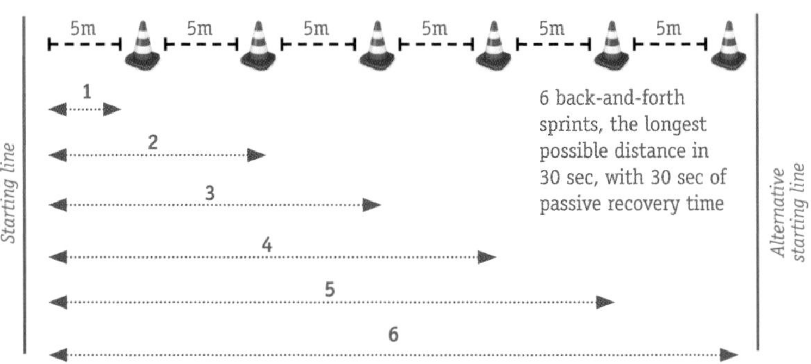

The idea here is to observe the loss of intensity during extremely lactic effort. The athlete shouldn't try to manage effort, but should instead try, in each set, to cover the longest possible distance; the first attempt will inevitably be the best. If blood tests are being performed, they should be done after the first attempt, 3 minutes after the first attempt, after the second attempt, then 3 minutes after the second attempt. It's also possible to check these lactic tests by taking blood at 5 minutes and then again at 8 minutes to observe the athlete's recovery.

- After an appropriate warm-up, the athlete gets into position at the starting line.
- At the signal, the athlete sprints toward the first cone, then returns to the starting line, sprints to the second cone, then returns to the starting line, sprints to the third cone, and so on. The goal is to run as far as possible in 30 seconds.
- At the 30 second mark, the first assessor stops the watch and the second notes the distance covered.
- After 30 seconds of passive recovery, the athlete again gets into position on the closest starting line (on either side) and begins sprinting upon hearing the signal. The athlete should do 6 sets of back-and-forth sprints under this protocol.

The different results are determined using the following calculations:

Lactic performance index

→ **Worst performance in 30 sec and best performance in 30 sec x 100**

The closer the index is to 100, the more the athlete's lactic profile is efficient and consistent.

Lactic power (in m/sec)

→ **Best performance/30**

Lactic capacity (in m/sec)

→ **Sum of the 6 sets/6 and then 30**

Performance in meters, first attempt

→ **Insufficient: 90 → Normal: 115 → Good: 130**

Total distance covered in 6 attempts

→ **Insufficient: 500 → Normal: 570 → Good: 680**

ENDURANCE

The aerobic energy production system is used in extra-long bouts and throughout competitions involving multiple bouts, but it is also the most important system during training. Finally, its impact on recovery following a lactic effort like judo is substantial.

LUC LÉGER'S BEEP TEST

• At each beep, the athlete being assessed must be at one of the two parallel lines, with one foot behind the line, before turning and heading back the same way.
• When the beeps get too fast for the athlete—that is, they sound when the athlete still has one or two meters to go, and the athlete cannot maintain the pace or catch up within the next few runs—the test is over.
• A voice on the beep test audio regularly announces the different stages. All the assessor has to do, then, is note the stage when the test ends, as well as the duration, to ascertain the estimated MAS.

Results

→ **Stage 6: Insufficient**
→ **Stage 11: Normal**
→ **Stage 14: Good**

EQUIPMENT

→ Cones, a flat surface, and CD and CD player (or MP3 player or beep test app).

OBJECTIVES

→ Estimate the athlete's $\dot{V}O_2$max and MAS.

→ Assess the athlete's general endurance.

→ Estimate the athlete's MAP.

→ Track the athlete's aerobic progress.

PREREQUISITE

→ Have sufficient running experience so that the locomotion technique is not a limiting factor.

SETUP

→ The idea here is for the athlete to perform a maximum, progressive, and continuous run.

→ Place the cones on a surface to create two parallel lines 20 m apart. The athlete runs back and forth inside this assessment area.

→ The CD/MP3 player or beep test app makes the beep sound that sets the pace of the run.

→ The speed increases by 0.5 km/h every minute. The starting speed is 8 km/h.

Test Your Speed

Speed is a multifaceted physical attribute that is essential for judo, especially for acceleration (short and intense movements). The engagement must be complete, with full recovery before each test.

ALERTNESS

An athlete's alertness manifests itself at the heart of notions of acceleration. This test comes from racket sports and features side steps, abrupt changes in direction, and short-distance runs, making it ideal for assessing alertness among judokas.

EQUIPMENT

→ Cones, a flat nonslip surface, and a tape measure.

OBJECTIVES

→ Assess the athlete's velocity, that is, their ability to accelerate and then slow down before counteraccelerating to change direction.

→ Assess the athlete's acceleration capacity.

→ Assess the athlete's speed.

→ Assess the athlete's alactic-anaerobic capacity.

SETUP

Place four cones on a flat surface so that they form a *T* shape. The distance between the base of the *T* and its cross is 10 yd (9.2 m). The cross also measures 10 yd and is divided into two equal parts.

_T_ TEST

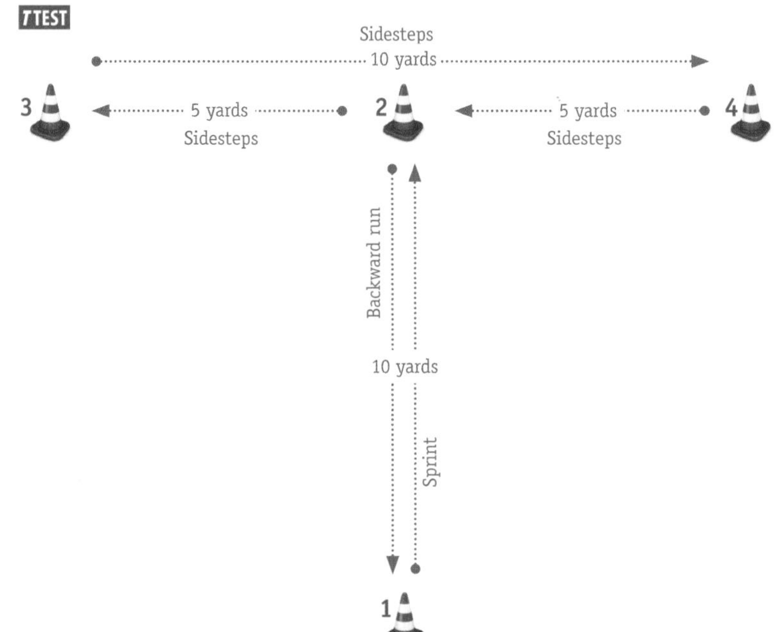

After warming up, the athlete gets into position at the bottom of the *T* shape, by the first cone.

- At the signal, they run to the second cone, in the middle of the cross of the *T*.
- They continue by sidestepping to the third cone, on the left, which they touch with their left hand.
- They then sidestep to the right until they reach the cone located on the far right of the *T*, which they touch with their right hand.
- They return to the middle cone, touch it, and then run backward to the starting point.

The athlete can make two attempts; the best time, to the nearest 0.1 sec, is recorded. The athlete should always face forward, never turning around, even when running backward. The athlete should never cross the legs.

Results

Alertness index

- → **Insufficient: 14 sec**
- → **Normal: 12 sec**
- → **Good: 10 sec**

MOVEMENT FREQUENCY

Movement frequency, or speed, can be measured in a judo-integrated manner thanks to an excellent tool we have at our disposal: *uchi-komi*. This test requires only a stopwatch. However, judokas will not be able to do this test without the expert and objective eye of their coach, who sets the engagement limits and is the only person who can ensure consistent quality of execution of movement, which is essential for the test to be valid. Since the results can vary by as much as threefold depending on the move selected, we have not suggested a scale (of course you must keep the same move for the entire set and only compare strictly identical moves from one set to another).

EQUIPMENT

→ Stopwatch

PREREQUISITE

→ Complete mastery of the move in question.

SETUP

→ Repeat as many moves as possible in 7 sec.

ACCELERATION, SPEED, AND MAINTAINING SPEED

The idea here is to time the athlete in a 10 m sprint for acceleration, a 30 m sprint for alactic anaerobic power (maximum intensity over an average distance), and an 80 m sprint for alactic anaerobic capacity (maintaining speed over a long distance). These tests require only a stopwatch.

Results

Acceleration
- → Insufficient: 2.5 sec
- → Normal: 2 sec
- → Good: 1.8 sec

Alactic anaerobic power
- → Insufficient: 5.5 sec
- → Normal: 4.5 sec
- → Good: 3.5 sec

Alactic anaerobic capacity
- → Insufficient: 12 sec
- → Normal: 11 sec
- → Good: 10.5 sec

PREREQUISITE

→ Just as in the Luc Léger beep test, you must have sufficient running experience so that the locomotion technique is not a limiting factor.

SETUP

→ The coach signals the start from the finish line and also controls the stopwatch.

10/10 *Uchi-Komi* Test

1	2	3	4	5	6	7	8	9	10	11	12	13	14	15	16	17	18	19	20	21	22	23	24	25
26	27	28	29	30	31	33	33	34	35	36	37	38	39	40	41	42	43	44	45	46	47	48	49	50

Total number of sets ______ **Total duration** ______

PRINCIPLE

Do as many sets as possible without losing the quick rhythm adopted from the outset or the quality of movement. The test should end in the event of overly high fatigue or as soon as the movement becomes too slow or mediocre. You should not exceed your limits despite signs of exhaustion; the key is to note the moment these signs appear.

Test Procedure

→ 10 repetitions of *ippon-seoi-nage*, with a throw in the 10th rep. Start facing Uke, turn around completely, and then return face-to-face again, with both feet aligned and your hand back on the other side. 10 sec of recovery time.

→ Continue doing sets for as long as possible without a decrease in performance. A set of 10 should be carried out in a maximum of 15 sec, plus 10 sec of rest (which cannot be shortened), so, 25 sec in total. A set of 100 should therefore be done at a base speed of approximately 4 min 30 sec. If you're over 5 minutes for the set of 100, it means that you are too slow.

Test Your Strength

MAXIMUM STRENGTH, MYOTYPOLOGY TEST

EQUIPMENT

→ Free weights or weight machines, depending on the physical trainer's equipment.

OBJECTIVES

→ Determine the distribution of muscle fibers (more slow-twitch fibers or more fast-twitch fibers) in an athlete based on two strength tests.

→ Determine an athlete's maximum repetitions for a given move.

PREREQUISITE

→ Have a large number of weights available.

→ Possess sufficient muscle-development experience and training. If the range of tests is being done at the beginning of the season, opt for the indirect maximal strength test instead.

SETUP

→ Determine the maximum weight that can be lifted once in a strength-training exercise during the one-rep max (e.g., bench press or deadlift).

→ Total rest: 10 min.

→ Adjust the weight to 85 percent of the maximum previously obtained and do the max number of repetitions.

This is the veritable gold standard of muscle strengthening; recording your maximum muscle-development performances allows you to work accurately on various ranges of strength throughout the season. But, while the concept of a test measuring how much weight you can lift in a single repetition is easily imaginable, it can be dangerous to carry out a maximal strength assessment right at the start of the season. In fact, the athlete is not, at that specific moment, physically, mentally, or technically ready for it. A possible alternative is to do the test indirectly and extrapolate the results. The simplest method involves ascertaining the heaviest load that can be lifted ten times. Bearing in mind that this load corresponds to 75 percent of the maximum load for a single repetition, the calculation is fairly straightforward. This solution, which is simpler to implement and certainly less risky, enables you to combine technical positioning work with strength work.

Results

→ 1 to 4 repetitions: **high ratio of fast-twitch fibers.**

→ 5 repetitions: **intermediate profile.**

→ 6 repetitions or more: **high ratio of fast-twitch fibers.**

In judo, strength is, more than ever, essential to performance, even if technique, body shape, and mobility are indisputably the framework of a judoka's effectiveness. The qualities of strength are manifold, and their proper development requires accurate assessment.

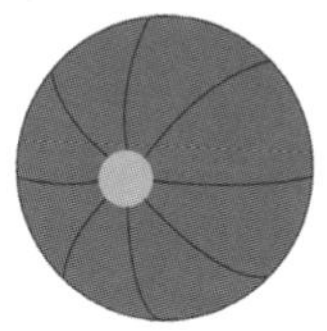

POWER

EQUIPMENT

→ Chalk, a tape measure, a chair, and a medicine ball.

SETUP

→ Sit on a chair and hold a medicine ball at chest height, then try to throw the ball as far as possible.

Power is the product of strength and speed of movement. Being powerful means developing maximum strength without a decrease in speed (or the other way around). This is a fundamental attribute in judo. We suggest two tests to assess it: one for the upper body and one for the lower body. For upper body power, the test is to throw a 6.6 lb (3 kg) medicine ball as far as possible.

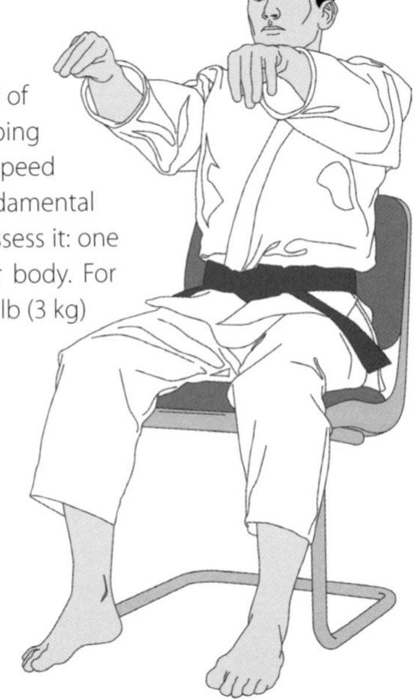

Results

→ **Insufficient: 4 m**

→ **Normal: 6 m**

→ **Good: 8 m**

SARGENT TEST

The Sargent Test, used to measure lower body power, is the simplest method to implement and the one that requires the least equipment. These days, it can be replaced with the new My Jump app, available for all smartphones that can film at high speed.

Since the data vary significantly from one individual to another and do not necessarily represent the complete range of judokas' power, we haven't provided a reference table. Still, the Sargent Test remains an effective monitoring tool.

EQUIPMENT

→ A rigid flat jumping surface, a tape measure or measuring stick, and chalk that is a different color than the wall.

OBJECTIVES

→ Assess an athlete's vertical spring.
→ Establish a vertical power index for the lower body.

PREREQUISITE

→ Measure the athlete with the arms up in the air.

SETUP

→ The athlete should rub chalk on his fingers.
→ The athlete stands up straight, with the shoulders about 6 in. (15 cm) from the wall and feet flat on the ground. The athlete lifts the dominant arm (the one used during the test) as high as possible and makes a first chalk mark on the wall.
→ Then, without changing position, the athlete immediately performs a counter movement and jumps as high as possible. At the highest point of the jump, the athlete touches the wall with the same hand.
→ The spring score is the difference in inches (centimeters), rounded up to the nearest inch (centimeter) between the two marks.
→ 3 attempts are permitted, and the best result is recorded.

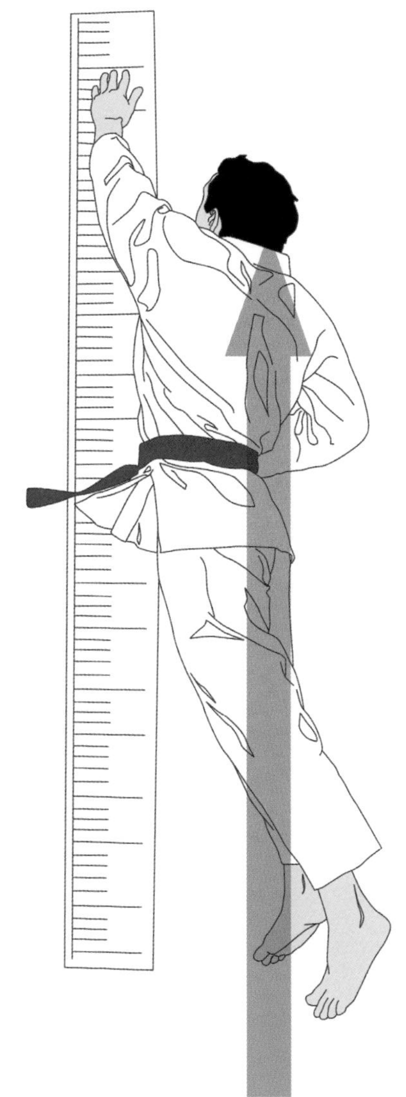

Overtraining

THIS COMPLEX BUT COMMON PHENOMENON THREATENS AMATEURS AS MUCH AS ELITE COMPETITORS. DIFFICULT TO DETECT, INSIDIOUS, AND EVEN DANGEROUS, OVERUSE IS DEFINITELY SOMETHING WE SHOULD TRY TO AVOID.

Overtraining is often rooted in the collective belief that the more you train, the more you progress, with no thought given to recovery. And yet, it's through effective recovery that we make progress. This phenomenon even has a name: dynamic overcompensation. During recovery, the various performance-enhancing systems reach higher levels to compensate for the stress put upon them.

If such an imbalance between overly intense training and incomplete or insufficient rest persists, then performance drops; this is overtraining.

Overtraining, Overload, Overstrain—What Are They?

Overtraining is an extended imbalance between training workload and recovery. It's characterized by continual fatigue, which builds up over several weeks, even after rest periods.

Performance gains from training are maintained up to a certain threshold, but beyond that, it becomes excessive. Below this threshold is the undertraining zone, or even deconditioning if the athlete remains at this point for too long. Above the threshold is the overtraining red zone. The athlete or the coach must be able to target this zone accurately through precise tailoring and adjustment of load. Overtraining can take many forms, which makes it difficult to diagnose exactly and pinpoint the source.

Who Falls Victim to Overtraining?

Contrary to popular belief, it's rarely the elite athlete, with exceptional training and recovery capabilities and supported by a solid team, who is the victim of overtraining. Rather, it's the young (or not so young), enthusiastic, busy amateur who's really in danger. Adults who love hitting the mat as they've been doing for over 20 years, but who do it irregularly, eat poorly, and sleep badly, may suffer from nervous system fatigue. Consequently, these enjoyable sessions end up exhausting them instead of doing them good.

The entire life of an elite athlete revolves around performance, but we sometimes forget that teenagers who train with a club often have to juggle their three weekly practices with sessions related to whatever sport they're doing in school, as well as their handball training, and so on. At this point, they're in a routine that is not unlike that of a professional athlete, while still having to worry about their next math quiz and what party they're attending on Saturday night. Young athletes selected for regional development programs, who are in great demand but are still inexperienced, are particularly susceptible.

What Causes Overtraining?

Preventing as well as curing overtraining involves pinpointing and removing the causes, to prevent it from becoming systematic. There are a variety of causes, and it may be a combination of one or more of the following:

- **Excessive training workload (volume and intensity)**
- **Insufficient recovery time**
- **Monotony of training type and workload**
- **Overly fast increase in training volume and intensity**
- **Medical problems**
- **Eating disorders**
- **Overly frequent elite-level competitions**
- **Unusual environmental stress (e.g., heat wave, harsh winter)**
- **Unusual psychological stress (e.g., personal worries, work-related concerns)**

GLOSSARY

tachycardia: A condition that makes your heart beat too quickly.
bradycardia: A heart rate that's too slow.
anemia: A condition in which you lack healthy red blood cells and suffer from a reduction in the concentration of hemoglobin. This shortfall leads to insufficient oxygen being carried by the blood to your body's tissues.

How Can We Detect Overtraining?

The first difficulty in making a diagnosis is actually distinguishing overtraining from simple fatigue—a normal consequence of training—and prolonged fatigue that might be pathological, such as that caused by overtraining.

Normal postexertion fatigue is due to traditional performance-limiting factors and can be identified through recovery periods:

→ Under 24 hours, if the exertion is habitual

→ Under 48 hours, if the exertion is unusual (very intense or very long)

Pathological fatigue arises from a disruption to the work-rest relationship balance. It can manifest itself, in concrete terms, through an abnormally long recovery time. When this fatigue is temporary and acute, it is known as overreaching. If recovery is incomplete, work capacity decreases as fatigue increases. When this warning sign is not respected, the athlete falls into a persistent state of fatigue, which can develop into chronic fatigue or overtraining.

The symptoms of overtraining vary widely. They can be objective (observable) or subjective (detectable, especially by a coach). The majority of them, which can also accumulate, are as follows:

→ Unexplained drop (gradual or sudden) in performance level

→ Increased need for sleep (and recovery time in general)

→ Disturbed sleep and mood (increased aggressiveness, irritability, cyclothymia [mood disorder], emotional instability, etc.)

→ Heavy legs

→ More frequent infections and illnesses (immunosuppression)

→ Loss of desire to exert oneself and loss of motivation, both in training and in competition

→ Decrease in the ability to concentrate

→ Loss of appetite; digestion trouble

→ Disturbed body function while at rest (heartbeat, cardiac output, breathing rate), but also sometimes during exertion and recovery

→ Decreased lean muscle mass

→ Progressive anemia

It's difficult to detect overtraining because no reliable criteria exist. Each indicator, be it biological or psychological (heart rate, immune system, testosterone levels, etc.) varies from one individual to the next and does not necessarily result only from overtraining. A combined analysis, through a medical checkup, regular communication with, and above all close monitoring of the athlete is the best way to refine the diagnosis. In short, the simplest tactic is still to prevent the emergence of the syndrome in the first place.

How Can We Prevent Overtraining?

It is possible to avoid the emergence of overtraining while continuing to train at the highest level you can manage, via rigorous work comprising three main areas.

• Plan your training sessions (frequency, schedules), adhering scrupulously to the set recovery periods. Follow the changes in performance through testing. Observe your psychological state and watch your diet. In a nutshell, streamline your training.
• Keep a training diary in which you note what you planned to do, what you actually did, your performance, and any observations that you feel are useful. This will help you to build a tailored training routine by adjusting the workload (and recovery time) to your level.
• Gauge your fitness: Implementing "alert" tools can be invaluable, especially with a large group of athletes. Although more accurate versions exist (these are longer and more difficult to use), here is a simple example, provided by Pascal Prévost.It is a fitness assessment rather than an overtraining detection system.

Before each session, the athlete assesses the following four elements (from 0 to 5, with 5 being the maximum):

→ **Fatigue level**

→ **Muscle pain**

→ **Sleep disruption**

→ **Stress**

The total constitutes a fatigue index, which, when close to 16, is normal during training periods.

A grade of 5 for longer than 5 days in one of the four categories necessitates a workload adjustment. Finally, during competitions, the index should be slightly lower (10 to 12). Again, this is an example. This assessment can be adapted to athletes' characteristics and to the environment.

What Can We Do if We Overtrain?

The treatment for overtraining is basically rest, which should be more or less active depending on the seriousness, with a duration that is proportional to that of the overtraining. Thus, early diagnosis is crucial. For overtraining maintained for a short period (3 weeks), 3 to 5 full recovery days will suffice. You should follow this with a few weeks of training that is light in volume and intensity, alternating a workout day with a rest day. Only after this long period of gradual resumption should you consider an increase in intensity. In the most serious cases, complete rest for a minimum of two weeks should be observed, followed by several months of very slightly active rest. During this phase, physical activities of moderate intensity, sometimes different from your preferred sport, are allowed as a way to combat the emotional weariness that is often associated with overtraining.

THE 3 GOLDEN RULES TO AVOID OVERTRAINING

1 Know your capabilities.

2 Manage the training workload.

3 Monitor the length and method of recovery.

REMEMBER THIS

→ A workload-recovery imbalance is often to blame.

→ This is a complex pathology with multiple triggers.

→ Diagnosis is challenging.

→ Questioning the athlete is vitally important.

→ A medical checkup is essential to confirm the syndrome and determine the causes.

→ Successful treatment is simple: rest.

→ An ounce of prevention is worth a pound of cure.

Recovery Cycle During Vacation

BETWEEN VACATIONS FROM SPORTS AND WELL-DESERVED RELAXATION, WHAT IS THE RIGHT EQUATION FOR A SUCCESSFUL RECOVERY CYCLE? WHILE SOME PEOPLE TAKE THEIR KIMONO WITH THEM "JUST IN CASE," OTHERS REPLACE JUDO WITH RUNNING OR MOUNTAIN BIKING FOR A FEW WEEKS. SOME DABBLE IN JUDO CLINICS WHILE OTHERS ESCAPE THE DOJO ALTOGETHER FOR A COMPLETE BREAK.

Vacations for Juniors and Seniors

Looking to relax and get a change of scenery by escaping the daily grind for a few weeks? That's good. But the return to the dojo is often unforgiving: extra pounds, slow and stiff *tai-sabaki*, lack of automatic reflexes, and so on. Sometimes you have to start from scratch. So, should we stay in touch with the sport during our vacation? How do we set up an effective program that can be run with a minimum of equipment, while respecting the body's need for rest? Here are my pointers for an active yet restorative recovery.

Prioritize Recovery (Every Day)

If you've trained seriously all year long, the main objective of your recovery cycle is rest, above all, for two principal reasons:

1. You'll regain a physical and mental freshness that is essential to good training resumption conditions when you return from vacation.
2. It's during recovery that a large part of the hard-won progress you made throughout the season will come to the fore. Clearly, it's through rest that you'll continue to make progress.

My general advice is the following:

→ Set aside a proper unloading period.

→ Do some active recovery, such as a light, 20-minute jog.

→ Sleep is still the most powerful recovery technique; use your vacation to catch up on some shut-eye.

→ If you train regularly during the year, don't stop the physical side of things altogether for longer than two weeks, or you'll pay the price when you return to the mat.

BE CAREFUL!

→ Waking up your muscles through progressive stretching is an essential prerequisite for flexibility exercises to avoid damaging the musculotendinous structures.

→ Stretching should be done gradually and smoothly. Exhale progressively until you reach the point of painful tension (don't go past it).

→ Stretching when you wake up, without a cardiovascular warm-up beforehand, allows you to prioritize tendon work rather than muscle work. Though this has less to do with the range of motion in the joints, it requires greater caution and gradual movement.

Maintain Flexibility (Twice a Week)

There are two types of judokas. There are the flexible ones who don't really think about this aspect too much, and there are those whose hard-won inches in range of motion during the year will almost completely disappear during a 3-week break.

How Can We Avoid Loss of Flexibility?

Stretch well twice a week, preferably in the morning when you wake up; otherwise, at any time during the day. There are several possible techniques, and I'm going to suggest the simplest one: passive stretching (see the photos of adductor muscle stretches, as well as the section of this book that deals with this specifically). After progressive muscle preparation though a gradual increase in the range of motion and varying the position (by opening up the foot, for example), hold the stretched position for 20 sec, 1 min, and then 2 to 10 min. Do not overstretch.

PASSIVE POSES

Keep the Cardio Going (Twice a Week)

Endurance is one of the easier things to maintain, but if you neglect it, the first month back in the dojo following your vacation is going to be difficult. I'd therefore strongly advise that you pay special attention to it. Maintaining your cardio will enable you to keep up a high level of general endurance, to resume practicing judo without any problems when you return, and to optimize your recovery, all without the need for special training equipment. The suggested routine is of the long intermittent type. This training model allows you to shorten your sessions while increasing the amount of time in which you work at high intensity (this is the most effective when you train year-round).

The idea here is to alternate phases of intense effort and moderate effort that is closer to active recovery.

→ **Number of sessions per week:** 2.

→ **Supporting activity:** mainly running, but also cycling and swimming.

→ **Session:** 10 min warm-up, 10 min at 60 percent of the maximum, 4 sets of 3 min of effort alternated with 3 min active recovery time, 10 min active recovery time (light jogging) at the end of the session.

→ **Intensity during sets:** around 70 percent of the maximum.

A few tips:

→ **If you opt for swimming,** it's essential that you are already a strong swimmer because otherwise you are just putting in unnecessary additional effort.

→ **Cyclists should divide their recovery time in half.**

→ **If you're running in the mountains**, select a place with little variation in height, especially for the descent, so that you can avoid unnecessary vibrations in the joints and musculotendinous structures. Do the 3 min of effort as you ascend and recover as you descend; this provides an easy framework for the intensity of work and avoids any loss of time at the start of the set.

→ **If you're running on the beach**, choose flat ground and hard sand to protect your ankles. Running on soft sand will almost certainly lead to painful stiffness. Don't forget that you're on vacation! Finally, avoid running barefoot if your stride isn't perfect.

Generally, try to avoid participating in sports in the midday sun. Practice instead in the early morning or in the late afternoon. Not only will it be more comfortable, but you'll avoid sunstroke, sunburn, or hyperthermia.

Maintaining Strength (Twice a Week)

While judokas use a great variety of strength, from maximum strength to explosive strength and power, strength endurance is the most beneficial for a large volume of work, which is very important in the run-up to competitions. In fact, here we're looking to fulfill a dual purpose: to maintain the strength levels acquired over the previous season and to prepare for the resumption of work. (We could also add the esthetics factor for those spending time on the beach.)

Strength endurance work allows you to maintain or improve your technical, muscular, and nervous system-related techniques, and paves the way for you to resume intense work as soon as vacation is over; it also contributes to muscle definition. This type of work is ideal for vacationers because it is based on the principle of long and varied sets, done slowly, with a light load. Most often, body weight is sufficient, and you can add a resistance band, which fits easily into your suitcase.

The goal of the session I recommend is to saturate the muscle's ability to contract, while varying as much as possible the movements, contraction protocols, and working angles to meet as many of a judoka's specific needs as possible.

BE CAREFUL!

The goal is to tire out the muscle as much as you can. At no time should you continue to work if your technique deteriorates. Don't do an additional repetition if your technique is faulty; that's a sign that the set is over. The muscle is tired, and that's the only objective.

This example is for push-ups, with or without a resistance band:

[A] 20 normal reps
[B] 10 reps with staggered hands
[C] 10 reps with a hold as you come down (5 sec)
[D] 10 static-dynamic reps, with a 3 sec hold and then 1 clap push-up
[E] 10 static-dynamic reps, with hands spread out more widely than in position [A]
[F] 20 normal reps

→ **Recovery time:** 1 min 30 sec as you stretch the antagonist muscles, especially the back muscles.
→ **Intensity during sets:** low, with slow and controlled movements (apart from the static-dynamic reps).

Vacations for Child and Adolescent Judokas

Coordination Games

Judo is a demanding discipline that requires, by its very nature, a high level of coordination. Two problems arise, then, for teenagers:

1. At this age, you change from week to week, as does your body. With summer behind you, you're going to be starting back at school at a different size and height. Maintaining control of your body is almost a daily job.
2. Athletes under 16 tend to take the simplest route during competitions so as to feel effective rapidly. You should quickly abandon this attitude; although it might pay dividends in the short term, it is clearly limiting in the medium term.

To maintain or develop coordination during vacation:

• Practice *tandoku-renshu* (judo moves without a partner) every day.

• Go enjoy yourself away from the judo mats! Rugby, gymnastics, surfing, and climbing are all sports that involve risk-taking and coordination, which are transferable to your sport.

• Coordination games are another option. These can be played with your friends, like the one shown here, a psychomotor game with two balls.

Psychomotor Exercise With Two Balls

Players position themselves in a circle. Players 1 and 2 each have a ball. Player 2 throws the ball up in the air, to him- or herself. At the same time, Player 1 passes Player 2 the ball at chest height. Player 2 then passes the ball received from Player 1 to Player 3, while his or her ball is still up in the air. When the ball belonging to Player 2 drops back down, he or she then passes it to Player 3, who has already thrown his or her ball up in the air and will pass the second ball onto Player 1, and so on (see illustration).

The ideal setup is to start with several players and eliminate someone each time a ball falls to the ground. The circle should get smaller and smaller, speeding up the game. When you have four or five players, you can change the direction following a signal or randomly. You can also add challenges, such as playing with exercise balls, or running around in a circle while the ball is in the air.

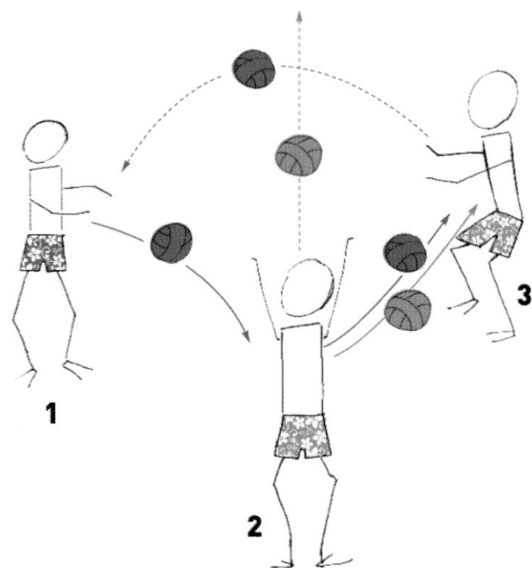

Speed

Vacation also provides an opportunity to develop a performance parameter that is often overlooked due to lack of time, and the golden age for which lies between 12 and 15: speed! The beach is even better suited for this because these is no need for equipment.

Plyometric and Sprinting Exercise

After 10 min of jogging on the beach, do some active stretching, then alternate between 3 exercises on the harder sand.

[Exercise 1] **6 jumping strides, then a 20 to 30 m sprint at maximum speed.**

[Exercise 2] **6 jump squats, switching leg positions, then a 20 to 30 m sprint at maximum speed.**

[Exercise 3] **Crazy hopscotch, that is, a ramped-up hopscotch that includes coordination challenges.**

Example: spins, backward steps (dropping to the ground, both feet on the ground, etc.), then a 20 to 30 m sprint at maximum speed.

Important Note

- → **Do each exercise once with 1 min of recovery time between exercises**
- → **Recover for 4 min and then repeat up to 4 times**

End the Session With

- → **2 × 30 m sprints on hard sand with 3 min of recovery time**
- → **2 × 60 m sprints on hard sand with 5 min of recovery time**
- → **15 min of jogging on the beach**

Endurance

Endurance is the foundation for judokas' range of physical attributes because it enables them to perform effectively (in competition, but also in training) and recover quickly. A sandy beach is often a good reason to go for a jog, but it would be a shame not to make the most of the sea, which can make exercising much more fun, especially if you're not used to jogging. Here's what you can do.

Aerobic Sand-and-Sea Exercise

After 10 min of a warm-up jog, do 3 gradual accelerations over 30 sec alternated with 30 sec of active recovery time, before beginning your actual workout. Run along the beach at a moderate pace for 30 sec. At the signal, sprint directly into the sea, trying to get as far as you can, and then run back, all within 30 sec, before doing a 30 sec recovery run.

Important

You can run or swim or both. You should spread out your effort so that you can make it out into the sea and back again in the allotted time. If you go over your time on the way back, you'll get less recovery time. If you come back too early, you'll have more recovery time, but you won't have gone as far as others.

Session Type

2 circuits of 10 sets of 30 sec of effort, 30 sec of recovery time.

3 min of recovery time between circuits.

End the session with some active recovery via a 10-min jog.

SHOULD YOU RUN BAREFOOT ON THE SAND?

A growing number of people seem to think it's fashionable to run barefoot. Be careful, because while it does offer certain benefits, such as improved proprioception, better sensory information received by the arches of the foot, and all the resulting technical adjustments, this technique is up for debate.

If you opt for a barefoot jog, here are some pointers:

- → Take things gradually and pay attention to any tendon pain.
- → Watch out for anything hidden in the sand, such as broken glass.
- → Select a flat route.
- → Pick hard sand for continuous and prolonged exercise and use soft sand for accelerations or to increase intensity at certain points of your jog.

Please note that running in badly fitting shoes can cause more problems than running barefoot and that suitable shoes can help to protect you from the impact of your feet hitting the ground.

What If You're in the Mountains?

Well, that's good: You can use those hills to your advantage! Choose a reasonable-looking hill so it doesn't slow you down too much. The same principle applies: Accelerate for 30 sec as you climb, and then unwind for 30 sec as you descend. Of course, this also works on flat ground. It just means that you have to run faster during the phases of effort.

If you have a heart monitor, try to stabilize yourself at 90 percent of your maximum heart rate.*

**Approximately 220 minus your age. If you really want to know: Do a maximum effort for 5 minutes and see how high it goes!*

Sample Weekly Program

	MONDAY	TUESDAY	WEDNESDAY	THURSDAY	FRIDAY
MORNING	**15 MIN STRETCHING** and *tandoku-renshu*	**ABDOMINAL MUSCLES** 20 normal sit-ups 20 slow sit-ups ×5 20 sit-ups with arms crossed 20 normal sit-ups 20 slow sit-ups ×5 2000 scissor kicks	**15 MIN STRETCHING** and *tandoku-renshu*	**PUSH-UPS** 6 sets of gradually decreasing push-ups, starting at 20 (then 19, 18, 17, etc.), with 15 sec of recovery time between sets. 6 series of pull-ups (as many as possible), with 1 min of recovery time	**15 MIN STRETCHING** and *tandoku-renshu*
AFTERNOON	ENDURANCE	SPEED	COORDINATION GAMES	ENDURANCE	Long, continuous jog on the beach

Returning to Training

AFTER A VACATION OR A RECOVERY PERIOD, IT CAN BE DIFFICULT TO ADJUST THE LOAD AND CHOOSE THE RIGHT TRAINING CONTENT. IF WE MAKE BAD CHOICES, WE RUN THE RISK OF LOSING VALUABLE TRAINING TIME OR, ON THE FLIP SIDE, RUSHING THINGS TOO MUCH.

No matter what form the cycle before a gradual resumption of judo takes, this training block should be given special attention.

If we consider what tends to be the longest break, a summer vacation (potentially 2 or 3 weeks), the resumption of training has a strong influence on the rest of the season. It really sets the tone for the fighter's training. Committing to this phase is essential for smooth progress in the season, both physically and technically. However, its implementation can be complex, torn between different training concepts and traditions, and constrained by the competitive judoka's busy and early schedule. Regardless of the judoka's choices, his or her level and fitness status will determine the content and the loads that they'll have to include in their training. Usually, it is customary to resume training with basic exercises, with a large volume of training at low intensity. But to what extent can we resume gently without feeling like we're wasting time? I prefer to focus on quality.

Quality as the Basis for Judo Work

The quality of work is the foundation of training and should be something that fighters are always thinking about. Qualitative work is the prerequisite for effectiveness, especially in judo, one of the most complex disciplines out there, and even more so during the resumption period. Here's what I mean by quality.

- **Quality of effort:** Training has a positive impact only if you work at limits that are close to the maximum at the time (not the maximum recorded at your peak fitness). Resuming gently and gradually is definitely necessary, but if it's below a certain threshold, it'll have zero effect. Making sure you don't sweat too much is a waste of time; the only limits are the means available to the athlete during this period.
- **Quality of movement:** Technical quality, especially in a sport like judo, is a top priority, and makes particular sense at the start of the season. This is the time to swiftly regain your automatic reflexes, and for nonexperts, to acquire them. It is through technique that physical attributes are developed in training, and so this aspect should be a primary concern.
- **Quality of mental commitment:** In order for your training to reach a certain quality, you have to put your vacation behind you. Judokas must be involved and committed from the get-go, focused on clearly established objectives, and motivated to achieve their goals.

Effective training hinges on high-quality work. During cardio and muscle-development exercises, just as in judo, the intensity, volume, complexity, and specificity of the training workload may vary, but the quality should not.

Intermittent Exercise as the Basis for Endurance Work

The resumption of so-called cardiovascular-pulmonary work tends to be the most problematic. In fact, judo, an intense sport involving short and fragmented effort, warrants particular attention in the resumption of cardio training. The tradition of basic work means that you would normally start with a long, low-intensity effort, such as a light, 45-minute jog. But as I explained in the section on endurance, it's a waste of time if you've trained regularly during the previous cycles, for the following reasons:

- **Judo does not require this type of effort** (you'll never be involved in a 45-min, low-intensity bout).
- **It's boring and time-consuming.**

Long and continuous work does, however, have its uses, in addition to the mental training benefits that some claim: It can help with weight loss, with—to a lesser extent—active recovery, and, of course, with adaptations to the central nervous system, if you're completely deconditioned.

Which types of exercises are best during this resumption period? There's no reason why you can't immediately start with dividing up your effort, which doesn't necessarily involve doing extreme sessions right from the outset. It's just essential to stick to the main principles of progressiveness (increase the difficulty gradually), variety (cover the range of the different types of effort encountered during a bout), and specificity, always based on a quality foundation. The main advantage is that we can sustain high-intensity work for longer than continuous work and get better results. This divided effort should be organized in a pyramid-like fashion.

A Typical Model for This Example

- **→ 2 min of effort, 2 min at low intensity**
- **→ 1 min 30 sec of effort, 1 min 30 sec at low intensity**
- **→ 1 min, 1 min**
- **→ 30 sec, 30 sec**
- **→ 30 sec, 30 sec**
- **→ 1 min, 1 min**
- **→ 1 min 30 sec of effort, 1 min 30 sec at low intensity**
- **→ 2 min of effort, 2 min at low intensity**

An example using running: After a custom warm-up, I recommend that you do intense work, followed by an active recovery period of the same duration. The choice of duration and intensity, as well as the number of sets, are up to you. This training block can be repeated during the session and should evolve from one session to the next. You can gradually double the stages (e.g., 2 × 30-30), increase the length, and make other additions. As the intensity increases, the pyramid can even be inverted (start with the short split, such as 30-30). The session must absolutely end with a gradual cool-down, taking the form of jogging, then walking, and then finishing off with light stretching. The final rule to follow is specificity, which means getting as close as possible, during training, to real judo. The choice of effort can be perfectly reproduced and expressed through judo. Refusing to start with judo itself at the start of the season under the guise of progressiveness is to attack the problem using the wrong reasoning.

And what if your break from the mat lasts for several months? In that case, you really will be deconditioned. You will have to find the minimal central nervous system functions necessary for the smooth operation of the aerobic system. Here I'm talking about central nervous system adaptations for aerobic training: sufficient cardiac output, thickness of the left ventricle, effectiveness of heart contractions (and therefore blood pumping efficiency), and even an increase in plasma volume. These adaptations represent essential prerequisites for the effectiveness of high-intensity work. In terms of training, you should take your time and start with 2 to 4 weeks of continuous exercise like long runs.

GLOSSARY

→ **training volume:** The amount and duration of work. An assessment of this can be done using the training time, the distance traveled, the number of sets or repetitions, and so on.

→ **training intensity:** The measure of an athlete's level of effort compared to his or her maximum performance capabilities. This is expressed as a percentage of maximum strength or speed.

→ **workload:** The organized series of exercises that helps you to improve.

→ **concentric contraction:** The two muscle insertions come together.

→ **eccentric contraction:** The muscle resists the load by stretching out.

→ **plyometric contraction:** Concentric and eccentric contractions alternate with no breaks (e.g., jumps with a controlled landing).

→ **isometric contraction:** A static contraction.

Strength Endurance as a Foundation for Muscle Strengthening

In muscle strengthening, the work is primarily focused on the following:

- **Technique and acquisition** (or recovery) of automatic reflexes
- **Hypertrophy work** (increase in muscle mass) building up a judoka's armor, and strength workouts with long, numerous sets with a reasonable load, prior to any intense work during the season

Example (note that the recovery time between stages is less than 1 min 30 sec)

→ Phase 1: resistance band pull 2 × 10

→ Phase 2: loaded pull

2 × 10 repetitions at 40 percent of your load capacity. Alternate pulling between the right and left arms

2 × 8 reps at 50 percent. Pull quickly and release slowly

2 × 6 reps at 60 percent. Hold halfway through as you release the load

4 reps at 65 to 70 percent. You can add holds, change the tempo, and so on.

More than ever, the notion of progressiveness is key, whether during a session (from the warm-up onward) or the season (the pursuit of progress from one session to another, or from one cycle to another, is essential). The work must also be specific, both in terms of the exercises and the working angles, contraction methods, and strength attributes.

Nevertheless, this type of training can quickly become long and tedious, forcing us to be creative and break with the routines originating from bodybuilding and athletic strength. Varied work will therefore aim to provide a range of different contractions (see previous glossary), as well as different strength-development methods, types of muscle engagement (voluntary or via electrostimulation), and types of movement, enabling you to prepare the muscle for the different scenarios it will face.

Resumption Cycle FAQ

Should you wait before resuming judo and just start with a general physical training workout?

No. Judo is a sufficiently varied and adjustable discipline that the difficulty, quantity, and intensity can be adapted to the more limited resources of the fighter at that particular moment. Put plainly, you should start back with judo as soon as possible, modifying the physical and technical demands accordingly. The pursuit of quality doesn't mean you should be looking to reproduce "the" move of the Olympics immediately, though!

I'm really overwhelmed physically. To get my spark back, I was thinking about doing some basic running work. Is that appropriate?

No, not if you have previously been training normally. Basic running work and other basic activities are most often associated with aerobic capacity effort, which is only useful for learning to appreciate and manage effort, weight regulation, adaptations of the central nervous system, or even recovery. In the case of a judoka who is resuming training, having previously trained seriously, it is best to opt for work that is divided into portions. It's certainly more difficult, but it's so much more effective! It's also more fun if you pick an activity other than running, like one of the racket sports. Once again, progression is the priority.

Yes, if you've not trained seriously for quite some time. In this case, you will need to try to recover the main adaptations of the cardiopulmonary system that you've lost with the passage of time. Without those, short-term effectiveness is not achievable in intensity-focused training sessions. Here, resuming via a gradual cycle of continuous, low-intensity effort is an excellent idea.

Should the competitive judo squad consider a serious military-style resumption training camp?

It depends. When judokas get back from vacation, two scenarios may emerge: competitors who kept up with their training, even moderately, over the summer, and others who stopped all activities for several weeks. In both cases, an intense resumption camp would serve the dual purpose of team building and getting the group back into a training rhythm right away.

In the first instance, where fighters are not deconditioned, a development cycle with an increasing load (gradually increasing each week) would be particularly suitable.

In the second example, the technical focus of the camp should be on the basics, and it should be physically varied and very progressive. The idea is for the athletes to get their appetite back for the rhythm and intensity of effort, and to regain their fitness within one week.

I'm stiff as a board. Do you have any particular advice about stretching?

Yes, indeed. Stretching should be an integral part of the resumption program, from the first training session onward, first through passive flexibility exercises done on your own, and then through prolonged postural work. Pairs exercises and more advanced methods combining contractions and stretching should be scheduled for later in the season.

I feel as though I have fragile joints and muscles. Which exercises should I choose to strengthen and protect my body during bouts?

Recovering strength levels is a secondary concern. The priority during this period is to rebuild the fighter's armor. This means strengthening structures locally that are traditionally fragile and susceptible to injury during the resumption period, such as the following:

- **The rotator cuff, especially through lateral raises** (and arm rotations once the arm is raised to 90 degrees) with dumbbells or resistance bands. Forward lunges, side lunges, and squats for the hamstrings, quadriceps, and adductors.
- **The dorsal-lumbar structure, the abdominal muscles, and the postural muscles can be worked through static core-strengthening exercises.** For example: facing the floor, balanced on your elbows and feet, with your legs straight, or on your back, with your hips raised, supported by your shoulders and feet, in a bridge position. You can devote one or two sessions during the week to this type of work in the weight room or fit it into a circuit at the end of a warm-up or the end of a session.

Is Training at Altitude Worthwhile?

TRADITIONALLY, IN EARLY SPRING AND THEN AGAIN, A LITTLE BIT LATER IN THE SUMMER, NUMEROUS JUDOKAS TRADE THEIR KIMONOS FOR HIKING BOOTS, BACKPACKS, OR SNOWSHOES FOR A BIT OF ALTITUDE TRAINING, REPUTED TO BE BENEFICIAL AND ULTRA-EFFECTIVE. BUT IT'S NOT SOMETHING THAT CAN JUST BE IMPROVISED.

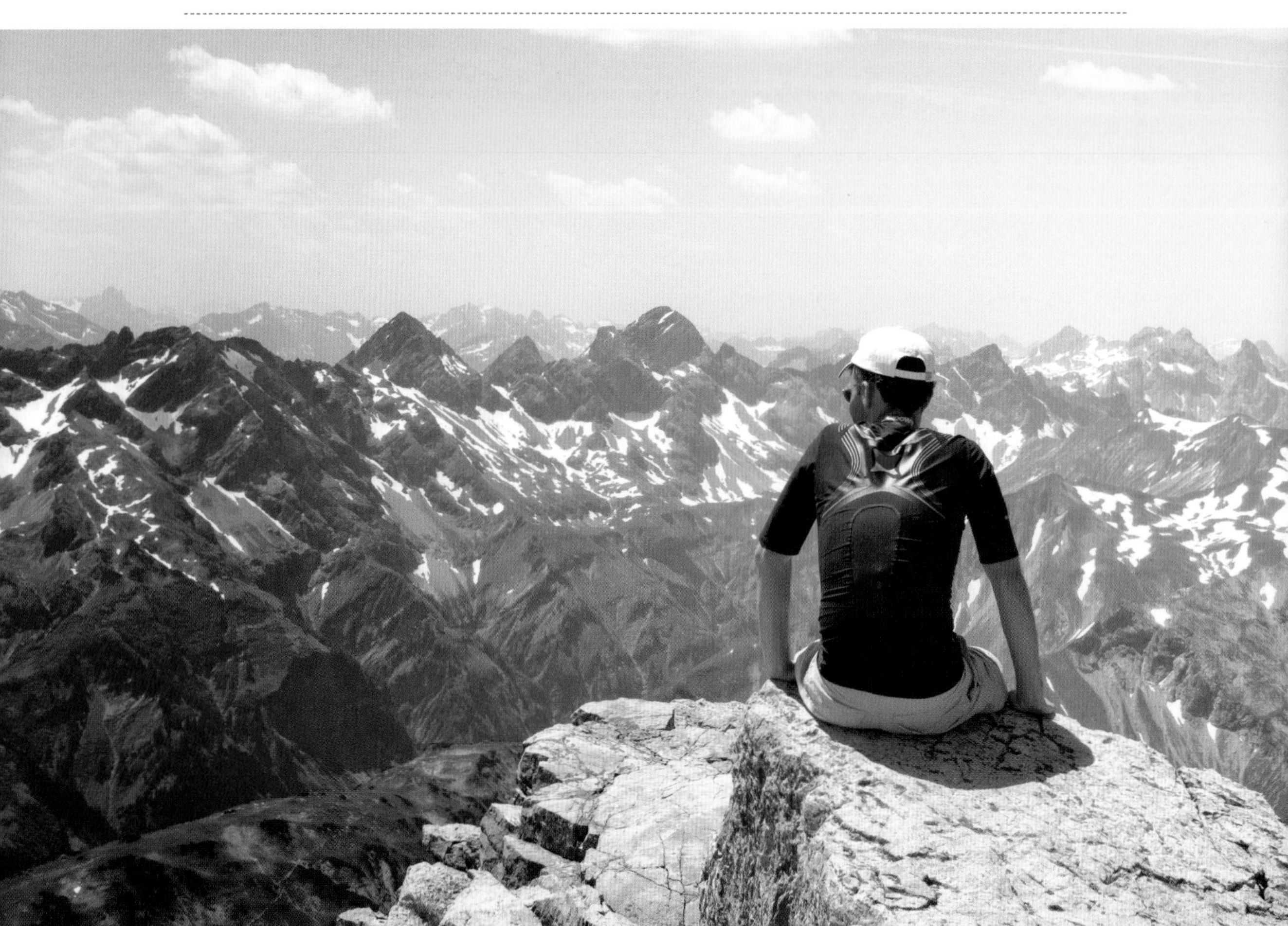

Mountain training has been fashionable for about 40 years now, and people swear by its benefits. Soccer players or track-and-field athletes do it to prepare for major events, and there is a considerable temptation for the average judoka to do the same. And there's no doubt that there's nothing nicer than being part of a group on a ski trip or doing judo in the mountains during awesome weather. Team spirit and the great outdoors guarantee good times. On the other hand, two questions remain: Can high-altitude training really improve your performance, and, if so, what do you need to do to make it happen? Here are my answers. Hold on tight, let's go!

Real Effects

This type of practice owes its reputation to hypoxia, the technical term for a reduction in the concentration of oxygen in the blood. The partial pressure of oxygen is lower in the mountains, which has a major influence on the transportation of oxygen in the body. The body reacts to this unusual situation by enhancing capabilities related to breathing (pushed to the limits at the start, the lungs adapt and subsequently ventilate better), the heart (increase in resting heartbeat and gradual adaptation), the blood (more red blood cells, which are oxygen carriers; this is the much-discussed hematocrit), and the muscles (increase in a certain number of processes linked to performance). When you return to sea level, some of the effects endure, thereby giving you, in theory, greater capabilities than the average athlete who did not spend time up in the clouds like you.

Effects on Recovery

At the muscular level, we have an accelerated rate of phosphocreatine resynthesis after spending time at 2,000 m, resulting in a real effect on recovery. If we stay at higher elevations, recovery after an aerobic effort will be as long, if not longer; however, if we return to lower elevations, it will, on the contrary, have a positive impact.

Short-Effort Work Possibilities

The low air density facilitates enhanced performance during short and intense effort. Mountains lend themselves very well to the development of speed (altitude is particularly excellent for overspeed), provided the recovery time is extended.

Effects on $\dot{V}O_2max$

While aerobic performance at altitude is diminished, the $\dot{V}O_2max$ increases when you return to lower ground. This is definitely the case for those with an average $\dot{V}O_2max$, which is the majority of judokas.

Watch Out for the Physical Risks

A number of risks related to the cold and the altitude can disrupt your group training: risk of altitude sickness, colds, flu, and so on. These are not that serious, and they can be prevented by using common sense and good equipment!

No Change in Performance or Slower Performance

There is no observable change to anaerobic performance at altitude, but there is a decrease in $\dot{V}O_2max$. The consequence of this is that a judoka does not perform as well in the mountains.

Adapting the Workload

At altitude, it is essential to increase the recovery time and to reduce the intensity of execution, which limits training possibilities for a large number of sports known for their level of engagement, like judo. This means that organized and intense camps for judokas, who may have two successive judo training sessions per day, interspersed with a day of skiing, are very risky and often ineffective.

A real drop in psychological performance is observable from 7,000 m upward. Of course, at that altitude, dojos tend to be rare. Seriously, though, working at rather low speeds, the time it takes the body to adapt, decreases in aerobic performance, the cold, and so forth, can all have a negative impact on confidence, even at medium altitude. We should keep this in mind during training periods close to competitions.

Time-Limited Effects

Lasting and usable adaptations at altitude take a minimum of two weeks, and you still require 2 to 3 days of acclimatization before and after the training, which makes a camp with a short duration irrelevant. When, then, should we schedule altitude training? A judoka wishing to properly reap the beneficial effects of altitude must be able to set aside between 2 and 3 weeks (no more, no less), and have a competitive event lined up 2 to 3 weeks after his or her return. It's important to note that the benefits gained only influence certain judo performance factors: recovery, aerobic power, and speed.

What Can We Do?

As you'll have understood, training in the mountains is not a miracle solution. It has strict implementation criteria and is best used only in specific circumstances. If your team's coach decides to arrange a camp at altitude, here are a few rules to follow. Four methods exist:

→ Train at high altitude, sleep at high altitude

→ Train at lower altitude, sleep at lower altitude

→ Train at high altitude, sleep at lower altitude

→ Train at lower altitude, sleep at high altitude

It would appear that living at a high altitude (where all the adaptations would occur, especially during recovery), combined with training at a moderate altitude (allowing for specific speed of movement and intensity), leads to the best results. This is exactly how the French and Norwegian national cross-country ski teams train.

Important Points for Altitude Training

→ Take a blood test 2 weeks before leaving to ascertain your ferritin levels (a blood cell protein that contains iron; the test provides a susceptibility index for altitude sickness).

→ Don't schedule any training on the first 2 days, which will be devoted to acclimatization. During the first week, you should strictly limit yourself to aerobic exercises, then very gradually increase your speed.

→ Divide your time at altitude in half by devoting 1 full day to rest (on the 7th or 8th day).

→ The second part of your getaway can be more intense ($\dot{V}O_2$max, maximum endurance, lactic capacity, speed).

→ At the end of the 2 weeks, any competition should still be at least 13 days away. A recovery micro-cycle of 5 to 6 days should be considered directly afterward, with intense training resuming only after that.

→ Your food plan should take into account the fact you're at altitude (fluid loss, iron, protein for amino acids, etc.).

GLOSSARY

→ **hematocrit:** The volume occupied by red blood cells in the blood.

→ **resynthesis:** The process that enables the body to re-create ATP (universal unit of energy) so that it can have energy available again.

→ **phosphocreatine:** An energy-rich molecule used by muscles in the seconds following intense effort.

→ **$\dot{V}O_2$max:** Maximal oxygen consumption during exercise.

→ **anaerobic:** When the body is deprived of oxygen.

→ **hypobaric:** Air pressure that is less than normal air pressure.

→ **O_2:** Oxygen.

The Tapering Cycle

THE APPROACH TO COMPETITION IS A DECISIVE MOMENT IN THE TRAINING PROCESS: YOU CAN GAIN A LOT, OR YOU CAN LOSE A LOT IF YOU ARE UNFAMILIAR WITH CERTAIN PRINCIPLES. SOME SIMPLE RULES WILL HELP YOU TO REACH AND OPTIMIZE THIS DELICATE PERIOD.

Should we train less or more? Harder or not? For more or less time? Correct our weaknesses or focus on automatic reflexes? All of these questions can plague a fighter in the days leading up to a competition.

The objective of this period is to get rid of the fatigue accumulated during your training—which hides the athlete's real performance potential—and to recharge your batteries. But what complicates a coach's task during this period, which guarantees the success of all your preparations, is the principle of training reversibility: Physical adaptations are temporary and cannot be maintained at a certain level without sustained, regular work. To put it plainly, there's only a small difference between tapering and deconditioning.

As usual, old habits die hard. We see, due to tradition, training that is done to death, as in a long sprint. Through anxiety, some fighters reassure themselves by giving their all, at the risk of actually putting in competitive performances before the competition even begins. Others believe that difficult training 24 to 48 hours before a competition will cause a surge in performance. In all these examples, the result is inevitable: The judoka will turn up to the competition in a physically diminished state. There is no reason to sacrifice the golden rule of tapering, which is to reduce the fighter's workload. The time for training is over, and the time for the accumulating resources has begun. But the specter of a decrease in performance still hovers over everyone. So the question is really about how much a judoka's workload should be reduced before he or she starts to regress.

When? Three Weeks Before

The moment where an athlete spirals into deconditioning is, even today, unclear. Nevertheless, recent research shows that there is a 3-week margin before a trained athlete starts to see any significant and lasting dip in performance during a workload reduction period.

This means that we can take our foot off the gas a little without worrying too much. Experts recommend 2 to 3 weeks for optimal tapering, which just goes to show the importance of this period. Several studies have shown that no decrease in endurance or muscle power is observable at this key moment; quite the opposite, in fact (Mujinka 2009).

How? Less Volume, More Intensity

There are many tapering methods, but one stands out today for its effectiveness in the world of modern training: nonlinear tapering in stages. You reduce the overall workload without the level of each stage being systematically lower than the previous one. There are several components that make up the training workload: volume, intensity, and—especially important for tapering—frequency. Consequently, the question of their specific configuration arises: Should they all be reduced together, or are there nuances that should be respected for each one of them?

Intensity seems to the be the key to successful tapering. Contrary to what you might think, it can be maintained or even increased in the run-up to competitions. So, it's sensible to include training content, such as speed or explosiveness, during this phase.

In addition, the tapering period usually sees a major decline in the volume of training. The correlation between a decrease in training volume and an increase in performance has been demonstrated several times. That leaves the thorny question of training frequency. If the volume can be reduced before a competition without affecting performance, it's important to note that the more technical the discipline (as is the case with judo), the more the training frequency should be maintained. In fact, accuracy of movement, as well as perception and anticipation abilities, can quickly go south. Some champions feel it necessary to schedule sessions right up to the night before the big day.

DECONDITIONING
A noticeable regression in the performance level of one or more physical factors.

Improve Strong Points or Correct Weaknesses?

Technically and physically speaking, this is no longer the time for development, but, rather, for optimization. It is certainly not a question of focusing on weaknesses that you won't end up using during competition, at the risk of underperforming. On the contrary, all of the technical work during tapering should be focused on actions that fighters will primarily use during a tournament: their strong points.

Weight Management

Weight management is a constant concern in judo. This is particularly the case during the tapering period, where the logic of losing weight, often up to the last few minutes before the weigh-in, might even contradict the reasoning presented in this section. The ideal scenario, then, is to control any body weight fluctuations completely during the 2 to 3 weeks leading up to the competition.

Should We Train the Night Before?

It all depends on the athlete. Reason would suggest that rest is a necessity, but some fighters need to reassure themselves and maintain their technical potential. Fortunately, it's possible to train in a short and intense manner the night before a competition.

Two Options

→ **Don't do anything the day before or on the day itself.**

→ **Schedule a very short speed and technique session (less than an hour) the night before.**

Suggested 3-Week Tapering Cycle

For a competitive judoka training every day, or even twice a day.

WEEK 1	MONDAY	TUESDAY	WEDNESDAY	THURSDAY	FRIDAY	SATURDAY	SUNDAY
MORNING	Speed Technique Lactic circuit	Technique *Randori* *Ne-waza*	Active recovery and mobility	Speed Strength			Active recovery and mobility Weight loss if necessary
AFTERNOON	*Randori*	MAP Jogging		*Randori*	*Randori*	Strength	

WEEK 2	MONDAY	TUESDAY	WEDNESDAY	THURSDAY	FRIDAY	SATURDAY	SUNDAY
MORNING	Speed Technique Lactic circuit	Strength	MAP Jogging	Strength	Speed Technique	Active recovery and mobility Weight loss if necessary	Active recovery and mobility Weight loss if necessary
AFTERNOON	*Randori*		*Randori*	Active recovery and mobility Weight loss if necessary	*Randori*		

WEEK 3	MONDAY	TUESDAY	WEDNESDAY	THURSDAY	FRIDAY	SATURDAY	SUNDAY
MORNING	Speed Technique	Active recovery and mobility Weight loss if necessary	Speed Technique	Strength	Speed Technique	Speed session or complete rest	Competition
AFTERNOON	*Randori*			Active recovery and mobility Weight loss if necessary			

Precompetition Speed Session

After a 15-minute warm-up, try this series of specific exercises:

6 burpees
at maximum speed
+
6 *uchi-komi* at maximum speed **[A]**
2 min of recovery time

5 tuck jumps at maximum speed
+
6 *uchi-komi* at maximum speed **[B]**
2 min of recovery time

4 burpees
and tuck jumps
+
6 *uchi-komi* at maximum speed
4 min of recovery time

Repeat this circuit 1 or 2 times

B

4 sec sprint in place
+
3 *uchi-komi*
+
1 *nage-komi* **[C]**
2 min of recovery time

4 sec of hip rotations in place **[D]**
+
3 *uchi-komi*
+
1 *nage-komi*
2 min of recovery time

4 sec of hip rotations in place and squats
+
3 *uchi-komi* **[D and E]**
+
1 *nage-komi*
4 min of recovery time

Repeat this circuit 1 or 2 times

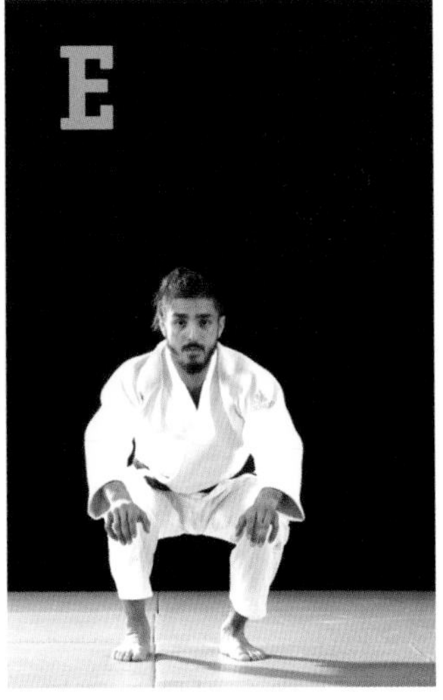

4 tuck jumps, as high as possible, keeping contact with the floor to a minimum.

+

2 full-speed *nage-komi* 2 times

3 min of recovery time

4 clap push-ups, keeping the contact your hands have with the floor to a minimum. **[F]** *(on knees for heavyweights and female judokas; this is about speed, not strength)*

+

2 full-speed *nage-komi* **[G]**

4 min of recovery time

Repeat this circuit 1 or 2 times

RECOVERY AND PREVENTION

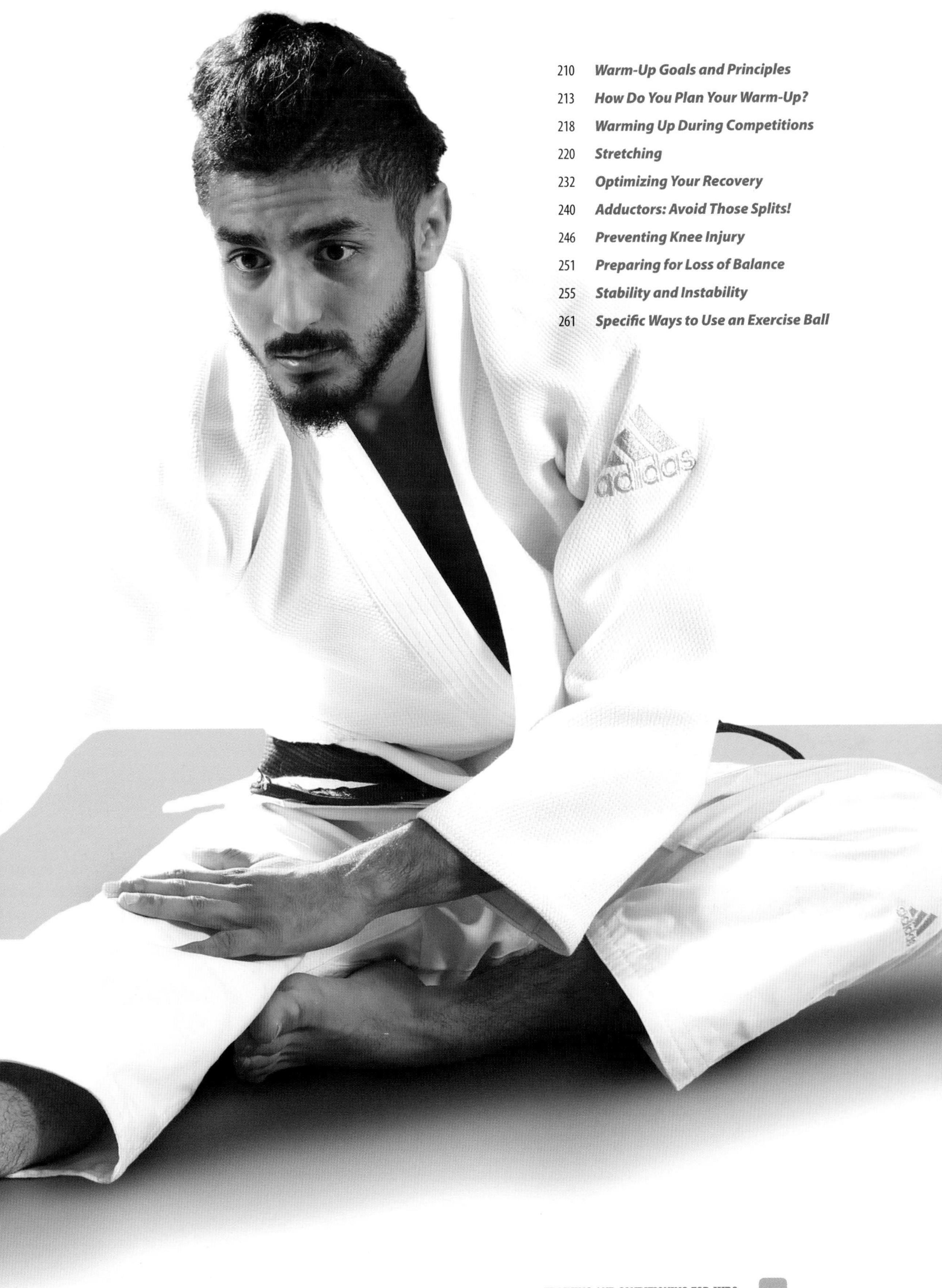

Warm-Up Goals and Principles

EVERYONE AGREES THAT WARMING UP IS ESSENTIAL. HOWEVER, THIS PROCESS OF LOOSENING UP CAN OFTEN BE PERFUNCTORY, ROUTINE, AND NONSPECIFIC, BOTH IN TRAINING AND DURING COMPETITIONS. THOSE THREE EVILS ARE GOOD REASONS FOR US TO TAKE A SERIOUS LOOK AT MODERN WARM-UP TECHNIQUES.

"5 × 10 *uchi-komi* and 2 *randori* on the floor!"

While some coaches do try to shake things up a bit, this is often the way in which sessions begin, with a mix of old habits and now-obsolete concepts. Shortened warm-up protocols are based on the assumption that judokas will progress when they get started on the actual judo part, and that they'll leave their pride in the locker room. In theory, it's possible to use *ne-waza* (or even *tachi-waza*) as a warm-up tool, but it should be done without any resistance, so that the focus can be on symbiosis and feeling. You need to relax and still maintain technical and mental control, which may be too much to ask!

Warm-ups are often incomplete (lacking a proper work phase or missing one particular area of the body), formulaic (always the same), or even inappropriate (for the circumstances, for the athlete, or for the session content). It's time we cleared up a few things, especially since a large amount of scientific research is now available to supplement the coach's methods and help to make the warm-up a success.

At club level, a comprehensive and well-organized warm-up can be done in about 20 minutes.

But why do we warm up in the first place? Although there are numerous warm-up methods out there, which may sometimes either converge or totally contradict each other, they are united by a common concern: raising the internal temperature of your muscles. Lullies, in 1973, made the following observation: A 1°C rise in body temperature corresponds to a cellular response speed increase of 13 percent (Goubel 1973)! The strength level increase, meanwhile, is 2 percent per degree, which, for competitive judo players, can end up being decisive, particularly for those in the heavyweight categories, for whom 2 percent can represent several kilograms. Since the temperature of the muscles and tendons at rest is 98.6°F (37°C), the goal is to raise the temperature to around 102°F (39°C). It's at this heat that they'll reach peak performance, as will the central nervous system and the joints. The physiological reactions function in the best possible manner; the biochemical reaction speed is at its maximum. It's worth remembering that as you initiate effort, several energy production systems are triggered to enable muscle contraction. The first efficient systems are those that do not use oxygen, preferring instead to use local muscle resources. The more intense the effort, the more prominent these so-called anaerobic systems will be. The aerobic system, which uses oxygen to produce energy, only starts up properly several minutes later and corresponds to a more modest intensity of effort. A badly calibrated warm-up, especially in terms of the way the intensity progresses, causes the body to incur an oxygen debt that it must deal with throughout the session and pay back at the end. This causes a longer and more difficult recovery.

THINGS TO AVOID

→ Extended static stages after a general warm-up, which can lead to the loss of all of the positive effects (e.g., running followed by stretching on the floor).

→ Training circuits with overly short or overly intense exercises, which cause a drastic increase in heart rate, but no (or very little) increase in cardiac output, which is actually the effect we want.

→ Warm-ups that are overly long or overly short.

→ Passive stretching in the guise of a warm-up.

→ Using a sports cream for a warm-up (external effect only).

Adjustments for the Younger and the Older

→ Young people respond well to fun. Their warm-up is often shortened because it competes with the judo activities themselves. We have to allow them to play as much as possible, and get them started on judo just as quickly, while educating them about the recipe for a successful warm-up, something they will retain for the rest of their careers.

→ More mature judokas should not hesitate to extend the progressiveness of the warm-up regarding judo-specific work, especially since their technical expertise allows for the use of specific release work such as *uchi-komi* in motion or *ne-waza*.

The Five Main Effects of a Successful Warm-Up

RAISE THE INTERNAL TEMPERATURE OF THE MUSCLE	INCREASE CARDIAC OUTPUT	INCREASE AIR INTAKE	IMPROVE MOTOR EFFICIENCY	PSYCHOLOGICAL PREPARATION
EFFECT	EFFECT	EFFECT	EFFECT	EFFECT
Optimize muscle contractions	Improve oxygen transportation and effort production	Optimize breathing during effort	Optimize breathing during effort	Optimal stimulation of mental activity depending on the situation
→ Better reaction speed → Reduction in muscle stiffness → Increase in contraction time → Greater muscle sensitivity → Quicker nerve impulses → Increase in strength production	→ Increased heart rate → Increased stroke volume → Optimization of blood pumping and circulation	→ Increased respiratory rate → Increased tidal volume → Optimization of gas exchange	→ Improved sensations → Protection of joints by a thickening of the cartilage → Better joint mobility → Improvement in muscle coordination	→ Confidence building → Enhanced motivation → Increased alertness

Warming up is therefore not only essential, psychologically, it's also an important psychological tipping point, a technical training method, and a teaching tool.

How Do You Plan Your Warm-Up?

YOU SHOULDN'T PUT YOURSELF UNDER UNNECESSARY PRESSURE, BUT A PROGRESSIVE AND SPECIFIC WARM-UP, FOCUSED PRIMARILY ON SENSORIMOTOR AWARENESS, USUALLY SUCCEEDS IN ACHIEVING ALL THE EFFECTS DESCRIBED IN THE PREVIOUS SECTIONS. HOWEVER, JUST TO BE CERTAIN YOU'RE ON THE RIGHT TRACK, HERE ARE SOME TIPS FOR CREATING YOUR OWN ROUTINE FOR THIS CRITICAL TRAINING COMPONENT.

Intelligent or Tailored Warm-Ups

Remember that there's no such thing as a one-size-fits-all warm-up. No warm-up meets every need or suits every person. So, the first rule is to vary things and constantly adjust the warm-up for the individual and the task for which he or she is training. Here are the key points to note.

In a Cold Location

→ Spend longer warming up to achieve a sufficient level of heat production to increase the internal temperature of your largest muscles.
→ Cover yourself up to keep in the generated heat, without which the warm-up is pointless. As a priority, you should cover up those areas of the body that will be working during the session.

In a Hot One

→ Hydrate regularly (before you feel thirsty).
→ Find a cooler spot for an outdoor warm-up (in the shade).
→ Let in fresh air and promote air circulation when working indoors (open windows and use a fan).
→ Make sure you avoid hyperthermia or sunstroke.

Time of Day

→ A warm-up in the early morning or evening should be longer and more thorough than one during the day.
→ Consider all external information (e.g., did you arrive on a bike).
→ Consider your personal psychological state (e.g., worries in your private life).

Type of Effort

→ For short-term, maximum-intensity effort, the warm-up should be in-depth, without tiring out the body, of course. An ideal length for a club session is often between 15 and 30 min.
→ As far as *randori* sessions are concerned, the warm-up should be particularly rigorous and last at least 20 min.
→ For prolonged, low-intensity effort as in technical sessions, a warm-up that lasts less than 10 min may suffice.

Four Key Rules

A warm-up will be effective and preventive if you follow these four rules.

Produce Real Heat

Body temperature only rises if the muscle power employed surpasses 50 watts. This means the intensity must be sufficiently high. Please note that the amount of visible perspiration, which varies hugely from one person to the next, is by no means a reliable marker. Heart rate is more relevant; it must gradually quicken and be maintained at between 130 and 160 beats per minute throughout the warm-up.

Preserve the Heat

The body cools through radiation (it emits infrared radiation and gets colder) and evaporation (perspiration). The colder the air is, the more important it is to cover yourself between activity phases. This often happens during competitions, where the cold and long wait times can be harmful.

Take a Gradual Approach

Without exhausting yourself, the combination of exercises should facilitate a gradual increase in intensity until the start of the actual session. This means you shouldn't start off with *randori*.

Alternate the Work

It's imperative, from both a physical and a psychological point of view, to alternate your exercises and vary your warm-up. It's important to mix drills that mobilize the cardiorespiratory system with those that engage different muscle groups and joints. Simple maneuvers like basic *uchi-komi* or *tandoku-renshu*, and more specific ones like a joint-focused warm-up or stretching, should be combined in varied ways.

Finally, in judo more than in any other discipline, the warm-up should begin with general mobility exercises, ideally carried out cold: backbends, full squats, lunges, torso rotations, shoulder movements, and so on.

HAMSTRINGS

Their particular function and structure warrant a specific approach:

→ Their contraction speed is slow

→ They have a strong tendency to stiffen up

I recommend taking your hamstrings very seriously:

→ Advance warm-up using butt kicks with varied stance: wide, narrow, then leaning forward (see photos)

→ Systematic stretching after the workout

Suggested Warm-Up for a Club Workout

A warm-up consists of three phases that should always be included. The choice of content and the duration, presented here as an example, do not represent the perfect combination. Your exercises should be systematically planned according to the situation while respecting the principles laid out earlier.

Warning! Though 10 to 15 minutes is enough for the temperature of the torso and the head to reach 102.2°F (39°C), it takes another 10 minutes for the arms and legs to reach 100.4°F (38°C) (mainly because of greater peripheral heat loss and the difference in blood flow between these two areas). This is why stretching makes sense, because it acts as a warm-up accelerator for distant muscles. It should be short (around 8 seconds) and combined with contractions and then movement so as to reactivate the stretched muscle. *Uchi-komi* and *tandoku-renshu* are particularly good for this purpose.

A WARM-UP IS NOT NECESSARILY A SERIES OF TRAINING CIRCUITS

These parts do not necessarily have to be divided up and may, depending on your needs, overlap and blend progressively, enabling feedback from one to the next, resulting in a gradual evolution of your warm-up as you get closer to the actual workout.

General Warm-Up → DURATION: 5 MIN

Following a short dynamic mobility intro (but without significant movement), this phase should activate the cardiopulmonary system through a gradual kick-start of the cardiac and respiratory systems. Thus, a low-intensity, whole-body exercise that is simple in motor terms is preferred here. I recommend exercises related to running and jumping (crossing steps, knee lifts, hopping, etc.). The complexity and intensity of the exercises increase gradually as they get closer and closer to judo *(tsugi-ashi, tai-sabaki,* etc.).

The following example can be freely adjusted to suit your needs:

→ Mobility sequence: forward lunge with a back extension, 5 sec at progressive intensity; crouching position, back straight and, ideally, feet flat, 5 sec; bend the torso over the legs, trying to reach the toes, 5 sec. Repeat 3 times, increasing your range of motion each time.

→ Running.

→ 10 knee lifts + 10 butt kicks. Repeat these exercises sideways and backward.

→ Continue running, adding changes of direction.

→ Jump in place, and then do different coordination exercises (lunges, legs apart, legs together, lift your arms in front of you and to the side, etc.). Don't hesitate to mix things up!

→ Continue running.

→ Jump in place.

→ Combine this with the next phase.

Supplementary Warm-Up → DURATION: 5 to 10 MIN

This phase, which reinforces the previous one, is based on the alternation of more specific (analytical) work while maintaining cardiopulmonary activity.

→ **Wake up and mobilize different joints (especially the neck, wrists, and ankles).**
→ **Run again at moderate intensity.**
→ **Do active, dynamic stretches: choose an area and stretch it for around 8 sec, contract it for about 8 sec, then do 6 *uchi-komi* in a row, before starting again with another muscle group. You can do this up to two times per muscle group, prioritizing the quadriceps, hamstrings, and hip flexors and extensors.**
→ **Run while varying the intensity (short accelerations).**

Specific Warm-Up → DURATION: 8 to 10 MIN

(Most of this can be combined with the technical content of the workout). This is the specific transition to judo, the essential step that leads from the general warm-up to the core of the workout, through specific reactivation of memory and motor patterns. It contains all of judo's basic exercises, like simple *tandoku-renshu* or *uchi-komi*, simple at first, and then in combination and in motion.

The variety of judo exercises is such that this final phase is limited only by your skills. You can, for example, use the following sequence:

Tandoku-renshu
→ **10 side steps + sweeps**
→ **10 lateral jumps + sweeps**
→ **10 *tsugi-ashi* (on each side)**
→ **10 *tai-sabaki* (on each side)**
→ **10 *tsugi-ashi* + *tai-sabaki* – 10 *ko-uchi* (on each side)**

Uchi-komi
→ **5 sets of 10**
→ ***Uchi-komi* in motion**
→ **4 sets of 30 sec**

GLOSSARY

→ ***tsugi-ashi:*** Walking in side steps.

→ ***tai-sabaki:*** Body movement.

→ ***tandoku-renshu:*** Training by yourself.

→ ***uchi-komi:*** Repetitive exercise.

→ ***nage-komi:*** Repetitive exercise with falls.

Warming Up During Competitions

WARM-UPS WHILE TRAINING SHOULD BE VARIED AND MUST AVOID BECOMING ROUTINE AT ALL COSTS TO REMAIN EFFECTIVE; HOWEVER, WARM-UPS DURING COMPETITIONS MUST BE FORMAL AND CONSTANTLY LOCKED INTO A ROUTINE. THEY GIVE YOU A POINT OF REFERENCE, BOOST YOUR CONFIDENCE, AND GET EVERYTHING IN ORDER AT JUST THE RIGHT MOMENT. HERE ARE A FEW TIPS FOR DESIGNING YOUR OWN COMPETITION WARM-UP.

Since it's longer—because it's adapted to the requirement for repeated effort throughout a day of competition—this warm-up almost takes the form of a proper workout. The main objective is to move gradually closer to the physical and psychological intensity of a competitive bout. To be truly ready for your fight, you have to understand that it starts well before the referee gives the *hajime* signal. When you bow to your opponent, you have to be well and truly present. The mistake athletes often make is believing that arriving as fresh as possible means that you save your strength. In reality, the opposite is true: if you've already been fighting for a minute, you're a minute ahead of your opponent. The difficulty is to properly adjust the warm-up so that you don't burn out before stepping out onto the mat.

During a day of competition (before your first bout), you should systematically go through the following phases:

- **General warm-up, waking up your muscles and mind, around 10 min**
- **Gradual rise in intensity, around 15 min**
- **Warm-up close to competition-level intensity, around 20 min**

The effects will be optimal for 20 minutes (if you cover yourself and remain active) and will disappear after 40 minutes (don't go take a nap in the bleachers, or you'll have wasted your time!). Then, before returning to the mat, do a short 15-minute warm-up. Each bout is followed by a period of active recovery, but the most important thing is to eat a snack as quickly as possible (energy bar) to maintain your energy reserves for the entire day.

In competition, your psychological performance is as important as your physical performance. In this regard, the difficulty of the warm-up lies in what psychologists call the *flow*, that optimal state of activation that fluctuates over time—not too relaxed, but not too frenzied either. But in judo, there's no way of knowing at what exact moment the preceding fight is going to end. So, you have to develop prefight routines, in which you repeat warm-up sequences that enable you to maintain an activation level that is as close as possible to the flow. These routines must be short and stable, and should alternate physical training phases (jumps, sweeps, *tai-sabaki*, etc.), and psychological phases (focusing attention, visualizing moves or attack combinations, tactics, etc.).

SAMPLE COMPETITION WARM-UP

- 10 to 15 min of jogging
- 10 min of dynamic stretching alternated with *tandoku-renshu*
- 5 × 10 explosive *uchi-komi* (30 sec of recovery)
- 2 min break
- 5 sets of 30 sec of *uchi-komi* in motion (30 sec of recovery)
- 2 min break
- 5 to 10 *randori* at 60 percent and *kumikata* for 20 to 30 sec (30 sec to 1 min of recovery)
- 3 min break
- 6 *randori* and *kumikata* at 90 percent resistance for 1 min (30 sec to 1 min of recovery)
- 3 min break
- 5 × 10 push-ups + jumps followed by 10 *uchi-komi* at maximum speed (30 sec of recovery)
- Walking around listening to music, hydrating, and focusing before the first bout

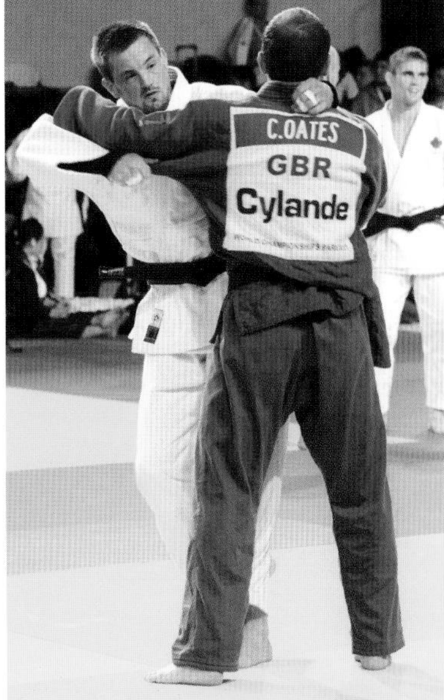

Colin Oates (GBR), two-time medalist at the European Championships and a fifth-place finisher at the 2011 World Championships, in the middle of his warm-up.

Stretching

THE RIGOR OF THE WARM-UP INCREASES IN TANDEM WITH AN ATHLETE'S AGE. WHILE YOUNG JUDOKAS CASUALLY SKIP SOME OF THESE STEPS (THIS IS A MISTAKE THAT MAY COST THEM LATER), STRETCHING IS A PARTICULARLY IMPORTANT PART OF THEIR OLDER COLLEAGUES' WARM-UPS. IF DONE REGULARLY FOR YOUR ENTIRE ATHLETIC CAREER, IT WILL ALLOW YOU TO PARTICIPATE IN YOUR SPORT FOR LONGER WITHOUT GETTING INJURED.

There are many stretching methods that meet specific needs and are suited to certain moments more than others. Faced with this range of possibilities and the controversy they fuel, a number of athletes have simply decided to give up stretching. The consequence of this is a whole generation of stiff judokas who hate stretching. That's the last straw!

Three types of goals can be pursued during stretching: preparation and prevention first and foremost (grouping together warm-up protocols, maintaining your level of alertness and activation during the workout, and protecting yourself), recovery, and finally, improving flexibility. For each goal, though the multitude of existing processes goes far beyond the scope of this section, I'll suggest a concrete and effective method, supported by different specific examples, for each of the main muscle groups.

If stretching is to be truly effective, we still have the lingering problem of making appropriate choices. How long, which method, at what time, and for what purpose?

Warming Up

Stretches used as a warm-up have long been a source of lively debate among sports enthusiasts: What technique do we use? How long do we do it for? And while we're at it, should we really be stretching at all?

Warming Up Is Hard!

The main purpose of the warm-up is now well known: raise the internal temperature of the muscle to make it more efficient. The trouble, as I mentioned in the previous section, is that it's a long process. So we have to find some shortcuts.

Stretching to the Rescue

Lengthening the muscle means placing a high internal tension on it, in the form of an isometric contraction. The consequence? A rapid rise in the temperature of the stretched muscle. It's therefore with complete confidence that enlightened coaches have long used stretching techniques to round off and accelerate the effects of their warm-ups.

Since 2000, however, scientific concern has been growing: What if stretching actually weakens the muscle by making it less alert?

Reactivate the Muscle After Stretching

In recent years, several research laboratories have focused on the problem of using passive stretching as a warm-up and confirmed that there is a real risk that your muscles will effectively fall asleep. When stretched, the muscle delays self-protecting reflex contractions during movements that are performed too quickly at risky angles. But since the impact of stretching on the muscle's internal temperature is indisputable, there is no question of doing away with it entirely!

Many authors have, therefore, considered alternatives by envisaging muscle reactivation protocols designed to counteract the negative effects of passive stretching.

A commonly agreed-upon technique consists of—after a traditional warm-up of 10 to 15 minutes—stretching, contracting, and then mobilizing the targeted muscle. Combining elongation with an isometric contraction and dynamic mobilization lets you prepare the muscle for effort, in training as well as in competition, all while maintaining muscular alertness.

This technique is often referred to as *active dynamic*, and it allows us to use, in the reactivation phase, a specific set of exercises. The goal is to prepare the muscle for effort by waking up the neuromuscular system, raising the internal temperature of the muscle, and accelerating blood circulation, which also prepares the muscle for the internal tensions it will experience during effort. Listening carefully to your body at this point allows you to create a connection between psychological and physical conditioning, and to strengthen proprioception.

BE CAREFUL!

While traditional postural stretching corresponds to a harmless isometric contraction, deep stretching designed to improve your flexibility imposes an eccentric contraction on the muscle, which weakens it in the short term and risks damaging it if the muscle is tired. It's important, then, to avoid stretching as a warm-up or after an intense workout. This type of technique could be done in a dedicated session or easily mixed in with a low-intensity technique workout.

Setup

→ **Stretch progressively, without sudden jolts. The length of the stretch should be moderate and should not go beyond the maximum elongation of the muscle. The idea is just to activate the muscle passively by gradually lengthening it.** *Duration: about 8 sec.*

→ **Intense isometric contraction (without movement). During this phase, try to produce an intense contraction and feel a warm sensation in the muscle in question.** *Duration: about 8 sec.*

→ **Dynamic mobilization of the muscle group being stretched in the form of active exercise (specific, if possible). The idea here is to link the stretch to the rest of the warm-up by specifically reenergizing this phase.** *Duration: about 8 sec.*

→ **Repeat this cycle 1 or 2 times per muscle group.**

ACTIVE-DYNAMIC HAMSTRING STRETCHES

STRETCHING

[A] Place one leg in front of the other and lean forward, balancing on your front heel, with your back straight and toes pointed upward. Bend your back leg and keep your feet parallel. *About 8 sec.*

CONTRACTION

[B] Slightly bend your front leg, balancing on your front heel, and push down into the ground and back, as if you were trying to straighten your leg. *About 8 sec.*

ACTIVATION

[C] 3 *tsugi-ashi/tai-sabaki.*

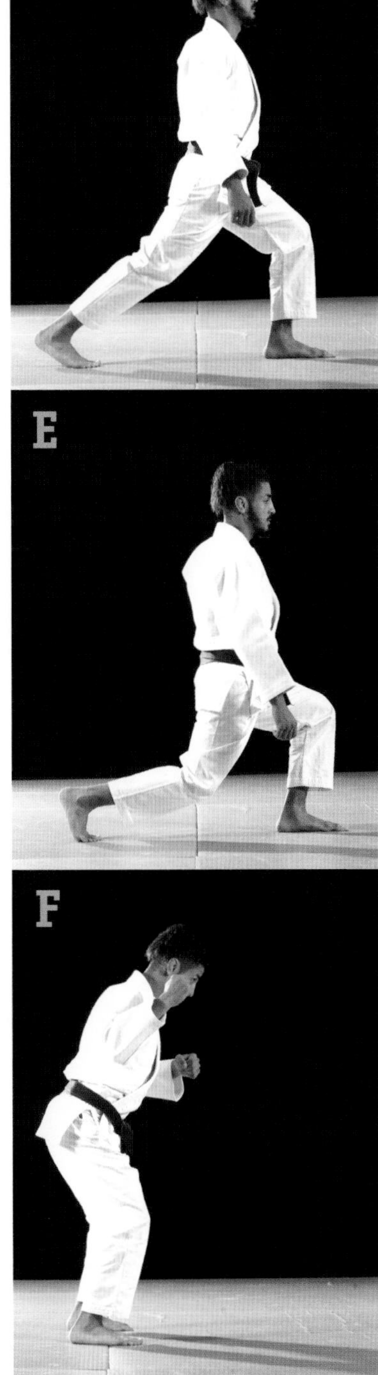

ACTIVE-DYNAMIC QUADRICEPS AND HIP FLEXOR STRETCHES

STRETCHING

[D] Do a forward lunge without arching your back or rotating your torso. Keep both feet parallel. *About 8 sec.*

CONTRACTION

[E] Slightly bend your front leg and tense your hip as if you were going to kick something. *About 8 sec.*

ACTIVATION

[F] 6 *seoi-nage/tan-doku-renshu.*

ACTIVE-DYNAMIC ADDUCTOR STRETCHES

STRETCHING

[G] Keeping your back straight, bend your legs (with your feet farther apart than your knees). The stretch comes from pushing down on your knees with your elbows and lowering your hips. *About 8 sec.*

CONTRACTION

[H] Hold the previous position and try to bring your knees together, resisting with your elbows. *About 8 sec.*

ACTIVATION

[I] 6 side steps and sweeps without a partner.

ACTIVE-DYNAMIC BACK STRETCHES

STRETCHING

[J] Put your elbow behind your head and grasp it with your other hand. Without leaning forward, bend your torso to one side. Keep your head upright. *About 8 sec.*

CONTRACTION

Push back against your hand with your elbow, contracting your back muscles as much as possible. *About 8 sec.*

ACTIVATION

[K] 6 *hiki-dashi*.

ACTIVE-DYNAMIC TRICEPS STRETCHES

STRETCHING

[L] Put your elbow behind your head and grasp it with your other hand. Then, without leaning forward, lower your head as if you were trying to sniff your armpit. *About 8 sec.*

CONTRACTION

Push back against your hand with your elbow, contracting your back muscles as much as possible. *About 8 sec.*

ACTIVATION

[M] 6 *uchi-komi/tsugi-ashi*.

ACTIVE-DYNAMIC SHOULDER STRETCHES

STRETCHING

[N] Grasp your shoulder and pull it toward you while keeping your back straight (don't bend or rotate the spine). Don't raise or lower the arm near the shoulder being stretched. This can be an uncomfortable position; please note that pain at the front or back of the shoulder is a sign of poor posture. Keep your head upright. *About 8 sec.*

CONTRACTION

Push back against your hand with your elbow, contracting your shoulder muscles as much as possible. *About 8 sec.*

ACTIVATION

[O] 8 square exercises on the floor.

ACTIVE-DYNAMIC PECTORAL MUSCLE STRETCHES

STRETCHING

[P] Ask a training partner to hold your wrist and pull your arm back. If necessary, position yourself perpendicular to a wall and stretch your pectoral muscles by playing with the angle. *About 8 sec.*

CONTRACTION

Push back against the wall with your hand (or against your partner's grasp), contracting your pectoral muscles as much as possible, as if you were about to slap someone. *About 8 sec.*

ACTIVATION

[Q] 6 *uchi-komi/tsugi-ashi*.

ACTIVE-DYNAMIC FOREARM STRETCHES

STRETCHING

[R] On your hands and knees, ease off on your body weight and support yourself on your hands, which are externally rotated. *About 8 sec.*

CONTRACTION

[S] With your palms placed together, push your fingers against each other. *About 8 sec.*

ACTIVATION

[T] Quickly open and close your fists. *About 8 sec.*

Recovery

Recent studies have shown what little effect stretching has on recovery (Hausswirth and Mujinka 2013). Even so, it is still regularly done at the end of a workout. In fact, no one questions its analgesic and psychological benefits. However, even in this case, you have to choose your method carefully because, when badly done, it can be harmful. It's worth noting that recent research has shown positive effects after a strength-training workout (10 minutes afterward, not immediately).

For recovery, passive stretching is preferred. Done in a comfortable position (usually on the floor), its first effect is to relax any muscles that have been mishandled by the physical effort, which shortens and contracts the muscle fibers. We should look to regain the range of motion lost during the effort and accelerate recovery to bring the body back to a steady state. This is a time to rebalance the tension between muscle groups.

Setup

→ End the session or competition with moderate activity during active recovery, enabling you to cool down and to enter the transition between high-intensity muscle engagement and the essential relaxation required for stretching.

→ Perform gradual and controlled stretching of the muscle, without any jolts or bounces, until you reach the maximum length.

→ Hold the position for a maximum of 30 sec, exhaling calmly.

→ This cycle can be repeated 2 or 3 times, varying the position slightly to cover the whole muscle (internal and external rotation).

Since most of these examples can be applied to all sports and are generally quite well known, no more needs to be said.

MISTAKES TO AVOID

→ Doing an intense stretching session on a damaged muscle (from soreness to tears).

→ Using stretches designed to increase flexibility as a warm-up or combining them with training content that uses the musculotendinous structures intensely.

→ Not gradually lengthening the muscle (abrupt stretching).

Flexibility

Too often, physical training priorities revolve around strength and speed, with many coaches believing that flexibility has very little impact on performance. However, judokas who put technical perfection at the core of their training and learning know that they cannot neglect the chief attribute of judo's deep meaning as a path to flexibility. More than just flexibility in the body, it's also a question of motor efficiency. In physical training terms, there are many reasons for including flexibility, including the following:

- better perception of the possibilities and limits of your body,
- increased intramuscular (muscle fibers within a single muscle) and intermuscular (different muscles working together) coordination, and
- enhanced sensitivity of proprioceptive receptors, because your muscles become more intelligent and provide more information to the central nervous system (about body position, condition, etc.).

Stretching is, of course, a preferred method for improving flexibility, knowing that the work is now focused more on increasing range of motion in the joints, and that it follows an essential cardiorespiratory and muscular warm-up. While passive stretching or techniques combining contractions and stretching are suitable for added flexibility, I also recommend a simple and very progressive technique: passive poses.

The goal is to lengthen, gradually and slowly, a joint that has a limited range of motion to recruit the joint's passive maintenance elements and to reduce the contraction of the muscle as much as possible.

The athlete should be comfortable and totally relaxed so as to avoid any reflex contraction or muscle defense reaction. You might need to massage the muscle beforehand to relax it.

Setup

To be done during a dedicated session or a low-intensity technical session.

→ Once you are comfortable, first do a gradual stretch, without abrupt jerks, very slowly, and try to increase the range of motion gradually for 30 seconds, using your own body weight or that of a training partner.

→ Repeat the exercise with a longer duration, around 2 minutes, but you can go up to 10 minutes if need be.

→ You can repeat up to 3 times for the same muscle group, varying your position to include the whole muscle (internal or external rotation).

We talk about passive stretching when a muscle group is subject to an elongation, via an external action (weight, for example). Conversely, active stretching is characterized by mobility that is achieved by joint-specific muscle action.

Since the postures are often similar in both cases, you can easily use recovery stretches for flexibility work.

What to Do During Training

Once training has started, some athletes yearn to stretch during recovery phases. Again, the use of passive stretching is not appropriate, because if the previous effort took place a short time beforehand, there is a risk of muscle damage. Conversely, if the upcoming effort is still some time away, the risk of decreased muscular vigilance is substantial. In fact, if athletes attempt to stretch, almost instinctively, it's because the muscle structure needs to remain under tension. A now well-known alternative is the contract-relax-stretch technique (passive-active stretching). While it is also used to increase range of motion in a joint, it has proved effective in maintaining nervous and muscle tension. In concrete terms, it's passive stretching followed by active stretching.

Depending on the circumstances, two separate strategies can be used:

1. Between very intense sets (strength-training exercises): passively stretch the antagonist muscle group, the one that relaxes during work. The antagonists of the hamstrings are the quadriceps. This is a classic stretch, so it's not necessary to use the contract-relax-stretch technique.
2. Between normal sets (during the judo session, for example): do alternate contractions lasting 10 seconds or so with 20-second stretches.

Setup

→ **Lengthen the muscle until you feel a twinge.**

→ **Contract the muscle by producing an intense isometric contraction.** *Duration: 10 sec.*

→ **Stretch passively and gradually without any jolts, and exhale slowly (place your elbows on your knees and lean forward).** *Duration: 20 sec.*

→ **Repeat this cycle 3 to 5 times, depending on how you feel.**

Usually focused on the lower limbs, this need for spontaneous stretching during training normally results in thigh, calf, and adductor stretches, and I've therefore used these for my examples. But of course you can stretch any muscle using the same principle.

ACTIVE-PASSIVE CALF STRETCHES

STRETCHING

[A] Get on all fours and push your toes against the floor.

STRETCHING

[B] Extend your legs from this position.

ACTIVE-PASSIVE HAMSTRING STRETCHES

STRETCHING

[C] Get on your back and bridge as if you were extricating yourself from under an opponent in *tate-shiho-gatame*.

STRETCHING

[D] Sit up and lean your torso forward over your straight legs.

ACTIVE-PASSIVE ADDUCTOR STRETCHES

STRETCHING

[E] From the floor grappling position that the Brazilians call the butterfly guard (cross-legged guard), squeeze your elbows in with your knees.

STRETCHING

[F] Now the other way around: try to push your knees (and open up your legs) with your elbows.

ACTIVE-PASSIVE QUADRICEPS AND HIP FLEXOR STRETCHES

STRETCHING

[G] Do a forward lunge that is long enough to cause a contraction of the quadriceps and the hip flexor.

STRETCHING

[H] Put both knees on the floor and lean back, contracting your abs and glutes to maintain the torso-hip-thigh alignment.

Optimizing Your Recovery

WHEN IT COMES TO RECOVERY, WE OFTEN GET CONTRADICTORY INFORMATION. TOOLS HAVE MULTIPLIED, AS HAVE COMPETITIONS, AND WE'RE NO LONGER SURE IF WE SHOULD BE GETTING A MASSAGE OR TAKING A COLD BATH. LET'S TAKE A LOOK AT THE OPTIONS.

Recovery is a consequence. The overloaded judo schedule has pushed it to the forefront, where it is seen as an end in and of itself, but don't be fooled: It is only the necessary consequence of applying a workload to the body. This workload-recovery pairing has to be taken as a whole in order to make progress; it's a serious methodological error to imagine that the more we train, the more we improve, just as we're not going to get any stronger by napping (sorry!). In fact, the physiology of exercise is a bit like farming: Sow the seeds, let them grow, then harvest. These are the components of a cycle where every step counts and recovery is your harvest. Indeed, most of the progress you make from a workout does not occur during the work, but during the recovery period.

Recovery is much more important than just simple rest.

Optimizing your recovery will do the following:

→ **Enable you to synchronize your peak form and competitions:** With a progressive "unloading" of the body, the hope is that you gradually recharge your batteries.

→ **Help your body to progress:** The vast majority of adaptations from training occur during recovery. After fluctuating for several hours, resources stabilize at rest at values higher than those observed before the application of an optimum load. This is what we call dynamic overcompensation.

→ **Repeat your efforts during a session, or during cyclical training:** Optimizing recovery is the foundation on which a judoka's endurance is built, from one set or workout to the next. This is what allows you to do a succession of *randori,* to take part in multiple bouts during a competition, and to handle training sessions week after week.

Trends and sport sciences have been driving an ever-growing debate on this topic: From compression stockings to cold baths and stretching, what really works?

Active Recovery

Active recovery has had its moment in the sun. Also known as *regeneration*, it consists of producing a low-intensity aerobic effort to activate the oxidative processes after intensive effort. The hope is that the tissue is oxygenated, increasing the blood supply necessary for its repair, reducing the acidity of the blood, and accelerating recovery while improving its quality. But here's the rub: This is effective only in the very short term, since the lactates are completely reused in a few hours. And what is even worse is that active recovery substantially increases the volume of aerobic work and mechanical load during a week in which your workload is already pretty high. 3 × 30 minutes of active recovery essentially equates to an extra session at the end of the day.

So, should we give it up? Thankfully, during a judo training session, the oxidative processes (which are necessary for the effectiveness of this protocol) are already activated or on the brink of being activated (they are activated after 10 minutes of effort). Thus, a 5-minute aerobic cool-down as soon as possible after the workout is still highly beneficial. To limit the mechanical load, you may wish to opt for a tool like the exercise bike.

Likewise, you should not overdo things just after a bout, because during a competition the day can easily turn into one long permanent effort.

What you need to stop: Active recovery sessions the evening of or the day after intense training or an intense competition. They inflate your training program unnecessarily with effects that are difficult to quantify.

Protocol

During competition: Keep a short, active recovery period immediately after prolonged bouts. The aerobic system is already partially engaged, so every minute you spend performing fluid movements as part of *tandoku-renshu*, engaging in floor maneuvers, or even running will be effective immediately. Don't go over 5 minutes (otherwise at the end of the day you'll have put in an effort that will be twice as long as that of other judokas) and maintain a constant but very low level of intensity. Combine this effort with gradual carbohydrate intake as soon as possible after the match. Be careful, though; if the bout is short, don't insist on active recovery.

During training: Immediately after *randori,* use judo exercises to prolong effort in the least intense way possible: *tandoku-renshu*, floor maneuvers, *yaku-soku-geiko*, *uchi-komi* in motion, and so on. Any low-intensity exercise with overall movement is particularly suitable.

Passive Recovery

Until now, passive recovery has not been very effective. Even certain tools that were thought to be impressive have ultimately proved disappointing. This is all the more unfortunate in that we are gradually moving back to active recovery approaches (see page 234). Thankfully, new tools have emerged that add to the physical trainer's arsenal for optimizing a judoka's recovery.

Passive Stretching

What we hope to gain by stretching at the end of a workout is, first and foremost, to produce so-called pumping or drainage that—by promoting venous return and rebalancing the tension between muscle groups—helps to combat muscle soreness. It's also a question of regaining a normal range of motion in the joints so as to accelerate recovery and a return to a normal state. Unfortunately, none of this seems to happen. The latest research on the topic has only found stretching to be mildly effective after intense muscle strength or alertness workouts, leaving enough relaxation time to avoid muscle damage. The analgesic effect persists, although a good nap seems to work just as well.

Does this mean we shouldn't stretch anymore? Of course, making the most of the analgesic effect is good, and organizing a specific recovery after alertness and strength workouts is relevant from a physiological point of view.

Psychologically, stretching facilitates relaxation and a cooldown with teammates. Finally, it's an opportunity to maintain flexibility and mobility, and the judoka should take advantage of it.

Protocol

After an alertness or maximum strength workout: In the shower or after a shower, 1-3 × 30 sec of passive stretching per muscle group on the muscles that are already relaxed (don't stretch a knotted muscle). Don't try to improve your flexibility—this is not the time or the goal. After any other workout, do free stretching and passive poses for 5 to 15 min with no intensity.

Sauna

When we're lucky enough to have a sauna in the dojo, and we take care to use it correctly, the effects on the body accumulate to assist in recovery: an analgesic and relaxing effect, lowering of heart and respiratory rates, better muscular regeneration, optimization of anti-infection defense mechanisms, elimination of intracellular waste, and (moderate) regulation of body weight. A sauna seems particularly effective for restoring flexibility and reducing muscle pain. These effects improve as you develop your sauna expertise, while harmful effects (slackening, central fatigue, etc.) seem to decrease. So there is, in fact, a place for the sauna in your training program. Although most studies recommend a maximum of two weekly sessions, you can, outside of competition periods, gradually train yourself to go in the sauna every day, like the Russians!

Protocol

The temperature should be about 176°F (80°C) to 194°F (90°C), with a moisture content not exceeding 15 percent. The session should not exceed 3 rounds of 10 min each, alternated with a phase of reacclimatization to ambient air, and then with cold water sprays. To end the session, you should relax in a cool room, lying down (covered) for around 20 min.

Mistakes to Avoid

→ Feeling tired or hungry in the sauna can cause discomfort.

→ Entering the sauna wet will delay perspiration.

→ Effort in the sauna increases your respiratory rate and circulation and, in fact, runs counter to the goals. Additionally, the risk of discomfort is high.

→ Excessive inhalation in the sauna and when exiting the sauna can bring about discomfort or epileptic fits.

→ Perspiring more after the sauna (in a hot bath, for example) could disrupt the body's rhythm.

→ Exerting yourself again after a sauna (gymnastics or swimming) can cause circulatory overload through an increase in the cardiac workload.

Cold Bath

Cold baths rose to prominence around 15 years ago. Since then, they've become popular with sports teams, but they have by no means been trouble-free. The initial protocols involved plunging into icy water at 39°F (4°C)! Thankfully, recent research has presented more reasonable protocols for these analgesic techniques encouraging muscle reconstruction and venous return (Hausswirth and Mujinka 2013). They are especially effective after endurance-type exertion, but you should not overuse them after speed sessions. Considering the number of impacts experienced during a *randori* session, it's perfectly natural to suggest this kind of protocol just after judo activity. You just need a big trash can full of cold water, and you're all set!

Protocol

2 or 3 stints of 5 min in water at 50°F (10°C) to 57°F (14°C).

Sleep

In all of the comparative studies carried out on the impact of different recovery methods, sleep usually comes out on top. A lack of sleep results in a decrease in physical, cognitive, and memory-related aptitudes, a disruption of hormonal balance, a decrease in concentration and motivation—as well as confidence and self-esteem—and increased irritability. Conversely, the effects of high-quality sleep on the body make it an essential part of an athlete's recovery. It helps to refuel energy reserves, secrete hormones (such as growth hormones involved in cell regeneration), regenerate brain cells, relax muscles generally, increase immune defenses, and improve memory ability (and thus, learning capacity).

It is, moreover, during the slow-wave sleep phase that these adaptations are the most pronounced. In concrete terms, it clears all of the physical and nervous fatigue from your body.

Protocol

Human beings are daytime creatures. Night living is not something we're all that comfortable with, and recovery will only be optimal during time slots adapted to our biological clock. Going to bed at 10 p.m. and waking up at 7 a.m., as well as an optional nap in the early afternoon, is recommended to obtain high-quality sleep. You can achieve the latter via good-quality bedding, a quiet environment that is as dark as possible, a moderate temperature, and set sleep times and lengths, if possible.

Mistakes to Avoid

→ Doing overly intense activity just before you go to bed increases excitability and psychological alertness, making it harder to fall asleep.

→ Training too early in the morning reduces the nocturnal recovery time and contributes to accumulating fatigue.

→ Irregular sleep times and amounts disrupt an athlete's biological clock, hindering their ability to fall asleep and reducing their sleep quality.

→ Disturbed or discontinuous sleep, in an environment with a harmful sensory impact, negatively affects the regeneration of the body during slow-wave sleep and prevents the body from completely relaxing.

→ To fall asleep more easily, you have to let the body cool down. An overly high room temperature can hinder sleep.

→ Intense light (stadium floodlights, UV light, etc.) sends deceptive information to the brain, making it believe that it's earlier in the day, and delaying sleep. The same goes for laptop screens and other blueish lights, which stimulate your eyes and brain. You should, therefore, limit this type of exposure before going to bed.

Massage

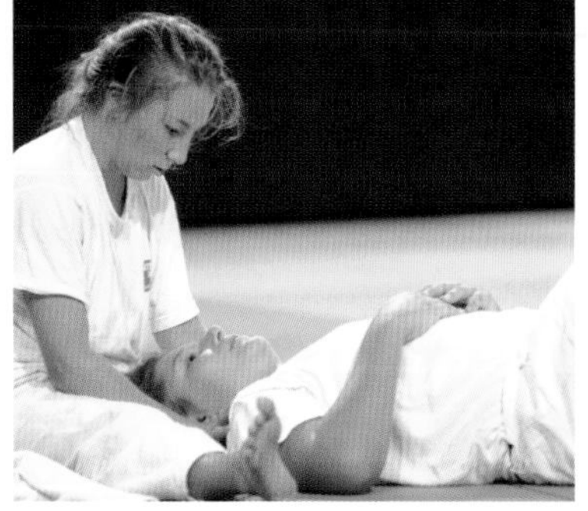

The prevalence of massage therapists and physiotherapists attests to the effectiveness of massages: general and localized relaxation, lower heart and respiratory rate, decrease in stress and muscle tension, vascularization of muscles, increase in venous return, and improved removal of waste from the body. The most conventional techniques are effleurage, petrissage, friction, and vibration, always starting in distal areas. They are also often combined with hydrotherapy, which reinforces the relaxing and vascularizing effects. Foam rollers are ideal for self-massage and maintaining mobility. Effective after strength-training workouts and useful in limiting muscle pain and stiffness, self-massages are especially popular in the sporting world at the moment.

Protocol

Use a foam roller to massage each of the muscles in your lower limbs as well as in your back. Spend 15 to 30 sec per muscle section.

Electrostimulation

Electrostimulation is now part of the array of tools used daily to help with recovery. As long as you follow the guidance provided by serious manufacturers (you should systematically avoid buying cheap equipment aimed at the general public), this technique will enable muscle drainage and localized active recovery through light activity that does not cause additional overall body fatigue. The oxygenation and vascularization of the muscle are thereby improved, allowing it to regain its original attributes more quickly. The effects are very pronounced after strength-training sessions.

Protocol

Normally done 15 minutes to 3 hours after training, electrostimulation works via a low-frequency current, without causing spasmodic contractions, which decreases during the session. It's best to place the electrodes on your forearms and calves.

Compression Socks

These long socks facilitate venous return and are now common among sports teams. Although they have not caught on as much in judo, they do encourage active and passive recovery. Comfortable and usable under any circumstances, they are particularly helpful during long return bus or plane rides, when judokas are seated for hours just after competing in tournaments. Optimizing venous return, they accelerate recovery, but they are not effective during training (while running, for example).

Protocol

Put on the socks as soon as possible after your shower and keep them on for 1 to 2 hours. Use them during travel to avoid the harmful effects of sitting in the same position for a prolonged period of time (especially after a competition).

Adductors: Avoid Those Splits!

THE TECHNIQUES AND MOVEMENTS USED IN JUDO INVOLVE A MUSCLE GROUP THAT IS OFTEN NEGLECTED IN PHYSICAL TRAINING: THE ADDUCTORS. HOWEVER, A SIMPLE GAP CAN SOMETIMES PROVE FATAL.

The adductors are a muscle group located inside the medial compartment of the thigh. This is where the adductor longus, adductor brevis, adductor magnus, pectineus muscle, and gracilis muscle are found. Together, these muscles enable adduction of the thighs (bringing the thighs together), as well as internal and external rotation. It's this muscle group, therefore, that is partly responsible for the effectiveness of fundamental judo maneuvers, such as the weight transfer and movement involved in side steps, leg attacks, sweeps, and ground grappling.

The problem is that their effectiveness is limited by their fragility; often underdeveloped, they lack the following:

→ **Flexibility.** This exposes them to powerful and sudden overstretching, creating an elongation that can end in a muscle strain.

→ **Strength.** They should be contracted more regularly and more intensely to obtain an effective result. However, you do run the risk of muscle knots.

→ **Proprioception** (which is the basis of dexterity-related attributes). Their ability to produce stretch reflexes to protect the joints is weak, increasing the risk of a sprain.

Beyond these direct risks (and that list is not exhaustive), we should add the dangers of an inflammation of the groin, which can often originate at the insertion of the adductor muscles. This type of inflammation is a common cause of pubalgia, which brings with it chronic pain that is grueling, disabling, and so difficult to get rid of that it may eventually require surgery. Strengthening this area is tricky, but the benefits gained by the athlete are manifold, both in terms of performance and prevention. This is why I've suggested a variety of exercises that will help prepare, protect, and strengthen your adductors.

Specific Adductor Warm-Up

Whether or not you are predisposed to inflammation in this area of the body makes no difference; it's important to prepare the adductors dutifully for any intense work. This is the case for activities like strength-training exercises, running, or judo itself. By now you know the techniques for stretches that prepare you for effort, often referred to as active-dynamic stretches.

What I'm recommending here is a specific version for the adductors and judo movement, which can easily be added to any warm-up.

[A] **Passively stretch the muscle for 8 sec by lightly pushing your elbows against your knees.**

[B] **Contract the muscle by pushing your knees in against your elbows for 6 to 8 sec.**

[C] **Dynamic movement in pairs: side steps down the length of the mat.**

Strengthen the Adductors Locally

Adductor strength deficit can be fixed easily with very little equipment. I recommend two exercises, one with a training partner and one without.

Without a partner: Wrap a resistance band around your ankle and attach the band to a wall or door. With a controlled sweeping movement and while maintaining your balance, slowly lift your leg up to the side then bring it back toward you, 12 to 15 times per set and 3 to 5 sets per leg.

With a partner: One works the adductors, while the other applies resistance through an action involving the abductor muscles. The resistance should be constant, limiting changes in applied strength. The movement should be slow and controlled. Repeat 12 to 15 times per set and 3 to 5 sets per leg.

In Practice

[D] Resistance band work, which is very effective, allows you to work on sweep moves, from the simplest to the most complex.

[E] Even without a band, you can still work with a training partner.

Create Synergy Between the Adductors and the Abdominal Muscles

Because inflammation of the abdominal and adductor muscles is the main cause of damage to the groin, strengthening them in a coordinated manner will allow for better intermuscular synchronization when performing high-risk movements.

In Practice

[F] **Start by contracting your abdominal muscles.**

[G] **Then do a series of sit-ups.**

Hold a medicine ball between your knees and squeeze it as hard as you can (see image). Suck in your stomach and strongly contract your abdominal muscles before you even start the exercise. Then do a set of sit-ups or torso rotations, in sets of 20 to 60 repetitions, depending on your level.

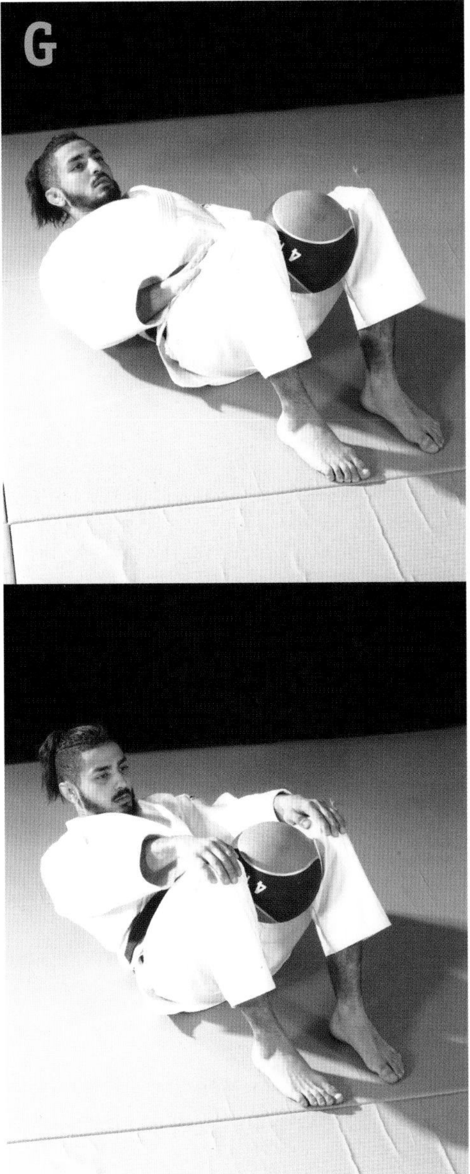

Enhance Local Flexibility

Flexibility is the range of motion in a joint. Being able to spread your legs apart wider significantly reduces the risk of muscle and joint injury and opens up new motor possibilities for the athlete.

In Practice

[H] **Contract for 10 sec.**

[I] **Then do the splits for 20 sec.**

Squeeze the medicine ball between your ankles for 10 sec, then move your legs apart, gradually trying to increase the range of motion for 20 sec. Repeat the exercise 3 to 5 times.

Link Adductor Dynamics to Holds

The preventive effectiveness of core strengthening has been amply covered in this book. Let's consider a specific approach for the adductors.

Keep your stomach flat and your legs, hips, and spine aligned. Then bring your free leg down to the floor and back up again.

As part of a warm-up, 10 of these leg lifts (per leg) will be enough to synchronize the adductor contractions effectively with the holding action that keeps the rest of the body in place.

For core-strengthening, you can repeat 4 sets of 20 repetitions per leg, without resting between sides but with 30 sec of recovery time before starting a new set with the first leg.

In Practice

[J] **Leg lifts with the legs on a bench is as much a warm-up drill as a core-strengthening exercise.**

Include the Adductors in a Comprehensive Warm-Up Requiring More Complex Motor Function

More broadly, a kind of giant-sumo-steps exercise offers a preventive warm-up for the adductors and hamstrings through dynamic and specific core strengthening. When you also push out your chest, by using your belt, you add shoulder injury prevention to the exercise.

Keep your back straight, with your shoulders back, your chest stuck out, and your head up. Spin on your supporting leg to reverse the position, lifting your free leg as high as possible. The more your mobility allows it, the lower you can go in squats.

If you do this in the middle of a warm-up, around 10 repetitions will generally suffice for transferring adductor activation in judo.

In Practice

[K] **Giant sumo steps require a specific overall motor function from the adductors**

PASSIVE STRETCHING

Holding the splits for over a minute as part of progressive passive stretching is only conceivable during well-run, dedicated sessions that include moderate tension in the muscles that are engaged during stretching. In fact, this type of stretching tends to relax the muscle. To avoid injuries, we strongly discourage doing this at the beginning of a standard training session. However, 10 minutes after the end of a workout, when dealing with tired muscles, stretching is useful in recovery (especially after strength training).

You shouldn't engage the muscle to its maximum, and you should hold the pose for about 20 seconds.

Preventing Knee Injury

AMONG THE MANY CONDITIONS AFFECTING JUDOKAS, ONE IN PARTICULAR IS WIDESPREAD AND GREATLY FEARED: AN ACL TEAR IN THE KNEE. HOWEVER, IT'S NOT A FOREGONE CONCLUSION. TAKE SOME SIMPLE PRECAUTIONS TO PROTECT YOUR KNEES.

Whether it's through wrapping your legs around an opponent, abruptly switching your supporting leg, or turning part of your leg while your foot remains rooted to the spot, the circumstances in which you can end up with a seriously sprained knee are numerous and are sometimes associated with a predisposition of certain fighters to joint weakness or natural instability, for instance. The problem is that we then become fatalistic, presuming that a tear in the knee is inevitable when we practice a high level of judo. This injury equates to long months away from the *tatami* mats (especially if you need an operation), as well as to pain, rehabilitation, doubts, and even a rejection of the sport altogether. However, it can be avoided.

Simple prevention work significantly reduces your risk. One of the principal causes of a tear of the anterior cruciate ligament (ACL) in judokas has now been clearly identified as a strength imbalance between the agonist and antagonist muscles in the thigh, which leads to joint fragility when the knee is engaged in an abnormal manner.

So what does that mean? All joints are held in place by a series of fibers that pull in one direction and by another series that pull in the opposite direction. For the thigh, the pairing consists of the quadriceps, the muscles at the front of the thigh that extend the knee (agonist action), and the hamstrings, the muscles at the back of the thigh that bend the knee (antagonist action).

Since judo requires greater quadriceps engagement (all of the knee-bending moves, such as *ippon-seoi-nage,* where the quadriceps muscles hold their position strongly), they are often overdeveloped in comparison with the hamstrings. Since judo's muscle-strengthening culture often promotes the squat (or press) as the key to lower body development, this exacerbates the imbalance. A second issue may also explain the large number of ACL tears in the judo world: the lack of work focusing on balance.

However, athletes who are regularly placed in situations involving instability will develop sensitivity in their various body receptors, and their various joints will develop the ability to respond to an unusual amount of pressure. Clearly, during a dangerous situation, the body will be more responsive and will more easily enter a protective mode by combining preventive reflex contractions and repositioning of the body segments.

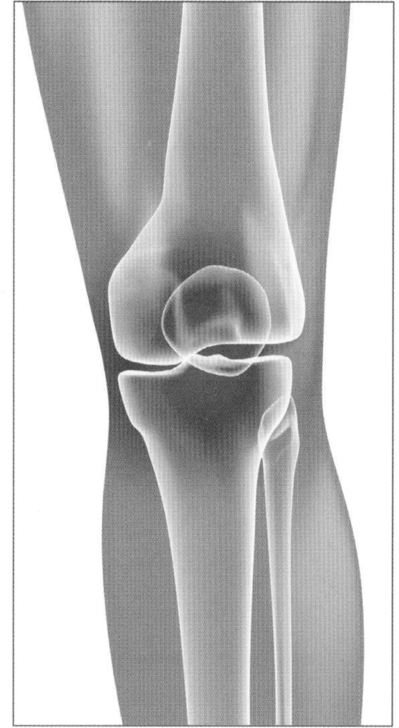

Two Priorities

1. **Rebalance the thigh muscles by strengthening the hamstrings.**
2. **Do balance work regularly so that the muscles and joints become "intelligent."**

Rebalancing Through Muscle Strengthening

The particular structure of the hamstrings calls for a special approach:

• The local warm-up should be extremely gradual and should explore all aspects and orientations of the muscle.
• The work should be done one leg at a time so as not to create (or maintain) any imbalance between the right and left legs.
• Since the hamstrings help support the joint, you should also consider strengthening them through isometric exercises.
• In the course of athletic activity, the hamstrings are mainly engaged during eccentric contractions, particularly in leg movements that involve a large range of motion.

Once you have mastered concentric and isometric work and can perfectly control the load and movement, you should also think about doing some eccentric strengthening exercises. Now that we've dealt with these principles, here are some exercises that are easy to implement.

An Athlete Strengthens the Hamstrings

Please note that correct pelvis positioning here is vitally important. Contract your glutes and tilt the pelvis forward. Avoid getting into a hollow back position.

[A] **Static position first, without a ball.**
[B] **Then with an exercise ball, still in a static position (vary the rotation of your legs by opening up your feet and then bringing them back together, to work all of the muscles).**
[C] **Roll the ball by bending and extending your legs (try to grip the ball with your toes).**
[D] **Work with the ball using just one leg.**

HOW AND WHEN?

→ A single program can really only be used for a few weeks because the body gets used to it, and the program loses its effectiveness. It's up to you to find or create other similar exercises to switch things up a little!

→ Proprioception and balance work exercises can be done anywhere and at any time, without any limits.

→ Muscle-strengthening work is effective when done twice a week, with at least one recovery day between 20-minute sessions. Long sets that require strength endurance, until the muscles are saturated, are best.

→ During a judo class, sequences can be incorporated into the warm-up phase (traditional muscle strengthening), or at the end of the session, if the workout wasn't too intense.

→ The tempo of the work gives prominence to the eccentric phase; take your time and slow down as you extend your knees during the dynamic exercises.

Awaken "Joint Intelligence"

The "intelligence" of a joint is its ability to take in direct information, which we call *proprioception* and *kinesthesia* (see glossary). Training proprioceptive and kinesthetic attributes leads muscles and joints to structure themselves during unusual situations so they can better protect themselves. So, it is a question of stimulating—by producing a variety of disruptions—the stability of different parts of the body in various configurations. Here are a few illustrations of preventive work involving unstable balance, either with or without equipment.

Practice

Weights rooms are often equipped with hamstring-strengthening machines. Whether or not they resemble the one in the photo, they are very simple to use. It's important, though, to remember how the hamstrings are used in judo; often the contraction is eccentric and occurs in only one leg.

After a preparatory concentric strengthening phase involving both legs (see opposite), or an alternate version (one leg after the other for each set), the muscles can be worked eccentrically, for example by pulling down a heavy load using one leg, and lightening the load a bit on the way up by using both legs.

Athletes should put themselves into positions where they are precariously balanced, in a situation as close as possible to their judo activity (in this case: in bare feet), and then try to stabilize themselves as best they can. The difficulty should gradually increase as follows:

→ First, without equipment, on both feet and then on one foot, transfer your body weight forward (to the balls of the feet), backward (to the heels), and sideways (to the inside and the outside of the feet).

→ Do the same exercise with your eyes closed, and then with your hands behind your back.

→ Do the same exercise but add equipment: gymnastics mats (vary the thickness by putting one on top of the other) or a balance cushion.

GLOSSARY

proprioception: The ability to position one or several parts of the body in space, to detect accelerations caused by body movements, and to trigger suitable motor adaptations.

kinesthesia: All of the sensations perceived by the nervous system: muscle tension, muscle relaxation, joint movement, positioning of different parts of the body, direction, dynamics, feeling of slowing down, stopping, balance, etc.

concentric muscle contraction: A contraction in which the muscle insertions shorten (when we bend the arms or legs, for example).

eccentric muscle contraction: A contraction in which the muscle insertions lengthen (when we straighten the arms or legs).

isometric muscle contraction: A contraction in which the muscle insertions do not move (when we hold the contraction without moving).

Preparing for Loss of Balance

A JUDO BOUT IS A GAME OF BALANCE IN A PERPETUAL STATE OF ORGANIZATION AND DISRUPTION WITH TWO OPPONENTS. THE GOAL IS TO DISRUPT YOUR OPPONENT'S BALANCE AND REGAIN YOUR OWN STABILITY, OR EVEN TO COMBINE THE TWO SIMULTANEOUSLY. IT IS LIKE WALKING A TIGHTROPE: THIS PRECARIOUS AND RANDOM BALANCE GAME IS THE HARDEST THING ABOUT JUDO, BUT ALSO THE MOST BEAUTIFUL. PHYSICAL TRAINING ALSO HAS A ROLE TO PLAY HERE. ARE YOU READY FOR THE BALANCE CHALLENGE?

The role of instability, a major principle of judo, is central to the application of techniques. But in the context of a movement, or, to a greater extent, a one-on-one confrontation, as in *randori* or *shiai,* the quest for this simple sensation requires complex technical development and great physical prowess. In concrete terms, an analysis of movement applied to judo reveals that the art of disrupting the opponent's balance requires fighters to take controlled risks, to continually flirt with their own balance limits, and to use their own body weight as the primary method of disrupting the other's positioning.

Climbing From the Ankles to the Hips

Studies show that the natural adaptation strategy adopted by the human body, when it finds itself in an unstable situation, is often based on balancing at ankle level. This is sufficient to stabilize the body on a sloped or slightly moving surface. But, in the battle against being unbalanced as well as unbalancing an opponent, the engagement created by the intense confrontations prevalent in judo requires the complete engagement of the body, the effectiveness of which stems from a new strategy that coordinates the hips and the other parts of the body. Judokas must structure their posture and movements around their hips, thus unlocking the different joint levels. Unlike the ankle strategy, which causes a rigidity in the overall body shape (fighters "set" their joints), the hip strategy develops the necessary mobility for an optimum way of coping with the imbalance. Moreover, it is the only strategy that includes the notion of balance-imbalance as a pair—when we grab and are grabbed, we can no longer manage our balance as if we were alone. How do we learn about and then master this game of hip-based organization-disruption, and how do we then include it in judo's comprehensive and complex motor functions, that is, simultaneous coordination (especially of the arms and legs)?

Please note that this progression, performed here with balance discs, can also be done with soft mats, balance boards, and the like. The idea is simply to increase the level of instability.

Simple Opposition From the Side

The goal is to make your opponent's back foot lift off the floor. This first stage allows you to feel the limits of ankle-based balancing. First, the fighter tenses up, leading to the loss of the support provided by the back leg. The ankle strategy may nevertheless suffice in this setup, where the unbalancing attempts are still not that daunting. First use the sleeves, then only work with the abdominal muscles; this works the upper part of the sub-umbilical muscles.

More than ever, physical training serves your technique, and in a fun way to boot. Here is a progression, developed with Jane Bridge (seventh dan), to make a smooth transition from specific physical training to technical seoi-nage *work.*

Distancing Yourself to Accentuate the Consequences of Instability

The idea here is to guide fighters to a second stage of balance control. By maintaining simple arm coordination (the interaction is limited to a rigid object like a stick), judokas should start to bend their knees to fight the growing instability. This increases mobility in the hips, eventually leading to the ability to structure their posture.

Specific Grips

This next stage enables fighters to structure their bodies while attempting to disrupt their opponents, incorporating hip mobility in the way in which they manage their own balance and attempt to generate imbalance, through arm-leg-hip coordination. The fine motor skills brought about by the kimono's total absence of rigidity forces athletes to keep their senses sharp and engage all their joints not only to maintain their own stability but also to try to knock the opponent off balance.

Specific Transfer Stage

In traditional *kumikata*, judokas put themselves in a state of total imbalance, where the only anchor is the counterweight provided by their partner's body. After a few repetitions where the body weights offset, push the controlled imbalance to the point where it causes your partner to fall.

In Practice

After this preparatory phase, the session can transition to *seoi-nage*-focused *nage-komi*, which will focus the attention on unbalancing the opponent.

Stability and Instability

JUDO IS A PERPETUAL BATTLE FOR STABILITY. BUT WHEN MODERN METHODS PLACE INSTABILITY AT THE HEART OF PHYSICAL TRAINING, THE TRAINER NEEDS TO KEEP HIS FEET ON THE GROUND.

In judo, there are two schools of thought: Making someone fall equates, first and foremost, to winning. But conversely, not falling equates to not losing. In this eternal confrontation between organization (of yourself) and disruption (of your opponent), judokas flirt with the limits of balance, alternating precarious stances with strong footholds, while as it were surfing on the *tatami* until the throw. This constant search for imbalance and balance is primarily a technical judo skill, but it is also worked on in physical training, an industry in which, over the past few years, functional trends have taken hold (any progress made is supposed to be more transferable to judo), bringing with them countless balance and proprioceptive tools.

The idea, as is often the case, is simple: By simplifying a specific, complex move from a technical viewpoint (replacing *seoi-nage* with a squat, for example), we can rely more accurately on a given physical attribute. Slide a Bosu disc, a creative instability platform, under the feet of a judoka performing such an exercise and you'll intensify the balance work. But remember, judo is as much about reacting and adapting to imbalance than it is about anchoring yourself to the ground to generate imbalance.

Unstable Surface or Unstable Load?

I've talked a lot about balance work on unstable surfaces. In judo, even though it's important to be able to structure yourself despite an increasingly unsteady stance (especially on a soft surface like a tatami), we shouldn't forget that handling unstable loads with a stable stance is also important. Research is still in its infancy regarding the transfer to physical and sporting activities, especially when it comes to unstable loads for the upper body, which is a relatively recent phenomenon in the sporting world (e.g., Aquahit, T1000 straps).

The benefits and limits of unstable loads in training are gradually becoming clear though; the study by Kholer and his team (2010) concludes that the more instability increases, the more the external load decreases. We can represent this another way: To manifest itself fully, strength requires great stability.

This means that a judoka will always be able to lift heavier weights on an Olympic bar in the bench press position than when doing the same exercise with dumbbells. This study is not exhaustive, however, because it did not use all of the available proprioceptive tools. We should remember that the activation of motor muscles is decreased in an unstable situation but that deep postural muscles like the erector spinae are more likely to be activated with loads or on unstable surfaces.

Thus, instability work seems unsuitable to develop strength or power, but it does make sense to help develop posture, to develop strength endurance, and for advanced core strengthening.

Training Ideas

Developing proprioception involves bringing about or optimizing various reflex adjustments, both in posture and in movement. It's a question of stimulating the stability of different parts of the body in various configurations by producing a variety of disruptions. Placed in a situation with unstable balance, the judoka will need to restore stability in one area while making use of the mobility of another area.

Appropriate Specific Exercises

→ Exercises focused on improving technique when in a balanced situation or when taking in unusual information, with variable range of motion and intensity.

→ Balance exercises, with or without equipment, with or without exteroceptive information, and with or without supplementary tasks.

→ Exercises that involve weight transfer and changes in stance. In addition to a transfer of weight, the change in stance may cause a total loss of balance.

→ Exercises that involve acquiring a position, repositioning, changes in direction, with or without rotations, with or without acceleration, with or without exteroceptive information.

→ Reeducation exercises.

GLOSSARY

→ proprioceptive: Refers to the sensitivity of the central nervous system to information related to body position and movement, originating in the muscles and joints.

→ exteroceptive: Stimulated by external factors (heat, pressure, etc.).

→ erector spinae: A group of three muscles located in the lower back that allow the spinal column to extend.

When Should You Do This Type of Exercise?

It all depends, of course, on the content of the judo or training session in question. Generally speaking, the final phase of the warm-up is good (10 to 15 minutes is sufficient). Although balance work in an unstable environment has supplementary goals, it can also be inserted between sets. So we could consider using it for simple tasks, during active recovery, or for more complex tasks, as if it were a pre- and postfatigue tool. So, in judo, specific balance work fits in with other training content in various ways, as in the case during games (we're constantly balancing, with different levels of fatigue, different scenarios on the ground, and different levels of alertness). At the end of the warm-up, paired with ball exercises, between games, as part of a circuit training exercises, during active recovery—the applications are infinite, since the intensity of the exercise is tailored to the situation and the goals.

For an athlete's long-term development, muscle strengthening in situations of unstable balance, along with more conventional strength-training techniques, is particularly well suited for young judokas. In fact, apart from the playful development of coordination and balance, muscle strengthening involving lighter loads aids progress while developing motor skills (Sparkes 2011).

BASIC EXERCISES

1

Keep the ball at a constant height, wedged between your chest and that of a training partner, while you both move forward, backward, or sideways. Keep your back as straight as possible throughout the exercise, with your head up and your shoulders back. If the ball slips a little, use your transverse abdominal muscle to control it, and not your hips, so that the position of your back doesn't change.

→ **Variation 1:** Close your eyes.

→ **Variation 2:** The coach calls out the directions you should move in.

→ **Variation 3:** Wedge the ball between your backs.

→ **Variation 4:** Wedge the ball between your heads (your back should stay aligned).

This type of exercise can be part of dynamic core building. It has the advantage of creating a situation where you have to cooperate but where you are also dueling with your partner. Note that the first exercise can be extremely demanding from a cardiovascular and muscular point of view. It should really only be used by experienced judokas who have warmed up thoroughly.

2

Keep the ball at the same height as in a core-strengthening exercise, shoulders on the ball, feet flat on the ground, and knees at 90°. Hold a medicine ball (MB) in each hand, or one MB that you'll switch from one hand to the other. Lower the arm to the side or backward while balancing the MB.

Variation 1: Close your eyes.

Variation 2: The coach creates an imbalance with the MB or the ball.

Variation 3: Do a bench press-type exercise and then arm circles. This is more than just balance work, we now find ourselves entering the sphere of dynamic core strengthening (proprioceptive).

This set of exercises is interesting because it facilitates the development of posterior muscles (hamstrings, glutes, and back), which coaches often neglect.

Progressive Squats

The squat is the exercise that engages the greatest number of muscles in the body. The intense recruitment of the lower limbs, as well as the upper body (controlling the bar and core strength) make it one of the physical trainer's most popular tools. Creating instability in squat work will allow us to do the following:

- Make technical progress in motor control in stable environments.
- Further engage deep and postural muscles, which are essential to core strength on the ground and in the air.
- Anticipate landings and recover stability following an imbalance of dangerous stances, by educating the body proprioceptively.

At the end of the cycle, the idea is, of course, to get back on stable footing on the floor to generate a maximum amount of strength and power.

Key Points

→ Back straight, maintained by controlling the pelvis (tilted slightly forward).
→ Knee trajectory in line with your toes.
→ Head up, focusing on a point above the horizon.
→ Chest stuck out, with elbows back, locking the bar in place on the shoulders.
→ Controlled descent over 2 sec (don't drop down suddenly).

STAGE 1

STABLE EXERCISE / FULL RANGE OF MOTION

CONVENTIONAL SQUAT

→ First cycle of 2 or 3 weeks with feet on the floor to gain confidence and to get used to controlling the bar with a light weight. 6 sets of 5 to 6 repetitions. Recovery: 1 min.

→ Gradually increase the weight, cycle after cycle: 3 to 5 sets of 5 to 7 repetitions, full range, heavier and heavier for 3 weeks. Recovery: 1 min 30 sec.

→ Alternate squats with the bar in front and squats with the bar behind your back.

STAGE 2

UNSTABLE WORK / VARIED RANGE OF MOTION

SQUAT ON BOSU BALL

➔ 2 or 3 weeks of squats on reversed Bosu balls, alternating with the bar in front and the bar behind your back from one session to the next or from one set to the next.

➔ Long sets, varying the range of motion: 3 reps using full range, 3 reps of parallel squats, 3 reps of half squats, then 1 min 30 sec of recovery time for 4 sets. If your range of motion is limited, increase the height of each squat.

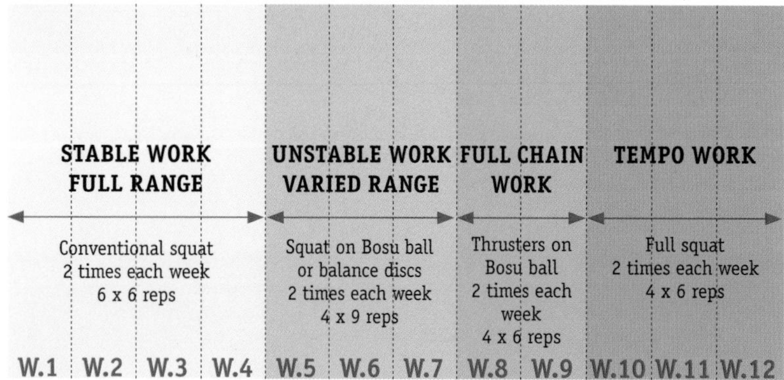

STAGE 3

FULL CHAIN WORK

THRUSTERS ON A BOSU

➔ 2 or 3 weeks of thrusters on reversed Bosu balls.

➔ 4 sets of 6 to 8 repetitions with 1 min 30 sec of recovery time.

➔ Change the weights on the bar without doing more than 8 repetitions. If you get too good at it, it's time to get your feet back on solid ground.

CYCLE 1

TEACHING PROGRESSION OVER 3 MONTHS *(to be followed)*

STABLE WORK FULL RANGE	UNSTABLE WORK VARIED RANGE	FULL CHAIN WORK	TEMPO WORK
Conventional squat 2 times each week 6 x 6 reps	Squat on Bosu ball or balance discs 2 times each week 4 x 9 reps	Thrusters on Bosu ball 2 times each week 4 x 6 reps	Full squat 2 times each week 4 x 6 reps
W.1 W.2 W.3 W.4	W.5 W.6 W.7	W.8 W.9	W.10 W.11 W.12

CYCLE 1

STANDARD DYNAMIC LOAD *(built up in three exercises)*

➔ **EXERCISE 1**
Warm-up, 2 sets of 8 to 10 reps. Squat on reversed Bosu ball, light load, slow tempo (recovery: 1 min)

➔ **EXERCISE 2**
Thrusters on a Bosu ball, 2 or 3 sets of 8 repetitions (recovery: 1 min)

➔ **EXERCISE 3**
Conventional squat using full range of motion, 3 or 4 sets, variable number of repetitions according to the work cycle (recovery: 1 to 3 min)

STAGE 3

TEMPO WORK

CONVENTIONAL SQUAT

➔ 2 or 3 weeks of squats using the full range of motion with your feet on the floor (4 sets of 6 to 8 repetitions, recover for 1 min 30 sec)

➔ During strength phases: 3 to 5 sets of 1 to 5 reps. Take 2 sec as you lower down and 2 sec as you come back up, with maximum load (recovery time: 3 to 5 min)

➔ During power phases: 4 to 6 sets of 4 to 6 repetitions using maximum range of motion. Aim for maximum acceleration as you come up (1 min max). Control the descent, 2 sec, using a medium load (recover for 1 to 2 min)

➔ During endurance phases: 3 to 5 sets of 8 to 12 repetitions using a varied range of motion, 3 to 4 sec as you lower down, 1 to 2 sec as you come up, using a medium to light load (recover for 1 min to 1 min 30 sec)

Specific Ways to Use an Exercise Ball

EXERCISE BALLS HAVE WELL AND TRULY ARRIVED IN DOJOS, WHERE THEY CAN BE USED IN A VERY ORIGINAL AND EXTREMELY SPECIFIC WAY.

The exercise ball, also known as the Swiss ball, takes its name from its country of origin, Switzerland, where it was developed and used for functional rehabilitation for adults with balance problems. Taking in information, situating your body in space, optimizing your balance in an unstable situation—what's all that for? To develop an attribute that is essential for the judoka, and for athletes in general: balance. And yes, balance does exist as a physical attribute, and it is fundamental to preventing injury and decisive in any sports performance, especially in judo. Cutting across all other physical attributes, it is balance first and foremost that influences your dexterity. Its improvement has an immediate effect on your technical quality, which hinges on continually managing imbalances. Exercise balls allow you to add instability to lots of traditional muscle-strengthening exercises, from static core strengthening to push-ups and abdominal exercises. I'd like to suggest some training drills with the ball that are specific for balance and strengthening work and that are effective, preventive, and fun, whether you do them as part of your warm-up or during the session.

Improve Your Balance

The improvement of instinctive balance mainly rests upon the way in which internal information is processed, which takes us into the domain of proprioception and kinesthesia. When you develop your proprioception, you improve your ability—even without a visual stimulus—to position your body (or some of its parts) in space, whether your body is moving or not. This information comes from a variety of receptors in different areas of the body. These receptors continually send information to the central nervous system, and more particularly, to the centers that control movement and posture, stimulating a number of muscle contraction and relaxation reflexes. It's partly through proprioceptive work that balance improves other physical and technical attributes. This is also how judokas develop intelligent muscles, capable of coordinating their actions as well as synchronizing muscle fiber stimulation to protect themselves or any joint during a high-risk situation.

For each exercise, start with external help (a training partner holding the ball or your hands), then try to find the balance point yourself.

Strengthen Your Body

Particularly effective for strengthening the body's core and deep postural muscles, exercise balls can be used in a specific way in judo. The idea involves alternating between locking and releasing different joint areas, as well as the scapular and pelvic girdles, for complete and preventive muscle strengthening, while using specific body shapes. The need to constantly stabilize your posture significantly increases the use of muscle fibers, because their engagement is faster, more comprehensive, and more specific than in any exercise performed on a stable surface.

BALANCE ON YOUR KNEES

First of all, climb on the ball, on your knees, and get your balance. Once you've mastered this step, try to sit up, pushing your hips out and keeping yourself as straight as possible.

FEET ON THE BALL

This is harder. Start by placing your hands on the ball, then put your knees on it and get your balance in the quadruped position (keep your back flat). From this position, try to bring your feet up onto the ball. Once both feet are up on the ball, crouch down.

STAND UPRIGHT ON THE BALL

The last step is to stand up. There are two options: support yourself against a wall (you can even wedge the ball into the corner of the dojo to make things easier) or use no support (with experience, you can achieve this).

MOVE FROM YOUR BACK TO YOUR FRONT BY ROTATING TO THE SIDE

→ The switch happens when you roll to the side, as if you were defending yourself from a hold-down attempt.

→ Start by rotating to the side by alternately supporting yourself on your right and then left elbows. Your shoulders should be completely locked.

→ In the second stage, you should try to get from your back to your front as quickly as possible without losing your balance.

MOVE FROM YOUR BACK TO YOUR FRONT BY GOING FORWARD AND BACKWARD

→ This time the switch occurs through forward movement. Part your legs, and from a sitting position, alternate between having your back on the ball and your front on the ball, and vice versa. This exercise is especially useful for improving upright to ground transitions in judo.

→ Reaching static stability on the ball in a seated position is a necessary step.

MOVE FROM YOUR BACK TO YOUR FRONT BY ROTATING YOUR HIPS

→ Start by finding your balance on the ball in a seated position with your feet raised (as in the guard position on the floor, facing your opponent).

→ Next, reverse the position of your legs by moving your hips. Use your hands for support at first, then try to remove your hands in what becomes an increasingly dynamic maneuver. This exercise is very useful for all movements requiring major hip mobility.

DON'T FALL DOWN!

→ In balance exercises, falling is part of the deal. Don't let that put you off; instead, do the exercises on a *tatami* mat and move any potentially dangerous objects out of the way. Falls constitute a balance breach that needs to be dealt with, which is very useful from a preventive and instructional point of view. Remember, you're a judoka. If the ball gets away from you, and you fall or roll, it's just like a sweep. Above all, don't stiffen your body or try to break your fall with your hands, because that's a surefire way to injure yourself.

References

Bailey, A. Donald, and Alan D. Martin. 1994. "Physical Activity and Skeletal Health in Adolescents." *Pediatr Exerc Sci* 6 (4): 330-47. https://doi.org/10.1123/pes.6.4.330.

Behm, David. 2010. "Training Adaptations With an 8-Week Instability Resistance Training Program With Recreationally Active Individuals." *J Strength Cond Res* 24 (7). https://journals.lww.com/nsca-jscr/Fulltext/2010/07000/Training_Adaptations_Associated_With_an_8_Week.32.aspx.

Blaak, E. 2001. "Gender Differences in Fat Metabolism." *Curr Opin Clin Nutr Metab Care* 4 (6): 499-502. https://journals.lww.com/co-clinicalnutrition/Abstract/2001/11000/Gender_differences_in_fat_metabolism.6.aspx

Docherty, D., and B. Sporer. 2000. "A Proposed Model for Examining the Interference Phenomenon Between Concurrent Aerobic and Strength Training." *Sports Med* 30 (6): 385-94. https://www.ncbi.nlm.nih.gov/pubmed/11132121.

Docherty, D., H.A. Wenger, and M.L. Collis. 1987. "The Effects of Resistance Training on Aerobic and Anaerobic Power of Young Boys." *Med Sci Sports Exerc* 19 (4): 389-92. https://www.ncbi.nlm.nih.gov/pubmed/3657487.

Falk, B. 1996. "Resistance-Training in Children and Adolescents." *Harefuah* 130 (11): 778-83. https://www.ncbi.nlm.nih.gov/pubmed/8794685.

Falk, B., and A. Eliakim. 2003. "Resistance Training, Skeletal Muscle and Growth." *Pediatr Edocrinol Rev* 1 (2): 120-7. https://www.ncbi.nlm.nih.gov/pubmed/16437017.

Goubel, Par F., and E. Pertuzon. 1973. "Évaluation De L Élasticité Du Muscle in Situ Par Une Méthode De Quick-Release." *Archives Internationales de Physiologie et de Biochimie* 81 (4): 697-707. https://www.tandfonline.com/doi/abs/10.3109/13813457309074474.

Hamill, Brian P. 1994. "Relative Safety of Weightlifting and Weight Training." *J Strength Cond Res* 8 (1): 53-7. https://crossfitatlanta.typepad.com/SoccerDangerous.pdf.

Hather, BM., P.A. Tesch, P. Buchanan, and G.A. Dudley. 1991. "Influence of Eccentric Actions on Skeletal Muscle Adaptations to Resistance Training." *Acta Physiol Scand* 143 (2): 177-85. https://www.ncbi.nlm.nih.gov/pubmed/1835816.

Hausswirth, Christophe, and Iñigo Mujinka, eds. 2013. *Recovery for Performance in Sport.* Champaign, IL: Human Kinetics.

Hetherington, MR. 1976. "Effect of Isometric Training on the Elbow Flexion Force Torque of Grade Five Boys." *Res Q* 47 (1): 41-7. https://www.ncbi.nlm.nih.gov/pubmed/1062827.

Kanehisa, H., and M. Miyashita. 1983. "Specificity of Velocity in Strength Training." *Eur J Appl Physiol Occup Physiol* 52 (1). 104-6. https://www.ncbi.nlm.nih.gov/pubmed/6686117.

Kohler, JM., S.P. Flanagan, and W.C. Whiting. 2010. "Muscle Activation Patterns While Lifting Stable and Unstable Loads on Stable and Unstable Surfaces." *J Strength Cond Res* 24 (2): 313-21. https://journals.lww.com/nsca-jscr/Fulltext/2010/02000/Muscle_Activation_Patterns_While_Lifting_Stable.4.aspx.

Krstulović, Saša. 2012. "Predictors of Judo Performance in Make Athletes." *Homosorticus* 14 (2): 5-11. https://www.researchgate.net/publication/330216204_PREDICTORS_OF_JUDO_PERFORMANCE_IN_MALE_ATHLETES.

Laurent, CM., L.S. Vervaecke, M.R. Kutz, and J.M. Green. 2014. "Sex-specific Responses to Self-paced, High-intensity Interval Training With Variable Recovery Periods." *J Strength Cond Res* 28 (4): 920-7. https://journals.lww.com/nsca-jscr/Fulltext/2014/04000/Sex_Specific_Responses_to_Self_Paced,.7.aspx.

Lillegard, WA., E.W. Brown, D.J. Wilson, R. Henderson, and E. Lewis. 1997. "Efficacy of Strength Training in Prepubescent to Early Postpubescent Males and Females: Effects of Gender and Maturity." *Pediatr Rehabil* 1 (3): 147-57. https://www.ncbi.nlm.nih.gov/pubmed/9689250.

MacDougall, JD., A.L. Hicks, J.R. MacDonald, R.S. McKelvie, H.J. Green, and K.M. Smith. 1998. "Muscle Performance and Enzymatic Adaptations to Sprint Interval Training." *J Appl Physiol* 84 (6): 2138-42. https://journals.physiology.org/doi/full/10.1152/jappl.1998.84.6.2138.

Malina, Robert M. 1994. "Physical Growth and Biological Maturation of Young Athletes." *Exerc & Sports Sci Reviews* 22 (1): 280-4. https://journals.lww.com/acsm-essr/Citation/1994/01000/Physical_Growth_and_Biological_Maturation_of_Young.12.aspx.

Mégrot, F., and B.G. Bardy. 2005. "Influence de l'expertise sportive sur le maintien de l'équilibre précaire : une étude dynamique." *Bulletin de Psychologie* 58 (475).

Mégrot, F., B.G. Bardy, and G. Dietrich. 2001. "Dimensionality and the Dynamics of Human Unstable Equilibrium." *Studies in Perception and Action* VI: 173-6.

Mégrot, F., G. Dietrich, Y. Kerlirzin, and S. Vieilledent. 2004. "Stratégies de maintien d'un équilibre dynamique: stabilisation d'un segment corporel ou du centre de masse?" *Cahiers dela Maison de la Recherche en Sciences Humaines, MRSH-Caen, CNRS,* 38: 171-85.

Mujinka, Iñigo. 2009. *Tapering and Peaking for Optimal Performance.* Champaign, IL: Human Kinetics.

Nielsen B., K. Nielsen, M. Hansen Behrendt, and E. Asmussen. 1980. "Training of 'Functional Muscular Strength' in Girls 7-19 Years Old." *Children and Exercise* IX.

Parlesbas, Pierre. 1990. *Activités physiques et éducation mortice.* Paris, France. Éditions EPS.

Pfeiffer, Ronald D., and Rulon S. Francis. 1986. "Effects of Strength Training on Muscle Development in Prepubescent, Pubescent, and Postpubescent Males." *The Physician and Sportsmedicine* 14 (9): 134-43. https://doi.org/10.1080/00913847.1986.11709173.

Sanal, E., F. Ardic, and S. Kirac. 2013. "Effects of Aerobic or Combined Aerobic Resistance Exercise on Body Composition in Overweight and Obese Adults: Gender Differences. A Randomized Intervention Study." *Eur J Phys Rehabil Med* 49 (1): 1-11. https://www.ncbi.nlm.nih.gov/pubmed/22569489.

Statuta, SM. 2020. "The Female Athlete Triad, Relative Energy Deficiency in Sport, and the Male Athlete Triad: The Exploration of Low-Energy Syndromes in Athletes." *Curr Sports Med Rep* 19 (2): 43-4. https://journals.lww.com/acsm-csmr/Citation/2020/02000/The_Female_Athlete_Triad,_Relative_Energy.2.aspx.

Vicente-Rodriguez, G., C. Dorado, I. Ara, J. Perez-Gomez, H. Olmedillas, S. Delgado-Guerra, and J.A. Calbet. 2007. "Artistic Versus Rhythmic Gymnastics: Effects on Bone and Muscle Mass in Young Girls." *Int J Sports Med* 28 (5): 386-93. https://www.ncbi.nlm.nih.gov/pubmed/17024630.

Weltman, A., C. Janney, C.B. Rians, K. Strand, B. Berg, S. Tippitt, J. Wise, B.R. Cahill, and F.I. Katch. 1986. "The Effects of Hydraulic Resistance Strength Training in Pre-Pubertal Males." *Med Sci Sports Exerc* 18 (6): 629-38. https://www.ncbi.nlm.nih.gov/pubmed/2946921.